Denney
Dec 74

A HISTORY
OF THE
LATER ROMAN EMPIRE

A Supplement containing:
The Emperors from Basil II to Isaac Komnenos
[A.D. 976-1057]
And Other Essays on Byzantine History

By
J. B. BURY

With an Appendix on:
THE PATRIARCHS OF CONSTANTINOPLE
By C. V. COBHAM

ARES   PUBLISHERS   INC.
CHICAGO   MCMLXXIV

Modified Reprint of the Editions:
Cambridge, 1930 and London, 1911.
Copyright © New Material by:
ARES PUBLISHERS INC.
150 E. Huron Street
Chicago, Illinois 60611
Printed in the United States of America
International Standard Book Number:
0-89005-028-7
Library of Congress Catalog Card Number:
74-77895

PREFACE

Only a few students of Byzantine history are aware of the fact that J. B. Bury was planning to complete his *History of the Later Roman Empire*. The two volumes of the first edition (London, 1899; Reprinted by Hakkert, Amsterdam, 1965) cover the period from Arcadius to Irene (395-800). The two volumes of the second edition cover only the period from the death of Theodosius I to the death of Justinian (London, 1923; Reprinted by Dover, New York, 1958). Long before this edition was published, Bury wrote a new volume which expanded his coverage of the Empire to 867 A.D. He changed the title, however, from "Later" to "Eastern" (*A History of the Eastern Roman Empire: From the Fall of Irene to the Accession of Basil I, A.D. 802-867*, London, 1912.)

Prior to 1889, the year of the first two-volume edition of *The Later Roman Empire*, Bury was preparing a third volume, which was never published. He must have planned to include in this the period from 802 until at least 867 A.D. and possibly more. He had completed the section from 976-1057 A.D. but had not organized his notes for the period 867-976 A.D. Thus he published *The Roman Emperors from Basil II to Isaac Komnenos* (976-1057 A.D.) as a prelude to the forthcoming volume in the *English Historical Review* (IV, 1889, pp. 41-64, 251-285.)

Obviously Bury later changed his plans and decided to continue his history on a larger scale. His 1912 volume gives us a good idea of what he intended this larger scale to be. However, it was not his destiny to produce any further volumes like this one. The two volumes of *The Later Roman Empire* published in 1923 present a revision of his larger scale original work. In 1923 he also published his *Survey of Byzantine History* (*cf.* pp. 19-31 of this *Supplement*)as an Introduction to the fourth volume of the

3

Cambridge Medieval History. This was his last work and it held but an echo of his plans to give the world a greater history of the Later or Eastern Roman Empire. Unhappily, these plans died with him in 1927 without any further additions to what he had already published.

In 1930, under the editorship of Harold Temperley,[1] a volume of Bury's *Selected Essays* was published (Cambridge, 1930; Reprinted by Hakkert, Amsterdam, 1964). This was the first time that the material was brought together, which we present here.

One of the reasons I decided to present this *Supplement* is that I am tired of hearing and reading that Bury did not write "one word (as a modern textbook historian recently wrote) about the Byzantine Empire after 867 A.D." In the years between the death of this great historian and the 1964 reprint of his *Selected Essays* only a few people had the opportunity to use this rare work. Still fewer people realized that his famous *Constitution of the Later Roman Empire* (publ. 1909) and the *Roman Emperors from Basil II to Isaac Komnenos* (publ. 1899) should be regarded as a "supplement" to his history. Now that this detail is established bibliographically for the first time, I hope that those who read *The Later Roman Empire* will be able to appreciate this work as the nucleus of what would have formed another, greater volume in Bury's series.

We have included Cobham's rare work, *The Patriarchs of Constantinople* as a worthwhile addition to this work. The listings Cobham gives are the best and most reliable for historical reference. I am sure that their reissue will be welcomed by all.

Al. N. Oikonomides

Loyola University of Chicago
June 1974

1. See note on p. 6.

CONTENTS

1. **Causes of the Survival of the Roman Empire in the East**   7-18

   Unity and vigour of the East 8 — Position, strength and population of Constantinople 9 — Reforms and ability of the fifth-century Emperors 9 — Religious discussion in the East and the responsibility of Justinian for the decline of the Empire 16 (Orig. Publ. 1900).

2. **Introductory Survey of Byzantine History** (Orig. Pub. 1923) 19-31

3. **The Constitution of the Later Roman Empire**   33-56

   Notes by Professor Bury (Orig. Publ. 1900)   56-59

4. **Roman Emperors from Basil II to Isaac Komnenos [A.D. 976-1075]** (Orig. Publ. 1899)   60-148

   Sources—Psellos 62. Attaleiates 67, Skylitzes 68, Zonaras 68 — *Basil II and Constantine VIII* [A.D. 976-1025] 70, revolt of Skleros 74-5, character and appearance of Basil 76 — Constantine VIII [A.D. 1025-8] 77—*Romanos III Argyros* [A.D. 1028-34] 79, Zoe's intrigue with Michael 82—*Michael IV the Paphlagonian* [A.D. 1034-41] 85, character 86, evil influence of his brothers, 88, Joannes 89, Zoe adopts Michael Kalaphates 94—*Michael V Kalaphates* [A.D. 1041-2] 96, revolution 100, deposition and blinding of Michael and Constantine 104, his real aims 105—*Zoe and Theodora* [A.D. 1042] 107, Zoe marries Constantine IX Monomachos 109—*Constantine IX* [A.D. 1042-54] 109, character 110, relations with Zoe 113, and Skleraina 114, Boilas 116, Constantine Leichudes chief minister [A.D. 1043] 118, Psellos 120, Xiphilinos 122, their resignations 125, military events 126, Maniakes—personal appearance, revolt and death 126, Russian naval engagement 128, abortive revolt of Leon Tornikios 128—*Theodora* sole Empress [A.D. 1054-6] 132—*Michael VI Stratiotikos* [A.D. 1056-7] 134, disgrace of Isaac Komnenos 135, assumes imperial state 138, deposition of Michael VI 140, character of revolution, a coalition between the Patriarch, the Senate and Isaac 141—*The Patriarch Michael Kerularios* 144, nepotism and his fall 148.

APPENDIX: C. V. Cobham, *The Patriarchs of Constantinople* (orig. ed. London 1911).

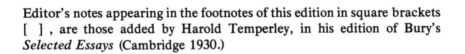

Editor's notes appearing in the footnotes of this edition in square brackets [ ] , are those added by Harold Temperley, in his edition of Bury's *Selected Essays* (Cambridge 1930.)

CAUSES OF THE SURVIVAL OF THE ROMAN EMPIRE IN THE EAST*

THE causes of decline did not operate equally in all parts of the Empire. Thus Egypt did not share in the general depopulation; and the Asiatic provinces seem not to have been affected to the same extent by the evils which led, in the West, to the destruction of the middle class and the growth of vast estates. In the fourth century, the commerce of the Mediterranean and the carrying trade of Western Europe were mainly in the hands of the Greeks; and, in general, the Eastern half of the Roman world was more prosperous and wealthy than the Western. Moreover—

the numbers of the Greek population in the Eastern Empire gave a unity of feeling to the inhabitants, a nationality of character to the government, and a degree of power to the Christian church, which were completely wanting in the ill-cemented structure of the West.[1]

This unity and quasi-nationality assumed some shape and substance when the Empire was finally divided after the death of Theodosius.

In the Western Empire, the people, the Roman aristocracy, and the imperial administration, formed three separate sections of society, unconnected either by religious opinion or national feelings; and each was ready to enter into alliances with armed bands of foreigners in the Empire in order to serve their respective interests or gratify their prejudices or passions.[2]

It is an essential moment in the situation that in the East there was no powerful pagan aristocracy. "The popular

[* This extract is given from the *Quarterly Review*, vol. cxcii, No. 383, pp. 146–55, by permission of the Editor. The article was written in 1900 and the theory of causation plays a large part in it. As has been indicated elsewhere, Bury's views as regards the fall of the Empire in the West were subsequently revised. There is however no such evidence that he altered his views about the survival of the Empire in the East, and they are given here as being an interesting pendant to his Byzantine studies.]

[1] Finlay, i, p. 147.   [2] *Ibid.*, p. 138.

element in the social organisation of the Greek people, by its alliance with Christianity, infused into society the energy which saved the Eastern Empire";[1] and the clergy in the East seem to have possessed more influence, and to have been able to protect the people to some extent against the oppression of the Government officials.

If we examine the resistance which the Illyrian peninsula presented to the barbarians, we are struck by the following points. European Greece, which had declined under the early Empire, had recovered in some measure its well-being and populousness, and though an invader might plunder it easily enough, it was so populous and homogeneous that a permanent occupation would not have been an easy matter. The task which faced an invader who aimed at permanent conquest was vastly increased by the number of strongly walled towns in the Illyrian peninsula. The cases in which even a small fortress successfully defied Goth or Hun illustrate this difficulty. Moreover, geographical configuration defended the Eastern Empire.

The sea which separated the European and Asiatic provinces opposed physical difficulties to invaders, while it afforded great facilities for defence, retreat, and renewed attack to the Roman forces, as long as they could maintain a naval superiority.[2]

The mountain ranges in the Balkan peninsula and in the Asiatic provinces, though not a safeguard against invasion, afforded the inhabitants a bulwark which rendered them more active and daring in resisting the invaders. It may be added that while the wealth of the Eastern Empire[3] invited the barbarians, "it furnished the means of repulsing their attacks or of bribing their forbearance".

In short, the East was more united and vigorous than the West, more populous, richer, and physically less easy for an invader to occupy. But with all these advantages it might not have escaped dismemberment if Constantine had not had the inspiration to plant a new capital of the Empire on the shores of the Bosporus. The advantages of its site

[1] Finlay, i, p. 138. [2] *Ibid.*, i, p. 163.
[3] Due especially to its commerce, and the gold and silver mines of Thrace and Pontus. Cp. Finlay, i, p. 167.

have been so often described that they are almost a common-place, but they have been put so strikingly and freshly by Mr A. van Millingen, in his recent scientific work on the walls and gates of Constantinople, that we need not hesitate to quote a part of his description (*Byzantine Constantinople,* p. 4).

No city owes so much to its site....Nowhere is the influence of geography upon history more strikingly marked. Here, to a degree that is marvellous, the possibilities of the freest and widest inter-course blend with the possibilities of complete isolation. No city can be more in the world and out of the world. It is the meeting point of some of the most important highways on the globe, whether by sea or land; the centre around which diverse, vast, and wealthy countries lie within easy reach, inviting intimate com-mercial relations, and permitting extended political control. Here the peninsula of Asia Minor, stretching like a bridge across the seas that sunder Asia and Europe, narrows the waters between the two great continents to a stream only half a mile across. Hither the Mediterranean ascends, through the avenues of the Ægean and the Marmora, from the regions of the south; while the Euxine and the Azoff spread a pathway to the regions of the north. Here is a harbour within which the largest and richest fleets can find a perfect shelter.

But no less remarkable is the facility with which the great world, so near at hand, can be excluded. Access to this point by sea is possible only through the straits of the Hellespont on the one side, and through the straits of the Bosporus on the other—defiles which, when properly guarded, no hostile navy could penetrate. These channels, with the Sea of Marmora between them, formed, moreover, a natural moat which prevented an Asiatic foe from coming within striking distance of the city; while the narrow breadth of the promontory on which the city stands allowed the erection of fortifications along the west, which could be held against immense armies by a comparatively small force.

This impregnable fortress was the palladium of the Balkan peninsula. We believe that its proximity was, above all others, the consideration which drove Alaric, Attila, and Theodoric to turn away from the Illyrian provinces. There was no city to do for the West what Constantinople did for the East. If Honorius had decided, like Valentinian I and Gratian, to make Trier the seat of empire, he might have saved Gaul, but he would have sacrificed Italy; by choosing Ravenna, he saved Italy and lost Gaul. If he had established his government at Rome he might have saved her from the humiliation of Alaric's sieges; but from a geographical point of view no city was less fitted to be the centre of her Empire, or even of the Western half of her Empire, than Rome herself. At this time she was equally unfitted from a political point of view; and this is the secret of the choice of Ravenna by Honorius. There was a distinct lack of sympathy between the Roman senators, most of whom were still devotedly attached to paganism, and the Christian court of the Emperor. This antagonism is in marked contrast with the state of things at Constantinople. There might be a pagan party there, but it was not an influential order, it was merely a handful of individuals. Arcadius was enveloped by a congenial atmosphere in Byzantium; at Rome Honorius could never have felt himself at home.

The population of Constantinople had increased so enormously since its foundation that it became necessary to extend its area by taking in the suburbs and erecting new fortifications. The enlargement had been foreseen in the reign of Theodosius the Great,[1] but was not carried out till the reign of Theodosius II. The able and experienced prefect Anthemius, who guided the helm of the Eastern Empire in the infancy of Theodosius, undertook this task and determined the future shape of the city. Anthemius did as much for the East as Stilicho did for the West, though the world has remembered Stilicho and forgotten Anthemius.[2] He had to face the Huns, who were now, under their chieftain Uldin, beginning to attack the Illyrian provinces. Anthemius beat them back beyond the Danube, and established upon that river a flotilla of two hundred and fifty vessels; he took care that the walls of the Illyrian cities, which had suffered through the Visigothic devastations, were rebuilt; and in planning the new walls of the capital he was preparing con-

[1] This is clear from a passage in an oration of Themistius quoted by Mr van Millingen, p. 42.

[2] Anthemius too was celebrated by a poet, named Theotimus; but the work of Theotimus is lost, and we may be sure that it did not approach the level of Claudian.

sciously for the Hunnic war which he foresaw, unconsciously for the assaults of successive hordes of barbarians, still beyond the Roman horizon, but destined to arrive one after another and vainly knock at the mighty gates for more than a thousand years. The inner of the two western walls is the wall of Anthemius, and it probably saved the city a siege by Attila. But violent earthquakes—Constantinople had no deadlier enemy—destroyed portions of this wall before the end of the same reign, and we may wonder that Attila did not seize the opportunity. The prefect Constantine met the crisis with an energy worthy of Anthemius, and his name, in Greek and in Latin, may still be read on one of the gates. He not only restored the Anthemian wall but he erected a second wall in front of it, outside of which was constructed a broad and deep moat. Thus the city was placed behind a triple line of defence.

The walls were flanked by 192 towers, while the ground between the two walls and that between the outer wall and the moat provided room for the action of large bodies of troops. These five portions of the fortifications rose tier above tier, and combined to form a barricade 190–207 feet thick, and over 100 feet high.[1]

The reign of Theodosius II was thus of the highest importance in the history of Constantinople, and thereby in that of the Eastern Empire. But the military fortification of the great citadel does not exhaust its importance. A university was founded at Constantinople, and the Theodosian code of laws was issued.

The Theodosian Code (says Finlay) afforded the people the means of arraigning the conduct of their rulers before fixed principles of law, and the University of Constantinople established the influence of Greek literature and gave the Greek language an official position in the Eastern Empire.[2]

The point which it here concerns us to insist upon is that these measures are significant of a steady desire for solid reform and the good of the people, a desire which is also shown in the alleviation which was afforded by two large remissions of arrears of taxation, wiping out the claims for unpaid taxes over a period of sixty years. Fortunately the

[1] van Millingen, p. 46.   [2] Finlay, i, p. 173.

reign of Theodosius did not stand alone. He was followed by a series of able sovereigns—Marcian, Leo, Zeno, Anastasius—who, whatever their faults may have been, were steadily bent on reform. They were "men born in the middle or lower ranks of society", and "appear to have participated in popular sympathies to a degree natural only to men who had long lived without courtly honours". It is certain that these strong intelligent men, who form such a striking contrast to the later Emperors of the West, contributed incalculably to the conservation of the Eastern Empire. They had no brilliant or showy qualities, and they are now well-nigh forgotten; but Leo, Zeno, and Anastasius were exceptionally able statesmen.

In the fifth century, then, a healthy spirit of reform, due to the fact that the Government was in touch with the people, manifested itself in the East, while in the West the pathetic and forlorn appeals of such Emperors as Majorian, seeking to arrest decay and suppress intolerable abuses, evoked no response. But there was another moment in the situation which, if we mistake not, had considerable significance. We have already referred to the fact that the chief ministers of Honorius and his successors were men of German race. We would not detract from the great services of Stilicho, or from the greater services of Aetius, but we would point out that these statesmen were sources of weakness, as well as strength. This will be readily admitted in the case of Count Ricimer, whose policy clearly paved the way for Odovacar; but it is also true of Stilicho and Aetius. If Honorius had been a strong ruler and had not consigned his power to Stilicho, or if Stilicho had not been a German, it is highly probable that the Empire would not have been divided by the revolt of Constantine, whose tyranny helped the successes of the barbarians. It has been said that the Vandals would never have occupied Africa if they had not been invited by Count Boniface; and though this statement is an exaggeration, the fact remains that the disasters of the reign of Valentinian III were partly due to the jealousy and antagonism which existed between Aetius, a minister of German stock, and Romans like Boniface. Now the Eastern Empire was also threatened by the ascendency of men of foreign extraction, first in the reign of Arcadius, and again in the reign of Leo. Each time the danger was averted. On the first occasion it took the form of an actual rebellion of Gothic troops under an ambitious leader named Gainas, whose programme was to revive the lost cause of Arianism. After the death of Marcian (A.D. 457) a powerful general of Alan race, named Aspar—an Arian, like most of the barbarians who embraced Christianity—assisted Leo to ascend the throne, and it might have seemed that he was destined to play in the East the same part, and to exercise the same authority, which had fallen to Stilicho, Aetius, and Ricimer in the West. But Leo apprehended the situation; he averted the immediate peril by assassinating Aspar, and he forestalled future dangers of the same kind by a reform of the military system. He began to recruit the army out of native troops, and ceased to rely, as his predecessors had relied, on foreign mercenaries. What Leo thus began, Zeno carried out. The great work of Zeno's reign, as Finlay observes, "was the formation of an army of native troops to serve as a counterpoise to the barbarian mercenaries who threatened the Eastern Empire with the same fate as the Western".

Within the limits of an article we have been unable to do more than indicate the various causes which determined the dismemberment of the Empire in the fifth century. Each, if it were to be illustrated fully, would almost demand an article to itself; but it may be of service to bring them together thus into a connected statement. We are now in a position to give a summary answer to the enquiry which we have attempted—an answer, however, which cannot be so briefly expressed as Professor Seeley's "depopulation". The Roman Empire as a whole was weakened by depopulation; Italy suffered eminently; and the original causes of this evil are not clear, though we can observe the forces—fiscal oppression, economic ignorance, the institution of slavery, and a new spirit of asceticism—which hindered the population from recovering itself. Like other ancient States, the Roman Empire suffered through ignorance of sound principles of economy; but to this universally prevailing evil it added a limitation of its own, which it inherited from the Republic, a certain antipathy or indifference to commerce. If an Adam Smith had arisen, the Empire might have been rescued from decline; but the only means which its rulers found to strengthen it was the settlement of barbarians in the provinces and the admission of barbarians into the legions.

This Germanising of the Empire (which was accompanied by a reciprocal process of Romanising the Germans) chiefly affected the European, Latin-speaking provinces; and it smoothed the way there for the ultimate ascendency of the German race. One of its immediate effects was a relaxation of military discipline, the upgrowth of a free spirit in the army; and without this the rebellions, revolutions, and usurpations of the third century would hardly have been possible. The disunion within the State at this period would have soon made it a prey for its enemies unless Diocletian had reorganised it and Constantine consolidated and completed the work of Diocletian. But though these statesmen restored the unity and defended the frontiers of the State, their new system aggravated, instead of removing, some essential weaknesses. The municipal classes declined in prosperity and were ultimately ruined; and this process was hastened by the incredible corruption of the collectors of revenue under the Constantinian system. Here again, however, the West suffered more severely than the more populous East. Neither Government did much for commerce and industries, but the industries and commerce which existed were mainly in the hands of the inhabitants of the Greek and Asiatic provinces. In these parts of the Empire men were better able to bear the fiscal burdens. Moreover Constantine, by his greatest work, the foundation of Constantinople, did for the East what he was unable to do for the West, and not only gave it a citadel but supplied a rallying-point for a sort of national unity. Christianity and the influence of the Church acted as a cement of such a unity, whereas in the West the members of the wealthy senatorial class were largely pagans and were out of touch both with their humbler fellow-subjects and with the Government.

In the same connexion it may be observed that there

existed in the Eastern Empire a public opinion which was able more easily to make itself felt than in the West. The Eastern provinces were also more favourably situated in point of geographical configuration. Accordingly it came about that, though the East had to bear the first brunt of the northern barbarians pressing in upon the Empire in the fourth century, and though it suffered severely from their devastations, yet the invaders saw that they would be unable to make good a permanently satisfactory lodgment in the East, and decided to divert their efforts to the feebler and distracted West, where men of their own race were influential in the State. Delivered of the presence of Alaric and his Visigoths, the Eastern Empire had escaped from its first great danger; and its future safety was confirmed and assured by a succession of able statesmen, from Anthemius to Anastasius I. It may be said that the strength of the East was a cause of calamity to the West, since Visigoth, Hun, and Ostrogoth turned successively from the Balkan lands to seek conquest in Italy, Gaul, or Spain; but this is no reproach to the rulers of Byzantium, who could reply that if the realm of Arcadius and Theodosius had been weaker, such weakness would assuredly not have saved the realm of Honorius and Valentinian. In the West all the causes of decline operated without check, and the ascendency of Germans at court was a source of division and discontent which led to rebellions. With the help of all these considerations we may be able to understand how the Latin half of the Empire was dismembered, while the Greek half held together and perpetuated the Empire of Rome.

Our enquiry, finished here, might naturally lead us on to meditate on the causes which brought about the subsequent dismemberment of the Eastern Empire by Persians, Saracens, and Bulgarians in the seventh century. Professor Seeley bracketed this later series of events with the events known as the fall of the Western Empire, and sought to embrace both under the same solution. We regard this view as completely erroneous. The causes which led to the success of the Saracens were wholly distinct from the causes which led to the success of the Germans. In one, but only in one, respect was there a continuity in the process. The ravages of Goths, Huns, and other barbarian hordes in the fifth century in the Illyrian provinces caused anew a decline in the population which facilitated the gradual infiltration of a new set of strangers, the Slavs. This influx began actively in the sixth century, and smoothed the way for the Slavonic and Bulgarian conquests in the seventh century—a repetition of the same process which we witnessed in the case of the German conquests. The Slavonic settlements were one cause of disintegration. A second, and perhaps the most vital and far-reaching, was the religious disunion of the Empire. The political importance of the theological controversies which raged in the fifth century as to the nature or natures of Christ can hardly be too highly estimated. In Egypt and Syria men's intellects did not move on the same lines as in the Greek provinces; and this fundamental divergence in spirit and modes of thought expressed itself in rival doctrines touching Christ's nature and personality. Never was the decree of an ecclesiastical council more fatal to the State than the wire-drawn formula issued by the Churchmen who met at Chalcedon. Egypt and Syria were alienated, and the tendency towards a quasi-national unity, which had been perceptible, was checked by this religious division. The mistake of Chalcedon must be largely imputed to the unfortunate influence of the Bishop of Rome; and when it had been committed, no more urgent problem faced the Government of Constantinople than to discover some means of rectifying it. Zeno and the able Patriarch Acacius, a Churchman exceptionally free from bigotry, grappled with the difficulty, and an Act of Union (Henotikon) was proclaimed, which recognised the doctrines of Nicæa and Ephesus and ignored the decision of Chalcedon. On this basis the Churches of Alexandria and Antioch were reunited in communion with Constantinople, and the religious peace of the East was restored. Statesmanship and tact could have maintained this union, but the disastrous policy of Justinian undid the work of Zeno and revived the political error of Chalcedon.

If any man can be regarded as distinctly, if partially, responsible for such a vast event as the dismemberment of the Eastern Empire, first by the Persians and then by the

Saracens, we say deliberately that it is the Emperor Justinian. We fear that this statement will appear startling and para- doxical; for we are accustomed to look upon Justinian's reign as an epoch of singular glory and brilliance. Two glorious achievements, beyond all blame or cavil, were accomplished under his auspices. Lawyers of unrivalled learning enriched the world with the *Digest*, the *Institutes*, and the *Code*; architects of matchless skill and soaring imagination built the church of St Sophia. But the famous conquests of the ambitious ruler were purchased at an exorbitant price. In the first place, seeing that in order to carry out his scheme of recovering Italy and the Western provinces from their German lords it would be of the highest importance to reconcile the Roman Church, which had been alienated by the policy of Zeno, he revived the doctrine of Chalcedon. Thus Rome was conciliated at the expense of the unity of the East, and the attempts which Justinian subsequently made to alleviate the consequences of his act only served to make the evil worse. The East was irrevocably disunited; Egypt and Syria were alienated from Con- stantinople. In the second place, Justinian's conquests were an enormous strain on the treasury. The grave struggle in which the Empire was then involved with the great Persian king Chosroes imposed such a heavy burden on the revenue that a ruler in Justinian's position was not justified in gratuitously undertaking other wars. If Justinian had merely spent the fund which had been accumulated by the economies of his predecessors, it might have been well; but in order to meet the expenses of his policy he overtaxed his subjects and revived financial oppression in its worst form.[1]* Allevia- tion of fiscal burdens had been one of the best features of the reigns of the Emperors who preceded him; and Anastasius had even reformed the curial system by doing away with the principle of joint responsibility. But the progress which their discreet policy inaugurated was un- done by Justinian; the merciless system of impositions, associated with the abominable name of John the Cappa-

[1] The evidence for this is treated in Panchenko's full and important study on the *Historia Arcana* of Procopius; [* published at St Petersburg: Press of Imperial Academy of Sciences].

docian, impoverished and ruined the people, and precipitated the Empire down that path of decline which ended in the disasters of the next century.

It would exceed the space and scope of this article to go on to show how within its diminished borders the Eastern Empire recovered its strength, so that during the eighth, ninth, and tenth centuries, as Mr Frederic Harrison observes in his eloquent Rede lecture, "the Emperors of New Rome ruled over a settled State which, if not as powerful in arms, was far more rich in various resources, more cultured, more truly modern, than any in Western Europe".* In the second decline, if we may so speak, which began in the eleventh century and culminated in the Latin capture of Constantinople (A.D. 1204), we see repeated some of those economic causes which induced the decay of the early Empire. We can mark especially the fatal growth of vast estates and the ruin of the small proprietors—a process against which the Emperors had legislated and struggled in vain. The day of doom came for the Younger as it had come for the Elder Rome. It is perhaps seldom realised how much longer the sway of Constantinople as an Imperial city endured than the rule of Rome herself. Even if we date the Empire of Rome from the conquest of Sicily, her first province, in the third century before our era, and extend the duration of her power to the subjugation of Italy by Odovacar (A.D. 476), her period amounts to little more than seven centuries. On the other hand, even if we omit to count the two hundred years of the restored Empire of the Palæologi, Constantinople, from her foundation to her capture by the Crusaders, reigned for little less than nine centuries. We are satisfied that this advantage which the daughter city enjoyed was due, above all, to the incomparable strength of her situation and her walls.

[* *Byzantine History in the Early Middle Ages*. The Rede Lecture, June 12, 1900, by Frederic Harrison, Macmillan & Co. (1900), p. 8.]

A SURVEY OF BYZANTINE
HISTORY *

The present volume carries on the fortunes of a portion
of Europe to the end of the Middle Ages. This exception
to the general chronological plan of the work seemed
both convenient and desirable. The orbit of Byzantium,
the history of the peoples and states which moved
within that orbit and always looked to it as the
central body, giver of light and heat, did indeed at
some points touch or traverse the orbits of western
European states, but the development of these on the
whole was not deeply affected or sensibly perturbed by
what happened east of Italy or south of the Danube,
and it was only in the time of the Crusades that some of
their rulers came into close contact with the Eastern
Empire or that it counted to any considerable extent
in their policies. England, the remotest state of the
West, was a legendary country to the people of Constantinople, and that imperial capital was no more than
a dream-name of wealth and splendour to Englishmen,
except to the few adventurers who travelled thither to
make their fortunes in the Varangian guards. It is thus
possible to follow the history of the Eastern Roman
Empire from the eighth century to its fall, along with
those of its neighbours and clients, independently of the
rest of Europe, and this is obviously more satisfactory
than to interpolate in the main history of Western

[* This is the Introduction from the *Cambridge Medieval History* (1923),
vol. IV, *The Eastern Roman Empire*, pp. vii–xiv. The references are to
chapters in the volume. It has been thought better to leave these just
as they stand.]

Europe chapters having no connexion with those which precede and follow.

Besides being convenient, this plan is desirable. For it enables us to emphasise the capital fact that throughout the Middle Ages the same Empire which was founded by Augustus continued to exist and function and occupy even in its final weakness a unique position in Europe—a fact which would otherwise be dissipated, as it were, and obscured amid the records of another system of states with which it was not in close or constant contact. It was one of Gibbon's services to history that the title of his book asserted clearly and unambiguously this continuity.

We have, however, tampered with the correct name, which is simply *Roman Empire*, by adding *Eastern*, a qualification which, although it has no official basis, is justifiable as a convenient mark of distinction from the Empire which Charlemagne founded and which lasted till the beginning of the nineteenth century. This Western Empire had no good claim to the name of Roman. Charlemagne and those who followed him were not legitimate successors of Augustus, Constantine, Justinian, and the Isaurians, and this was tacitly acknowledged in their endeavours to obtain recognition of the imperial title they assumed from the sovrans of Constantinople whose legitimacy was unquestionable.

Much as the Empire changed after the age of Justinian, as its population became more and more predominantly Greek in speech, its descent from Rome was always unmistakably preserved in the designation of its subjects as Romans ('Ρωμαῖοι). Its eastern neighbours knew it as Rūm. Till the very end the names of most of the titles of its ministers, officials, and institutions were either Latin or the Greek translations of Latin terms that had become current in the earliest days of the Empire.[1] Words of Latin derivation form a large class in medieval Greek. The modern Greek language was commonly called *Romaic* till the middle of the nineteenth century. It is only quite recently that *Roumelia* has been falling out of use to designate territories in the Balkan peninsula. Contrast with the persistence of the Roman name in the East the fact that the subjects of the Western Empire were never called Romans and indeed had no common name as a whole; the only "Romans" among them were the inhabitants of the city of Rome. There is indeed one district in Italy whose name still commemorates the Roman Empire—*Romagna*; but this exception only reinforces the contrast. For the district corresponds to the Exarchate of Ravenna, and was called Romania by its Lombard neighbours because it belonged to the Roman Emperor of Constantinople. It was at the New Rome, not at the Old, that the political tradition of the Empire was preserved. It is worth remembering too that the greatest public buildings of Constantinople were originally built, however they may have been afterwards changed or extended—the Hippodrome, the Great Palace, the Senatehouses, the churches of St Sophia and the Holy Apostles—by Emperors of Latin speech, Severus, Constantine, Justinian.

On the other hand, the civilisation of the later Roman Empire was the continuation of that of ancient Greece. Hellenism entered upon its second phase when Alexander of Macedon expanded the Greek world into the

---

[1] Examples: (1) ἀσηκρῆτις (*a secretis*), δούξ, κόμης, μάγιστρος, πατρίκιος, δομέστικος, πραιπόσιτος, πραίτωρ, κουαίστωρ, κουράτωρ; ἰδίκτον, πάκτον; κάστρον, φοσσάτον, παλάτιον, βῆλον (*velum*), ἀπληκεύειν = (*castra*) *applicare*, πραιδεύειν, δηριγεύειν; μοῦλτος=(*tu*)*multus*; (2) (ancient equivalents of Latin terms) βασιλεύς, αὐτοκράτωρ (*imperator*), σύγκλητος (*senatus*), ὕπατος (*consul*), ἀνθύπατος (*proconsul*), ὕπαρχος (*praefectus*), δρόμος (*cursus publicus*).

east, and on its third with the foundation of Constantine by the waters where Asia and Europe meet. Christianity, with its dogmatic theology and its monasticism, gave to this third phase its distinctive character and flavour, and *Byzantine* civilisation, as we have learned to call it, is an appropriate and happy name. Its features are very fully delineated in this volume by Professor Diehl (Chapter xxiv).* The continuity which links the fifteenth century A.D. with the fifth B.C. is notably expressed in the long series of Greek historians, who maintained, it may be said, a continuous tradition of historiography. From Critobulus, the imitator of Thucydides, and Chalcocondyles, who told the story of the last days of the Empire, we can go back, in a line broken only by a dark interval in the seventh and eighth centuries, to the first great masters, Thucydides and Herodotus.

The development of "Byzantinism" really began in the fourth century. The historian Finlay put the question in a rather awkward way by asking, When did the Roman Empire change into the Byzantine? The answer is that it did not change into any other Empire than itself, but that some of the characteristic features of Byzantinism began to appear immediately after Constantinople was founded. There is, however, a real truth in Finlay's own answer to his question. He drew the dividing line at the accession of Leo the Isaurian, at the beginning of the eighth century. And, in fact, Leo's reign marked the consummation of a rapid change which had been going on during the past hundred years. Rapid: for I believe anyone who has studied the history of those centuries will agree that in the age of the Isaurians we feel much further away from the age of Justinian than we feel in the age of Justinian from

[* Chap. xxiv, *Byzantine Civilisation.*]

22

the age of Theodosius the Great. Finlay's date has been taken as the starting point of this volume; it marks, so far as a date can, the transition to a new era.

The chief function which *as a political power* the Eastern Empire performed throughout the Middle Ages was to act as a bulwark for Europe, and for that civilisation which Greece had created and Rome had inherited and diffused, against Asiatic aggression. Since the rise of the Sasanid power in the third century, Asia had been attempting, with varying success, to resume the rôle which it had played under the Achaemenids. The arms of Alexander had delivered for hundreds of years the Eastern coasts and waters of the Mediterranean from all danger from an Asiatic power. The Sasanids finally succeeded in reaching the Mediterranean shores and the Bosphorus. The rôles of Europe and Asia were again reversed, and it was now for Byzantium to play on a larger stage the part formerly played by Athens and Sparta in a struggle for life and death. Heraclius proved himself not only a Themistocles but in some measure an Alexander. He not only checked the victorious advance of the enemy; he completely destroyed the power of the Great King and made him his vassal. But within ten years the rôles were reversed once more in that amazing transformation scene in which an obscure Asiatic people which had always seemed destined to play a minor part became suddenly one of the strongest powers in the world. Constantinople had again to fight for her life, and the danger was imminent and the strain unrelaxed for eighty years. Though the Empire did not succeed in barring the road to Spain and Sicily, its rulers held the gates of Europe at the Propontis and made it impossible for them to sweep over Europe as they had swept over Syria and Egypt. Centuries passed, and the Comnenians guarded Europe from the Seljūqs.

The Ottomans were the latest bearers of the Asiatic menace. If the Eastern Empire had not been mortally wounded and reduced to the dimensions of a petty state by the greed and brutality of the Western brigands who called themselves Crusaders, it is possible that the Turks might never have gained a footing in Europe. Even as it was, the impetus of their first victorious advance was broken by the tenacity of the Palaeologi— assisted it is true by the arms of Tīmūr. They had reached the Danube sixty years before Constantinople fell. When this at length happened, the first force and fury of their attack had been spent, and it is perhaps due to this delay that the Danube and the Carpathians were to mark the limit of Asiatic rule in Europe and that St Peter's was not to suffer the fate of St Sophia. Even in the last hours of its life, the Empire was still true to its traditional rôle of bulwark of Europe.

As a civilised state, we may say that the Eastern Empire performed three principal functions. As in its early years the Roman Empire laid the foundations of civilisation in the West and educated Celtic and German peoples, so in its later period it educated the Slavs of eastern Europe. Russia, Bulgaria, and Serbia owed it everything and bore its stamp. Secondly, it exercised a silent but constant and considerable influence on western Europe by sending its own manufactures and the products of the East to Italy, France, and Germany. Many examples of its embroidered textile fabrics and its jewellery have been preserved in the West. In the third place, it guarded safely the heritage of classical Greek literature which has had on the modern world a penetrating influence difficult to estimate. That we owe our possession of the masterpieces of Hellenic thought and imagination to the Byzantines everyone knows, but everyone does not remember that those books would not have travelled to Italy in the fourteenth and fifteenth centuries, because they would not have existed, if the Greek classics had not been read habitually by the educated subjects of the Eastern Empire and therefore continued to be copied.

Here we touch on a most fundamental contrast between the Eastern Empire and the western European states of the Middle Ages. The well-to-do classes in the West were as a rule illiterate, with the exception of ecclesiastics; among the well-to-do classes in the Byzantine world education was the rule, and education meant not merely reading, writing, and arithmetic, but the study of ancient Greek grammar and the reading of classical authors. The old traditions of Greek education had never died out. In court circles at Constantinople everyone who was not an utter parvenu would recognise and understand a quotation from Homer. In consequence of this difference, the intellectual standards in the West where book-learning was reserved for a particular class, and in the East where every boy and girl whose parents could afford to pay was educated, were entirely different. The advantages of science and training and system were understood in Byzantine society.

The appreciation of method and system which the Byzantines inherited both from the Greeks and from the Romans is conspicuously shewn in their military establishment and their conduct of war. Here their intellectuality stands out in vivid contrast with the rude dullness displayed in the modes of warfare practised in the West. Tactics were carefully studied, and the treatises on war which the officers used were kept up to date. The tacticians apprehended that it was stupid to employ uniform methods in campaigns against different foes. They observed carefully the military habits

of the various peoples with whom they had to fight—
Saracens, Lombards, Franks, Slavs, Hungarians—and
thought out different rules for dealing with each. The
soldiers were most carefully and efficiently drilled. They
understood organisation and the importance of not
leaving details to chance, of not neglecting small points
in equipment. Their armies were accompanied by am-
bulances and surgeons. Contrast the feudal armies of
the West, ill-disciplined, with no organisation, under
leaders who had not the most rudimentary idea of
tactics, who put their faith in sheer strength and courage,
and attacked all antagonists in exactly the same way.
More formidable the Western knights might be than
Slavs or Magyars, but in the eyes of a Byzantine officer
they were equally rude barbarians who had not yet
learned that war is an art which requires intelligence as
well as valour. In the period in which the Empire was
strong, before it lost the provinces which provided its
best recruits, its army was beyond comparison the best
fighting machine in Europe. When a Byzantine army was
defeated, it was always the incompetence of the general
or some indiscretion on his part, never inefficiency or
cowardice of the troops, that was to blame. The great
disaster of Manzikert (1071), from which perhaps the
decline of the Eastern Empire may be dated, was caused
by the imbecility of the brave Emperor who was in
command. A distinguished student of the art of war has
observed that Gibbon's dictum, "the vices of Byzantine
armies were inherent, their victories accidental",* is

[* *v.* Bury's *Gibbon* [1898], vol. v, pp. 59–60, "The genius of Belisarius
and Narses had been formed without a master, and expired without
a disciple. Neither honour, nor patriotism, nor generous superstition,
could animate the lifeless bodies of slaves and strangers, who had
succeeded to the honours of the legions—their vices were inherent, their
victories were accidental, and their costly maintenance exhausted the
substance of a state which they were unable to defend".]

precisely the reverse of the truth. He is perfectly right.

Military science enabled the Roman Empire to hold its own for many centuries against the foes around it, east and west and north. Internally, its permanence and stability depended above all on the rule of Roman law. Its subjects had always "the advantage of possessing a systematic administration of justice enforced by fixed legal procedure"; they were not at the mercy of caprice. They could contrast their courts in which justice was administered with a systematic observance of rules,. with those in which Mohammedan lawyers dispensed justice. The feeling that they were much better off under the government of Constantinople than their Eastern neighbours engendered a loyal attachment to the Empire, notwithstanding what they might suffer under an oppressive fiscal system.[1]

The influence of lawyers on the administration was always great, and may have been one of the facts which account for the proverbial conservatism of Byzantine civilisation. But that conservatism has generally been exaggerated, and even in the domain of law there was a development, though the foundations and principles remained those which were embodied in the legislation of Justinian.

The old Roman law, as expounded by the classical jurists, was in the East considerably modified in practice here and there by Greek and oriental custom, and there are traces of this influence in the laws of Justinian. But Justinianean law shews very few marks of ecclesiastical influence which in the seventh and following centuries led to various changes, particularly in laws relating to marriage. The law-book of the Isaurian Emperor, Leo III, was in some respects revolutionary, and

[1] Compare Finlay, *History of Greece*, II, 22–4; I, 411–12.

although at the end of the ninth century the Macedonian Emperors, eager to renounce all the works of the heretical Isaurians, professed to return to the pure principles of Justinian, they retained many of the innovations and compromised with others. The principal reforms of Leo were too much in accordance with public opinion to be undone. The legal status of concubinate for instance was definitely abolished. Only marriages between Christians were recognised as valid. Marriages between first and second cousins were forbidden. Fourth marriages were declared illegal and even third were discountenanced. It is remarkable however that in the matter of divorce, where the differences between the views of State and Church had been sharpest and where the Isaurians had given effect to the un-Roman ecclesiastical doctrine that marriage is indissoluble, the Macedonians returned to the common-sense view of Justinian and Roman lawyers that marriage like other contracts between human beings may be dissolved. We can see new tendencies too in the history of the *patria potestas*. The Iconoclasts substituted for it a parental *potestas*, assigning to the mother rights similar to those of the father. Other changes are mentioned below in Chapter XXII, pp. 709–10.[1]

In criminal law there was a marked change in tendency. From Augustus to Justinian penalties were ever becoming severer and new crimes being invented. After Justinian the movement was in the direction of mildness. In the eighth century only two or three crimes were punishable by death. One of these was murder and in

[1] It has been commonly held that the codes known as the Rhodian (Maritime) Law, the Farmer's (Rural) Law, and the Military Law were the work of the Isaurian Emperors, and this view is taken below in Chapter I (pp. 4–5) and Chapter XXII (pp. 708, 710). In the opinion of the present writer the investigations of Mr Ashburner have rendered it quite untenable, at least in regard to the two first.

this case the extreme penalty might be avoided if the murderer sought refuge in a church. On the other hand penalties of mutilation were extended and systematised. This kind of punishment had been inflicted in much earlier times and authorised in one or two cases by Justinian. In the eighth century we find amputations of the tongue, hand, and nose part of the criminal system, and particularly applied in dealing with sexual offences. If such punishments strike us to-day as barbaric (though in England, for instance, mutilation was inflicted little more than two centuries ago), they were then considered as a humane substitute for death, and the Church approved them because a tongue-less or nose-less sinner had time to repent.* In the same way, it was a common practice to blind, instead of killing, rebels or unsuccessful candidates for the throne. The tendency to avoid capital punishment is illustrated by the credible record that during the reign of John Comnenus there were no executions.

The fact that in domestic policy the Eastern Empire was far from being obstinately conservative is also illustrated by the reform of legal education in the eleventh century, when it was realised that a system which had been in practice for a long time did not work well and another was substituted (as is explained in Chapter XXII, p. 719).** That conception of the later Empire which has made the word Byzantine almost equivalent to Chinese was based on ignorance, and is now discredited. It is obvious that no State could have lasted so long in a changing world, if it had not had the capacity of adapting itself to new conditions. Its administrative machinery was being constantly modified

[* This subject is carried further by Bury in *R.P.A. Annual*, 1918, "The influence of Christianity on Roman Criminal Law".]

[** Chap. XXII, *Byzantine Legislation* 565–1453, by Professor Paul Collinet.]

by capable and hardworking rulers of whom there were many; the details of the system at the end of the tenth century differed at ever so many points from those of the eighth. As for art and literature, there were ups and downs, declines and renascences, throughout the whole duration of the Empire. It is only in quite recent years that Byzantine literature and Byzantine art have been methodically studied; in these wide fields of research Krumbacher's *Byzantine Literature* and Strzygowski's *Orient oder Rom* were pioneer works marking a new age. Now that we are getting to know the facts better and the darkness is gradually lifting, we have come to see that the history of the Empire is far from being a monotonous chronicle of palace revolutions, circus riots, theological disputes, tedious ceremonies in a servile court, and to realise that, as in any other political society, conditions were continually changing and in each succeeding age new political and social problems presented themselves for which some solution had to be found. If the chief interest in history lies in observing such changes, watching new problems shape themselves and the attempts of rulers or peoples to solve them, and seeing how the characters of individuals and the accidents which befall them determine the course of events, the story of the Eastern Empire is at least as interesting as that of any medieval State, or perhaps more interesting because its people were more civilised and intellectual than other Europeans and had a longer political experience behind them. On the ecclesiastical side it offers the longest and most considerable experiment of a State-Church that Christendom has ever seen.

The Crusades were, for the Eastern Empire, simply a series of barbarian invasions of a particularly embarrassing kind, and in the present volume they are treated merely from this point of view and their general significance in universal history is not considered. The full treatment of their causes and psychology and the consecutive story of the movement are reserved for Vol. v.

But the earlier history of Venice has been included in this volume. The character of Venice and her career were decided by the circumstance that she was subject to the Eastern Emperors before she became independent. She was extra-Italian throughout the Middle Ages; she never belonged to the Carolingian Kingdom of Italy. And after she had slipped into independence almost without knowing it—there was never a violent breaking away from her allegiance to the sovrans of Constantinople—she moved still in the orbit of the Empire; and it was on the ruins of the Empire, dismembered by the criminal enterprise of her Duke Dandolo, that she reached the summit of her power as mistress in the Aegean and in Greece. She was the meeting-place of two civilisations, but it was eastern not western Europe that controlled her history and lured her ambitions. Her citizens spoke a Latin tongue and in spiritual matters acknowledged the supremacy of the elder Rome, but the influence from new Rome had penetrated deep, and their great Byzantine basilica is a visible reminder of their long political connexion with the Eastern Empire.

8. THE CONSTITUTION OF THE LATER ROMAN EMPIRE*

THE forms of government which are commonly classified as absolute monarchies have not received the same attention or been so carefully analysed as those forms which are known as republics and constitutional monarchies. There is a considerable literature on absolute monarchy considered theoretically, in connexion with the question of Divine Right, but the actual examples which history offers of this kind of government have not been the subject of a detailed comparative study. Montesquieu, for instance, treats them indiscriminately as despotisms. Probably the reason lies in the apparent simplicity of a constitution, by which the supreme power is exclusively vested in one man. When we say that the monarch's will is supreme, we may seem to say all there is to be said. The Later Roman Empire is an example of absolute monarchy, and I propose to show that so far as it is concerned there is a good deal more to be said.

The term absolute monarchy is applied in contra-distinction to limited or constitutional monarchy. I understand the former to mean that the whole legis-lative, judicial, and executive powers of the state are vested in the monarch, and there is no other inde-pendent and concurrent authority.[1] The latter means that besides the so-called monarch there are other political bodies which possess an independent and effective authority of their own, and share in the sovran power. These terms, absolute and constitutional mon-

[* The Creighton Lecture, University College, London, November 12, 1909, Cambridge University Press, 1910, 49 pp. The spelling of proper names will be found to differ in these essays, but in each case Bury's own forms have been retained.]

archy, are unsatisfactory, from a logical point of view. For they group together these two forms of government as subdivisions of the class monarchy, implying or suggesting that they have much more real affinity to one another than either has to other constitutions. This is evidently untrue: a constitutional monarchy is far more closely allied to a republic like France than to an absolute monarchy like Russia. The English constitution, for instance, in which legislation is effected by the consent of three independent organs, the Crown, the Lords, and the Commons, might be described more correctly as a triarchy than as a monarchy; and it seems to be unfortunate that monarchy should have come to be used, quite unnecessarily, as a synonym for kingship. "Limited monarchy", as Austin said long ago, "is not monarchy";[2] monarchy properly so called is, simply and solely, absolute monarchy. We have however an alternative term, "autocracy", which involves no ambiguities, and might, I venture to think, be advantageously adopted as the technical term for this form of government in constitutional discussions. And "autocracy" has a special advantage over "absolute monarchy". Autocracies are not all alike, in respect to the power actually exercised by the autocrat. Although not limited by any bodies possessing an independent authority, he may be limited effectually in other ways. Now we can properly speak of more or less limited autocracies, whereas it is an impropriety of language to speak of more or less absolute monarchies, as "absolute" admits of no degrees.

Originally, and during the first three centuries of its existence, the Roman Empire was theoretically a republic. The Senate co-existed with the Emperor, as a body invested with an authority independent of his; but the functions which it exercised by virtue of that authority were surrendered one by one; it became more and more dependent on him; and by the end of the third century the fiction of a second power in the state was dropped altogether, although the Senate was not abolished.[3] From that time forward, under the system established by Diocletian and Constantine, until the fall of the Empire in the fifteenth century, the government was simply and undisguisedly an autocracy.

Now one broad distinction between autocracies may be found in the mode of accession to the throne. The sovranty may be hereditary or it may be elective. If it is elective, the sovranty is derived from the electors who, when the throne is vacant, exercise an independent and sovran authority in electing a new monarch. If it is hereditary, if the right of the autocrat depends entirely and indefeasibly on his birth, then we may say that his sovranty is underived; the succession is automatic, and there is no moment at which any other person or persons than the monarch can perform an act of sovran authority such as is implied in the election of a sovran. This difference may involve, as we shall see, important consequences.

In the case of the Roman Empire, the Imperial dignity continued to be elective, as it had been from the beginning, and the method of election remained the same. When the throne was vacant a new Emperor was chosen by the Senate and the army. The initiative might be taken either by the Senate or by the army, and both methods were recognised as equally valid. It was of course only a portion of the army that actually chose an Emperor—for instance, if the choice were made in Constantinople, the guard regiments; but such a portion was regarded as for this purpose representing all the troops which were scattered over the Empire. The appointment did not take the formal shape of what we commonly understand by election. If the soldiers took the initiative, they simply proclaimed the man they wanted. If the choice was made by the Senate, the procedure might be more deliberate, but there seems to have been no formal casting of votes, and the essential act was the proclamation.[4] It sufficed that one of these bodies should proclaim an Emperor to establish his title to the sovranty; it only remained for the other body to concur; and the inauguration was formally completed when the people of Constantinople had also acclaimed him in the Hippodrome—a formality always observed and reminiscent of the fact that the inhabitants of the new capital of Constantine had succeeded to the position of the old *populus Romanus*.[5]

The part which the Senate played in the appointment of an Emperor, whether by choosing him or by ratifying the choice of the army, is constitutionally important. The Senate or *Synklêtos* of New Rome was a very different body from the old Senatus Romanus. It was a small council consisting of persons who belonged to it by virtue of administrative offices to which they were appointed by the Emperor. In fact, the old Senate had coalesced with the Consistorium or Imperial council, and in consequence the new Senate had a double aspect. So long as there was a reigning Emperor, it acted as consistorium or advisory council of the sovran, but when there was an interval between two reigns, it resumed the independent authority which had lain in abeyance and performed functions which it had inherited from the early Senate.

But it was not only when the throne was vacant that it could perform such functions. The right of election might be exercised by the Senate and the army at any time. It was a principle of state-law in the Early Empire that the people which made the Emperor could also unmake him, and this principle continued in force under the autocracy. There was no formal process of deposing a sovran, but the members of the community had the means of dethroning him, if his government failed to give satisfaction, by proclaiming a new Emperor; and if anyone so proclaimed obtained sufficient support from the army, Senate, and people, the old Emperor was compelled to vacate the throne, retiring into a monastery, losing his eyesight, or suffering death, according to the circumstances of the situation or the temper of his supplanter; while the new Emperor was regarded as the legitimate monarch from the day on which he was proclaimed; the proclamation was taken as the legal expression of the general will. If he had not a sufficient following to render the proclamation effective and was suppressed, he was treated as a rebel; but during the struggle and before the catastrophe, the fact that a portion of the army had proclaimed him gave him a presumptive constitutional status, which the event might either confirm or annul. The method of deposition was in fact revolution, and we are accustomed to regard revolution as something essentially unconstitutional, an appeal from law to force; but under the Imperial system, it was not unconstitutional; the government was, to use an expression of Mommsen, "an autocracy tempered by the legal right of revolution".

Thus the sovranty of the Roman autocrat was delegated to him by the community, as represented by the Senate, and the army, and, we may add, the people of Constantinople.[6] The symbol of the sovranty thus delegated was the diadem, which was definitely introduced by Constantine. The Emperor wore other insignia, such as the purple robe and the red boots, but the diadem was preeminently the symbol and expression of the autocracy. The dress only represented the Imperator or commander-in-chief of the army, and no formalities were connected with its assumption. It was otherwise with the crown, which in the Persian Kingdom, from which it was borrowed, was placed on the king's head by the High-priest of the Magian religion. In theory, the Imperial crown should be imposed by a representative of those who conferred the sovran authority which it symbolised. And in the fourth century we find the Prefect, Sallustius Secundus, crowning Valentinian I, in whose election he had taken the most prominent part. But the Emperors seem to have felt some hesitation in thus receiving the diadem from the hands of a subject; and the selection of one magnate for this high office of conferring the symbol of sovranty was likely to cause enmity and jealousy. Yet a formality was considered necessary. In the fifth century, the difficulty was overcome in a clever and tactful way. The duty of coronation was assigned to the Patriarch of Constantinople. In discharging this office, the Patriarch was not envied by the secular magnates because he could not be their rival, and his ecclesiastical position relieved the Emperor from all embarrassment in receiving the diadem from a subject. There is some evidence, though it is not above suspicion, that this plan was adopted at the coronation of Marcian in A.D. 450, but it seems certain that his successor Leo was crowned by the Patriarch in A.D. 457. Henceforward this was the regular practice. In the thirteenth century we find Theodore II postponing his coronation until the Patriarchal throne, which happened to be vacant, was filled. But although it was the regular and desirable form of coronation, it was never regarded as indispensable for the autocrat's legitimate inauguration. The last of the East Roman Emperors, Constantine Palaeologus, was not crowned by the Patriarch; he was crowned by a layman.[7] This fact that coronation by the Patriarch was not constitutionally necessary, though it was the usual custom, is significant.

For it shows that the Patriarch, in performing the ceremony, was not representing the Church. It is possible that the idea of committing the office to him was suggested by the Persian coronations which were performed by the High-priest, but the significance was not the same. The chief of the Magians acted as the representative of the Persian religion, the Patriarch acted as the representative of the State.[8] For if he had specially represented the Church, it is clear that his co-operation could never have been dispensed with. In other words, no new constitutional theory or constitutional requirement was introduced by the assignment of the privilege of crowning Emperors to the Patriarch. It did not mean that the consent of the Church was formally necessary to the inauguration of the sovran.

I will make this point still more evident presently in connection with another important feature of the constitution to which we now come. If you look down the roll of Emperors, you will find that only a minority of them were actually elected in the ways I have described. In most cases, when an Emperor died, the throne was not vacant, for generally he had a younger colleague, who had already been invested with the Imperial dignity, so that no new election was necessary. This practice[9] by which a reigning Emperor could appoint his successor modified the elective principle. The Emperor used to devolve the succession upon his son, if he had one; so that son constantly succeeded father, and the history of the Roman Empire is marked by a series of hereditary dynasties. The constitution thus combined the elective and the hereditary principles; a device was found for securing the advantages of hereditary succession, and obviating its disadvantages by preserving the principle of election. The chief advantage of hereditary monarchy is that it avoids the danger of domestic troubles and civil war which are likely to occur when the throne is elective and there are two rival candidates. Its chief disadvantage is that the supreme power in the State will inevitably devolve sometimes upon a weak and incapable ruler. The result of the mixture of the two principles, the dynastic and the elective, was that there were far fewer incapable sovrans than if the dynastic succession had been exclusively valid, and fewer struggles for power than if every change of ruler had meant an election. It would be interesting to trace, if we had the material, how the inhabitants of the Empire became more and more attached to the idea of legitimacy—the idea that the children of an Emperor had a constitutional right to the supreme power. We can see at least that this feeling grew very strong under the long rule of the Macedonian dynasty; it is illustrated by the political rôle which the Empress Zoe, an utterly incompetent and depraved old woman, was allowed to play because she was the daughter of Constantine VIII.* But the fact remained that although a father invariably raised his eldest son, and sometimes younger sons too, to the rank of Augustus, the son became Emperor by virtue of his father's will and not by virtue of his birth. The Emperor was not in any way bound to devolve the succession upon his son.[10] Now what I ask you to observe is that when a reigning sovran created a second Emperor, whether his son or anyone else, there was no election. The Senate, the army, and the people expressed their joy and satisfaction, in the ceremonies which attended the creation, but the creation was entirely the act of the Emperor. The constitutional significance is evident. The autocratic powers conferred upon an Emperor by his election included the right of devolving the Imperial dignity upon others. It was part

[* v. infra references p. 112 note.]

of his sovranty to be able to create a colleague who was potentially another sovran.

This difference between the appointment of an Emperor when the throne is vacant and the appointment of an Emperor as colleague when the throne is occupied is clearly and significantly expressed by the difference between the coronation acts in the two cases. In the former case the act is performed by a representative of the electors, almost always the Patriarch; in the latter case it is regularly performed by the reigning Emperor. It is he who, possessing the undivided sovranty, confers the Imperial dignity and therefore with his own hands delivers its symbol. Sometimes indeed he commits the office of coronation to the Patriarch, but the Patriarch is then acting simply as his delegate.[11] This difference is a confirmation of the view that the Patriarch, in discharging the duty of coronation, acts as a representative of the electors, and not of the Church. For if the coronation had been conceived as a religious act, it must have been performed in the same way, in all cases, by the chief minister of the Church.

But now you may ask, is the term autocracy or the term monarchy strictly applicable to the Empire? Monarchy and autocracy mean the sovran rule of one man alone, but, as we have just seen, the Emperor generally had a colleague. Both in the early and in the later Empire, there were constantly two Emperors, sometimes more. In the tenth century, for instance, in the reign of Romanus I, there were as many as five— each of them an Augustus, each a Basileus.[12] This practice is derived from the original collegial character of the proconsular Imperium and the tribunician power, on which Augustus based his authority. But, although the Roman Imperium or Basileia was collegial, the sovranty was not divided. When there were two

Emperors only one exercised the sovran power and governed the State; his colleague was subordinate, and simply enjoyed the dignity and the expectation of succession. Though his name appeared in legislative acts and his effigy on coins, and though he shared in all the Imperial honours, he was a sleeping partner. With one exception, which I will notice presently, the only cases of Imperial colleagues exercising concurrent sovranty were in the period from Diocletian to the death of Julius Nepos, when the Empire was territorially divided. Diocletian and Maximian, for instance; the sons of Constantine, Arcadius, and Honorius; were severally monarchs in their own dominions. But except in the case of territorial division, the supreme power was exercised by one man, and monarchy is therefore a right description of the constitution. In the reign of Constantine IV, the soldiers demanded that the Emperor should crown his two brothers. "We believe in the Trinity", they cried, "and we would have three Emperors". But this must not be interpreted as a demand that each member of the desired Imperial trinity should exercise sovran authority. Such a joint sovranty was never tried except in one case, and a clear distinction was drawn between the Basileus who governed and the Basileus who did not govern. The exceptional case was the peculiar one of two Empresses, who ruled conjointly for a short time in the eleventh century. I will mention this case again, in a few minutes, when I come to speak of the position of Empresses.

And here I must dwell for a moment on the name *Basileus* and another Greek name *Autokrator*, which were employed to designate the Emperor. In the early Empire, Basileus was used in the East and especially in Egypt, where Augustus was regarded as the successor of the Ptolemies, but it was not used officially by the Emperors; it was not the Greek for Imperator. The Greek word adopted to translate Imperator was Autokrator, and this is the term always used in Imperial Greek inscriptions. By the fourth century Basileus had come into universal use in the Greek-speaking parts of the Empire; it was the regular term used by Greek writers; but it was not yet accepted as an official title. Nor was it adopted officially till the seventh century in the reign of Heraclius. It has been pointed out by Bréhier[13] that the earliest official act in which an Emperor entitles himself Basileus is a law of Heraclius of the year 629. In the earlier diplomas of his reign he uses the old traditional form Autokrator. Bréhier, however, has failed to see the reason of this change of style, but the significant date A.D. 629 supplies the explanation. In that year Heraclius completed the conquest of Persia. Now, the Persian king was the only foreign monarch to whom the Roman Emperors conceded the title Basileus; except the Abyssinian king, who hardly counted. So long as there was a great independent Basileus outside the Roman Empire, the Emperors refrained from adopting a title which would be shared by another monarch. But as soon as that monarch was reduced to the condition of a dependent vassal and there was no longer a concurrence, the Emperor signified the event by assuming officially the title which had for several centuries been applied to him unofficially. The Empire was extremely conservative in forms and usages; changes were slow in official documents, they were slower still in the coinage. It is not till more than a century later that Basileus begins to be adopted by the mint. By this change Basileus became the official equivalent of Imperator; it took the place of Autokrator; and it was now possible for Autokrator to come into its own and express its full etymological significance. Thus we find a strongly marked tendency in later times to apply the term specially to the Basileus who was the actual ruler. Though he and his colleague might be acclaimed jointly as Autokrators; yet Autokrator is distinctly used to express the plenitude of despotic power which was exercised by the senior Emperor alone.[14] Thus we may say that in early times Basileus was the pregnant title which expressed that full monarchical authority which the system of Augustus aimed at disguising, and Autokrator was simply the equivalent of the republican title Imperator; while in later times the rôles of the two titles were reversed, and Autokrator became the pregnant title, expressing the fulness of authority which the familiar Basileus no longer emphasised.

Before we leave this part of our subject, a word must be said about the rights of women to exercise autocracy. From the foundation of the Empire the title of Augusta had been conferred on the wives of Emperors, and we find in early times the mothers of minors, like Agrippina and Julia Domna, exercising political power. But this power was always exercised in the name of their sons. At the beginning of the fifth century the Augusta Pulcheria presides over the government which acted for her brother Theodosius II while he was a minor. On his death without children, it is recognised that although she cannot govern alone, she nevertheless has a right to have a voice in the election of a new Emperor, and the situation is met by her nominal marriage with Marcian. Similarly, forty years later, when Zeno dies without a son, his wife, the Augusta Ariadne, has, by general consent, the decisive voice in selecting her husband's successor; her choice falls on Anastasius, and he is elected. But it is not she who confers the Imperial authority on Anastasius, it is the Senate and army, who elect him, in accordance with her wishes. In the following century, the political importance of Empresses is augmented by the exceptional positions occupied by Theodora the consort of Justinian, and Sophia the consort of Justin II. But so far, although an Empress may act as regent for a minor,[15] may intervene in an Imperial election, may receive honours suggesting that she is her husband's colleague rather than consort, she never exercises independent sovran power, she is never, in the later sense of the word, an Autokrator. Passing on to the close of the eighth century, we come to the Empress Irene, the Athenian lady who is famous as the first restorer of Image-worship. When her husband died, her son Constantine was too young to rule, and she governed in the same way as Pulcheria had governed for Theodosius. When Constantine was old enough to govern himself, Irene was unwilling to retire into the background, and although the son succeeded in holding the power in his own hands for some years, the mother was continually intriguing against him. The struggle ended in her triumph. She caused her son to be blinded, and five years she reigned alone with full sovran powers as Autokrator. This was a considerable constitutional innovation, and the official style of her diplomas illustrates, in an interesting way, that it was felt as such. She was, of course, always spoken of as the Empress, but in her official acts she is styled not "Irene the Empress" but "Irene the Emperor" (*Basileus*).[16] It was felt that only an Emperor could legislate, and so the legal fiction of her masculinity was adopted.

It was said in Western Europe, for the purpose of justifying the Imperial claim of Charles the Great, that the sovranty of the Empire could not devolve on a woman, and that Irene's tenure of power was really an interregnum; but the Byzantines never admitted this constitutional doctrine. Nevertheless they had a strong objection to the *régime* of women, except in the capacity of regents, and the precedent established by Irene was repeated only in the case of Zoe and Theodora, the two nieces of Basil II. We find each of these ladies exercising the sovran authority alone for brief periods, and we also find them ruling together. This is the instance, which I mentioned already, of the experiment of government by two autocrats. Their joint rule might have been protracted, if they had been in harmony, but Zoe was extremely jealous of Theodora, and in order to oust her she took a husband, who immediately assumed the autocratic authority, and Zoe fell back into the subordinate position of a consort.*

We may now pass to the consideration of the nature and amplitude of the Imperial supremacy. The act of proclamation conferred his sovran powers upon the Emperor. In early days the Imperial powers were defined explicitly by a law, the *lex de imperio*. We have the text of the law which was passed for Vespasian. But the practice of passing it anew on the accession of a new Emperor was discontinued, and under the autocracy, when all the legislative, judicial and executive powers were vested in the autocrat, there was no reason to define what those powers were. In the sixth century, however, in the legislation of Justinian, it is recognised that by the *lex de imperio* the people transferred its sovranty to the Emperor. In the eighth century we may be pretty sure that no one from the Emperor downwards had ever heard of the *lex de imperio*.[17] But although there was no constitution of this kind defining or limiting the monarch's functions, I will proceed to show that his power, legally unlimited, was subject to limitations which must be described as constitutional.

[* *v.* for the joint rule *pp.* 168–75, and for Theodora's sole rule *pp.* 198–200.]

For his legislative and administrative acts, the monarch was responsible to none, except to Heaven; there was no organ in the state that had a right to control him; so that his government answers to our definition of autocracy. But when the monarch is appointed by any body or bodies in the state, the electors can impose conditions on him at the time of election, and thus there is the possibility of limiting his power. In other words, an elective autocracy, like the Roman Empire, is liable to the imposition of limitations. The case of the Emperor Anastasius I is in point. The Senate required from him an oath that he would administer the Empire conscientiously and not visit offences upon anyone with whom he had had a quarrel. This exhibits the principle, which was constantly and chiefly applied for the purpose of preventing a new Emperor from making ecclesiastical innovations.

It was a recognised condition of eligibility to the throne that the candidate should be a Christian, and an orthodox Christian. The latest pagan Emperor was Julian. After him it would have been virtually impossible for a pagan to rule at Constantinople. After the Council of Constantinople in A.D. 381, which crushed the Arian heresies, it would have been impossible for an Arian to wear the diadem. This was expressly recognised in the situation which ensued on the death of Theodosius II. The most prominent man at the moment was Aspar, but he was an Arian, and on that account alone his elevation was considered out of the question. Up to that period it may be said that such conditions of faith were political rather than constitutional; but when the coronation ceremony was attended with religious forms, we may say that Christianity was coming to be considered a constitutional condition of eligibility. By religious forms, I do not mean the part which the Patriarch played in the act of coronation, which, as we have seen, had no ecclesiastical significance, but other parts of the ceremony, such as prayers, which were introduced in the fifth century. It was at the accession of Anastasius I that a religious declaration was first required from an Emperor. Anastasius was with good reason suspected of heterodoxy; he was in fact a monophysite. He was not asked to make any personal confession of faith, but at the Patriarch's demand, he signed a written oath that he would maintain the existing ecclesiastical settlement unimpaired and introduce no novelty in the Church. We are ignorant whether such a written declaration was formally required at all subsequent elections; probably not; but it was, we know, imposed in a number of cases where there was reason to suspect a new Emperor of heretical tendencies. Ultimately, we cannot say at what time, this practice crystallised into the shape of a regular coronation oath, in which the monarch confesses and confirms the decrees of the Seven Ecumenical Councils and of the local synods, and the privileges of the Church, and vows to be a mild ruler and to abstain as far as possible from punishments of death and mutilation.[18]

The fact that such capitulations could be and were imposed at the time of election, even though the Emperor's obligation to submit to them was moral rather than legal, means that the autocracy was subject to limitations and was limited. But apart from such definite capitulations, the monarch's power was restricted by unwritten principles of government which bound him as much as the unwritten part of the English constitution binds our king and government. The autocrat was the supreme legislator; personally he was above the laws, *solutus legibus*;[19] there was no tribunal before which he could be summoned; but he was bound by the principles and the forms of the law which was the great glory of Roman civilisation.[20] He could modify laws, he could make new laws; but no Emperor ever questioned the obligation of conforming his acts to the law or presumed to assert that he could set it aside. Although theoretically above the law, he was at the same time bound by it, *alligatus legibus*, as Theodosius II expressly acknowledges.[21] Basil I, in a legal handbook, explicitly affirms the obligation of the Emperor to maintain not only the Scriptures and the canons of the Seven Councils, but also the Roman laws. And the laws embraced the institutions. Though changing circumstances led to adaptations and alterations, the Byzantine conservatism, which is almost proverbial and is often exaggerated, attests the strength of the unwritten limitations which always restrained the Imperial autocracy.

The Senate, too, though it had no share in the sovranty, might operate as a check on the sovran's actions. For there were various political matters which the Emperor was bound by custom to lay before it. We have not the material for enumerating what those matters were, but among the most important were questions of peace and war and the conclusion of treaties. The Senate would obediently concur in the views of a strong sovran, and probably its meetings were generally of a purely formal nature, but it is significant that in the case of a weak Emperor (Michael I) we find the Senate opposing the autocrat's wishes and the autocrat bowing to its opinion.[22]

It is implied in what I have said that the Church represented a limit on the Emperor's power. From the ninth century onward, the Decrees of the Seven Councils were an unalterable law which no Emperor could touch.[23] At the same time, the relation of the State to the Church, of which I must now speak, illustrates the amplitude of his power. The Byzantine Church is the most important example in history of a State-Church.

Its head was the Emperor. He was considered the delegate of God in a sphere which included the ecclesiastical as well as the secular order. The Patriarch of Constantinople was his minister of the department of religion, and though the usual forms of episcopal election were observed, was virtually appointed by him. It was the Emperor who convoked the Ecumenical Councils, and it was the Emperor who presided at them either in person or, if he did not care to suffer the boredom of theological debates, represented by some of his secular ministers.[24] Canonical decrees passed at Councils did not become obligatory till they were confirmed by the Emperor; and the Emperors issued edicts and laws relating to purely ecclesiastical affairs, quite independently of Councils. The Patriarch Menas asserted in the reign of Justinian that nothing should be done in the Church contrary to the Emperor's will, and Justinian, who was the incarnation of sacerdotal monarchy, was acclaimed as High-priest Basileus ($\dot{a}\rho\chi\iota\epsilon\rho\epsilon\dot{v}s$ $\beta a\sigma\iota\lambda\epsilon\dot{v}s$). It is true that the voices of prominent ecclesiastics were raised from time to time protesting that ecclesiastical matters lay outside the domain of secular authority and advocating the complete freedom of the Church. But this idea, of which Theodore of Studion was the latest champion, never gained ground; it was definitely defeated in the ninth century, and the Emperor continued to hold the position of a Christian caliph. Thus the theory of State and Church in the Eastern Empire is conspicuously contrasted with the theory which in Western Europe was realised under Innocent III. In both cases Church and State are indivisible, but in the West the Church is the State, whereas in the East it is a department which the Emperor directs. In the West we have a theocracy; the Church represented by the Pope claims to possess the supreme authority in temporal as

well as spiritual affairs. In the East relations are reversed; instead of a theocracy, we have what has been
called caesaropapism. A papalist writer, who endeavours
to demonstrate the Pope's universal supremacy, remarks that in point of jurisdiction a layman might be
Pope; all the powers and rights of a Pope, in spiritual as
well as secular affairs, would be conferred upon him by
election.[25] This hypothesis of Agostino Trionfo was
realised in the Eastern Empire.

There were occasional struggles between the Emperor
and the Patriarch, usually caused by an attempt on the
Emperor's part to introduce, for political reasons, some
new doctrine which the Patriarch considered inconsistent with the Decrees of the Councils or the Scriptures.
In such cases the Patriarch was defending the constitution against innovation; he was not disputing the Emperor's position as head of the Church. And in such cases
the usual result was that the Patriarch either yielded or
was deposed, the Emperor had his way, and the orthodox doctrine was not reinstated until another Emperor
reversed the acts of his predecessor. Some Patriarchs
might suggest that the Emperor, not being an expert in
theology, ought not to interfere in matters of doctrine;
but the normal relations were generally accepted as
fundamental and constitutional.

The Patriarch had indeed one weapon which he might
use against his sovran—the weapon of excommunication.
He might refuse, and direct his clergy to refuse, to communicate with the Emperor. It was a weapon to which
recourse was seldom taken. Another means of exerting
power which the Patriarch possessed was due to the part
which he took in the coronation. He might make terms
with the new Emperor before he crowned him. Thus
the Patriarch Polyeuktos forced John Tzimiskes to consent to abrogate a law which required the Imperial

approbation of candidates for ecclesiastical offices before they were elected.

The constitutional theory which I have delineated is implied in the actual usages from which I have drawn it; but it was never formulated. Constitutional questions did not arise, and no lawyer or historian expounded the basis or the limits of the sovran power. In fact, the constitution was not differentiated in men's consciousness from the whole body of laws and institutions. They did not analyse the assumptions implied in their practice, and the only idea they entertained, which can be described as a constitutional theory, does not agree, though it may be conciliated, with the theory that I have sketched. If you had asked a Byzantine Emperor what was the basis of his autocracy and by what right he exercised it, he would not have told you that it had been committed to him by the Senate, the army, or the people; he would have said that he derived his sovranty directly from God. I could produce a great deal of evidence to illustrate this view, but it will be enough to refer to the words of the Emperor Basil I in his Advice to his son Leo: "You received the Empire from God"; "You received the crown from God by my hand".[26] Such a doctrine of the monarch's divine right naturally tended to reflect a new significance on the part which the Patriarch played in the Emperor's inauguration. But it found an explicit symbolic expression in the new custom of unction, which perhaps was practised (though opinions differ on this point)[27] as early as the ninth century. In crowning, the Patriarch expressed the will of the State; in anointing, the will of the Deity. This theory, logically developed, implies the view which Dante expresses in his *De Monarchia*, that the Electors when they choose the Emperor are merely voicing the choice of the Deity. It was quite in accordance with the prevailing religious sentiments; it enhanced the Emperor's authority by representing that authority as a divine gift, and perhaps it sometimes enhanced his sense of responsibility. But although calculated to place the sovran above criticism, this theory of divine right did not affect the actual working of the constitutional tradition which determined the appointment of Emperors and the limitations of their power. Its chief interest lies in its relation to the political theories which were evolved in the Middle Ages in Western Europe. It has been observed by Mr Bryce,[28] as a striking contrast between the Eastern and Western Empires, that, while the West was fertile in conceptions and theories, displaying abundant wealth of creative imagination, in the East men did not trouble themselves to theorise about the Empire at all. The inspiration, in the West, came in the first place from the fact that the Holy Roman Empire was always an ideal, never fully realised, "a dream" (to use Mr Bryce's words), "half theology and half poetry". The Eastern Roman Empire, on the other hand, was always an actual fact, adequate to its own conception; there it was—there was no mistake about its being here and now; there was much in it to cause pride, there was nothing to stir imagination. In the second place, there was no need, in the Eastern Empire, to evolve theories, as nothing was in dispute. In the West a great constitutional question arose, of far-reaching practical importance, touching the relations of the two rival authorities, the Pope and the Emperor. It was to solve the political problem set by their rival pretensions that Dante wrote his *De Monarchia*, William of Ockham his *Dialogue*, Marsilius of Padua his *Defensor pacis*. In the East no such problem arose, inasmuch as the Emperor was recognised as the head of the Church, and there was therefore no stimulus to evolve political theories. Yet if a similar problem or need had arisen, I cannot help thinking that the medieval Greeks, though they were incapable of producing a Dante, would have proved themselves not less ingenious than Western thinkers in political speculation. But it is instructive to observe that the claim of the Eastern Emperor to derive his sovranty directly from God is the same theory of Divine Right which was asserted by the Western Imperialist writers. Dante affirmed this theory most forcibly; William of Ockham and Marsilius affirmed it too, but they tempered it by the view that the Empire was originally derived from the people, thus combining, as it were, the Divine pretensions of the later autocrats of Constantinople with the democratic origin of sovranty which is asserted in the lawbooks of Justinian.

I have endeavoured to show how the autocracy of the later Roman Empire was a limited autocracy. Every autocracy, every government, has of course natural limitations. The action of the monarch is limited by public opinion; there will always be some point beyond which he is afraid to venture in defying public opinion. It is also limited by the fact that he has to employ human instruments, and their personal views and qualities may modify or compromise or thwart the execution of his will. Further, if he rules over a highly organised society, he may be restrained from sweeping measures by the knowledge that such changes will involve other consequences which he does not desire.[29] These natural limitations affect all autocracies, all governments, in various modes and degrees. But apart from them, the Roman autocracy had definite restrictions which must be described as constitutional.[30] In what is miscalled a limited monarchy, the king may have legal rights which it would be unconstitutional to exercise. The action of the English crown, for instance, is restricted not merely by the statutory limits, such as are imposed on it by the Bill of Rights or the Act of Settlement, but by unwritten constitutional usage, which is obligatory. In the same way the action of the Roman autocrat was limited by a tradition and usage which were felt by him and by the community to be absolutely binding. The sanctions in the two cases are different. An English king is hindered from exceeding the constitutional bounds of his authority by the power which Parliament possesses of bringing the government to a standstill, as it can do by refusing to grant supplies or to pass the Mutiny Act. The more powerful Roman monarch was forced to conform to the institutions, customs, and traditions of his society by the more drastic sanction of deposition. The Russian autocrat, Peter the Great, abolished the Patriarchate of Moscow; it would have been an impossibility for the Roman Emperor to abolish the Patriarchate of Constantinople or to introduce any serious change in the organisation of the Church. The integrity of the Church was indeed secured against him not merely by this moral force, but by capitulations which, in consequence of the elective character of the monarchy, he could be obliged to swear to at his accession and which were finally embodied in a coronation oath. Here there was a religious sanction superadded.

The limitations tended to maintain the conservative character for which Byzantium is often reproached, and were in fact one of the results of that conservatism. They were efficacious, because the autocrat himself was usually imbued deeply with this conservative spirit, being a child of his age and civilisation; whilst the complex and elaborate machinery, furnishing the channels through which he had to act, was a powerful check on his freedom. It must, I think, be admitted that the autocracy of the Eastern Empire suited the given conditions, and probably worked better than any other system that could have been devised. The government was not arbitrary, and the evils from which the subjects of the Empire suffered were due (apart from the calamities of war) to economic ignorance and bad finance, such as prevailed everywhere alike in the ancient and the middle ages, and would have pressed as heavily under any other form of government. The freedom and absence of formality in the method of appointing the sovran made it possible to meet different situations in different ways; and if we examine the roll of Emperors from Constantine the Great in the fourth to Manuel Comnenus in the twelfth century, we must admit that the constitution secured, with a few dark but short intervals, a succession of able and hard-working rulers such as cannot, I think, be paralleled in the annals of any other state during so long a period.

NOTES

1 This differs somewhat from Sidgwick's definition, in *Development of European Polity*, p. 10: "What is meant by calling him [an Absolute Monarch] 'absolute' is that there is no established constitutional authority—no human authority that his subjects habitually obey as much as they obey him—which can legitimately resist him or call him to account".

2 *Lectures on Jurisprudence*, I, 241 (ed. 1885).

3 The *Roman* Senate however seems to have retained some nominal sovranty; for under the *régime* of Theodoric it had the power, like the Emperor, *constituere leges* (a power which Theodoric did not possess). Cp. Cassiodorus, *Variae*, 6, 4, § 1, 2 (p. 177, ed. Mommsen).

4 This (ἀναγόρευσις) is the technical word applied to the whole procedure of inauguration.

5 In the early Empire, the Roman people took the initiative in proclaiming Pertinax; they forced the Praetorians to proclaim him; but undoubtedly it was the proclamation of the latter that conferred the Imperium. In the later Empire we find a section of the people of Constantinople taking the initiative in proclaiming the

nephews of Anastasius, on the occasion of the Nika revolt against Justinian.

6 Cp. for instance Leo Diaconus, II, 12, where Polyeuktos says that the sons of Romanus II were proclaimed Emperors "by us (the Senate) and the whole people".

7 Nicephorus Bryennius, who was proclaimed Emperor in the reign of Michael VII (11th cent.) and was suppressed, placed the diadem on his own head, Anna Comnena, *Alexiad*, I, 4.

8 This is brought out by W. Sickel in his important article "Das byzantinische Krönungsrecht bis zum 10 Jahrhundert", in the *Byzantinische Zeitschrift*, VII, 511 *sqq.* (1898), to which I must acknowledge my obligations. For the details of the coronation ceremonies see F. E. Brightman's article in the *Journal of Theological Studies*, II, 359 *sqq.* (1901).

9 It was introduced by the Augustus in the form of the co-regency, for a full discussion of which see Mommsen, *Staatsrecht*, II, 1145 *sqq.* (ed. 3).

In the Hellenistic kingdoms (Macedonia, Syria, Egypt) there is material for instructive comparisons in regard to the combination of the elective and dynastic principles, and co-regencies.

10 This principle was asserted by Andronicus II who endeavoured to exclude his grandson (Andronicus III) from the throne. The civil wars which resulted represent, from the constitutional point of view, a struggle between this principle and the idea of legitimacy to which the Byzantines had become strongly attached.

11 The regular form of phrase is ἔστεψε διὰ τοῦ Πατριάρχου (cp. Theophanes, 417_{25}, 426_{27}, 480_{11}, 494_{26}). More explicitly Kedrenos, II, 296; Romanus I was crowned by the Patriarch ἐπιτροπῇ τοῦ βασιλέως Κωνσταντίνου (who was a minor). In the normal ceremony of crowning a colleague, described in Constantine Porph. *De Cer.* I, 38, the Patriarch hands the crown to the Emperor, who places it on the new Emperor's head (p. 194).

12 The colleague is often designated as ὁ δεύτερος βασιλεύς, or as συμβασιλεύς (and we may suppose that the description of Otto II as *co-imperator* of his father was borrowed from this); if a child, he is distinguished as "the little Emperor" (ὁ μικρὸς βασιλεύς), and this, no doubt, explains why Theodosius II was ὁ μικρός. The description, applied to him when a minor, survived his boyhood, because it served to distinguish him from his grandfather and namesake, Theodosius the Great. In one case, we find the term *rex* strangely applied to a second Emperor. It occurs on a bronze coin of the year 866-7, in which Basil I was colleague of Michael III.

The obverse has *Mihael imperat(or)*, the reverse *Basilius rex* (Wroth, *Catalogue of the Imperial Byzantine Coins of the British Museum*, II, 432). I do not know how to explain this eccentricity which is contrary to all the principles of the Roman Imperium. The western title *Romanorum rex*, which in the eleventh century began to be assumed by Western Emperors before they were crowned at Rome and was afterwards appropriated to their successors, cannot be compared.

13 *Byzantinische Zeitschrift*, XV, 151 *sqq.* (1906).

14 It came into official use in the eleventh century, as a reinforcement of Basileus (β. καὶ αὐτ.), and in Latin diplomas we find it translated by *moderator*, Basileus by *Imperator*. A colleague could only use the title Autokrator by special permission of the senior Emperor (Codinus, *De Officiis*, c. 17, pp. 86, 87, ed. Bonn). But the distinction was drawn as early as the ninth century, for in Philotheos (A.D. 900), *Kletorologion* (*apud* Const. Porph.' *De Cerimoniis*, p. 712), we find ὁ αὐτοκράτωρ βασιλεύς explicitly contrasted with ὁ δεύτερος βασιλεύς.

15 If an Emperor foresaw his approaching death and his colleague was a minor, he could make arrangements for the regency in his will. This was done, *e.g.* by Theophilus and by Alexander.

16 Zacharia von Lingenthal, *Jus Graeco-romanum*, III, 55 (Εἰρήνη πιστὸς βασιλεύς). The point is brought out in the *Chronicle* of Theophanes (p. 466, l. 25, ed. De Boor): Constantine VI causes the Armeniac soldiers to swear not to accept his mother Irene εἰς βασιλέα. The later force of the term αὐτοκράτωρ comes out in the same passage (l. 15).

17 In this connexion, however, may be noted the remarkable notion of establishing a democracy, attributed to the Emperor Stauracius (A.D. 811) by the contemporary chronicler Theophanes (ed. De Boor, p. 492). He was on his deathbed at the time and wished to be succeeded by his wife, the Athenian Theophano (a relative of Irene) as sovran Empress. He threatened democracy as an alternative. We should like to know what his idea of a democracy was.

18 Codinus, *De Officiis*, c. 17.

19 *Digest*, I, 3, 31; *Basilica*, II, 6, 1.

20 *Basilica*, II, 6, 9, καὶ κατὰ βασιλέως οἱ γενικοὶ κρατείτωσαν νόμοι καὶ πᾶσα παράνομος ἐκβαλλέσθω ἀντιγραφή. The meaning of *lex generalis* (briefly, an edict promulgated as applicable to the whole Empire) is explained *ib.* 8, which is based on *Cod. Just.* I, 14, 3. The Emperor could not enact a special constitution—applicable to a section, district, or town—which was contrary to the provisions of a *lex generalis*.

21 *Cod. Just.* I, 14, 4, digna vox maiestate regnantis legibus alligatum se principem profiteri: adeo de auctoritate iuris nostra pendet auctoritas.

22 The functions of the Senate seem to have closely resembled those of the Synedrion in the Hellenistic kingdoms. Compare the account of a meeting of the Synedrion of Antiochus in Polybius, v, 41–42. It may be noticed that during the minority after the death of Romanus II, it is the Senate that appoints Nicephorus II to the supreme command of the Asiatic troops (Leo Diaconus, II, 12). The importance of the Senate is illustrated by the political measure of Constantine X who "democratised" it: see Psellos, *Historia*, p. 238 (ed. Sathas, 1899); C. Neumann, *Die Weltstellung des byzantinischen Reiches vor den Kreuzzügen*, p. 79.

23 This principle had been already laid down by Justinian in regard to the first four Councils, the decrees of which he places on the same level as Holy Scripture: *Nov.* 151, α′, ed. Zachariä, II, p. 267.

24 The best general account of the relation of State and Church in Byzantium will be found in the late Professor Gelzer's article in the *Historische Zeitschrift*, N.F. vol. L, 193 *sqq.* (1901). At the Seventh Ecumenical Council (A.D. 787) the presidency was committed to the Patriarch Tarasios, evidently because he had been a layman and minister, not (like most of his predecessors) a monk.

25 Augustinus Triumphus, *Summa de potestate Ecclesiastica*, I, 1, p. 2, ed. 1584 (Rome): si quis eligatur in Papam nullum ordinem habens, erit verus Papa et habebit omnem potestatem iurisdictionis in spiritualibus et temporalibus et tamen nullam habebit potestatem ordinis.

26 *Paraenesis ad Leonem*, in Migne, *P. G.* CVII, pp. xxv, xxxii.

27 See Photius, in Migne, *P. G.* CII, 765 and 573. Cp. Sickel, *op. cit.* 547–8, and on the other hand Brightman, *op. cit.* 383–5.

28 *The Holy Roman Empire* (last ed. 1904), 343 *sqq.*

29 This is noted by Sidgwick, *Development of European Polity*, p. 10.

30 For an analysis of the conception of *unconstitutional* as distinguished from *illegal* see Austin, *Jurisprudence*, I, 265 *sqq.* (ed. 1885).

ROMAN EMPERORS FROM BASIL II TO ISAAC KOMNÊNOS*

PART I

The eleventh century is the turning point in the Middle
Ages; in it new currents are beginning to flow and old
currents are beginning to ebb. It was in the eleventh
century that Normans founded their kingdom in
southern Europe and conquered England; it was in the
eleventh century that Gregory VII introduced a new
spirit into western Christendom; it was in the eleventh
century that the crusade movement began. The mere
mention of the Crusades, Gregory VII, and the Normans
sufficiently indicates the new currents that flowed in
western Europe. A change was taking place at the same
time in the Eastern Roman Empire, a change which
implied and led to its decline; and if we do not mis-
understand the system of medieval Europe, unduly
isolating the Byzantine world from the occidental kingdoms as if they did not act and react upon one another,
we must assume that the new tide in the West was
causally, or rather reciprocally—for reciprocity is
generally the right category in history—connected with
the ebb in the East. The most obvious indication of this
connection is the commercial change which resulted in
the transference of trade from the Greeks, who had
hitherto almost monopolised it, to the rising republics
of Italy. The chief external event in the Eastern Empire
was the succession of the house of Komnênos to the
house of Basil the Macedonian, whose descendants had
worn the purple for two centuries. This change of

[* I.e. A.D. 976–1057. Reprinted from *English Historical Review*, vol. IV,
part I, pp. 41–64, part II, pp. 251–85 (1889).]

dynasty meant the triumph and preponderance of the wealthy aristocratic families of Asia Minor; it was the outward sign of a great inward change which had been taking place since the reign of Basil II. The final separation of the Greek and Latin churches occurred at this period (1054); but as they were really alienated long before, this is an event of only second-rate importance. Of much more interest are the projects of the patriarch Kêrularios to make the Church independent of the State, in fact to do what Hildebrand did in the West. Another movement of the time which deserves attention is the revival of literature under the auspices of Michael Psellos, who reclaimed Greek prose from the barbarism into which it was falling.

There is a plentiful lack of contemporary authority for the last years of the Macedonian dynasty. For a few events at the beginning of the reign of Basil II (976–1025) we have a page or two of a contemporary author, Leo Diakonos; but for the rest of his long reign and for that of his brother Constantine VIII we have only the later chronographers, Kedrênos and Zônaras. For the following Emperors, until the accession of Isaac Komnênos, Finlay's only Greek sources were Kedrênos and Zônaras, for we need hardly take into account such writers as Glykas or Manassês. But since Finlay wrote his history the labours of M. Constantine Sathas have rendered a new source accessible, the contemporary history of Michael Psellos.[1] This history was so diligently utilised by Zônaras that the original does not supply us with any new facts of great importance; but nevertheless it is invaluable, as we learn a large number of inter-

[1] *Bibliotheca Græca Medii Ævi*; vol. IV, *Pselli Historia Byzantina et alia opuscula* (1874). The opuscula are three Ἐπιτάφιοι λόγοι, on Michael Kêrularios, Constantine Leichudês, and Joannes Xiphilinos, three personages of whom we shall have more to say. Vol. V of this series contains other "words" of Psellos, including a large collection of letters.

esting details, not to mention that the work of a contemporary has always a flavour which no compilation
can have. There may be sufficient foundation for the
paradoxical statement of M. Amédée Thierry that details are the soul of history, to warrant us in collecting
and recording the new points which may be gleaned
from Psellos. Accordingly, as the subject has not been
worked up, I propose to give a sketch of Byzantine
history from Basil II to the deposition of Michael VI,
confining myself almost entirely to what Psellos has recorded, and consequently omitting altogether some important wars of which Finlay, reproducing Kedrênos
and Zônaras, has given so full an account, that a repetition here seems unnecessary. It will be advisable at the
outset to say something more of Psellos and the nature
of his history, and also to notice briefly our other
authorities.

1. *Sources.* The history of Psellos is a Ἑκατονταετηρίς;
it embraces a period of one hundred years, beginning
with the accession of Basil II (976) and ending with the
accession of Nikêphoros Botaneiatês (1077). For the
first three reigns (of Basil, Constantine, and Rômanos)
it is a short and meagre record of things which he had
not witnessed, though he had doubtless heard many facts
on first-hand authority, but with the accession of
Michael IV in 1034 it becomes more complete and
detailed, and at the same time assumes the value of
contemporary history. In order to understand and
appreciate its value we must give a short outline of
the author's career.[1]

He was born in 1018, and thus at the accession of

[1] M. Sathas has prefaced his edition with a full biographical account
of Psellos. His original name was Constantine; he was renamed Michael
when he took the monastic vows. How little is generally known of
Psellos and his works is apparent in the short notice in the *Encyclopædia
Britannica*.

Michael the Paphlagonian was sixteen years old. He had seen the Emperor Rômanos in a public procession not long before his death. Thus for the reign of Rômanos he may be considered a contemporary writer in the same sense that Cicero's authority might be called contemporary for the history of Livius Drusus. His father's fathers had been consuls and patricians; his mother was of good family and herself a clever woman who used to assist her son, when a boy, in preparing his lessons. He studied rhetoric and philosophy, giving the preference to the latter, and in his studies "chummed" with an older friend, Joannês Xiphilinos, whom he assisted in philosophy and in return received help in jurisprudence. Under Michael IV he was appointed judge at Philadelphia, and in the short reign of Michael V held the post of under-secretary ($\dot{v}\pi o\gamma\rho a\mu\mu a\tau\epsilon\dot{v}\varsigma$), through the influence probably of his friend Constantine Leichudês, whom that Emperor appointed chief minister. Leichudês did not fall with his master; Constantine IX retained his services, and Psellos won the marked affection of that impressionable sovran and became his trusted confidant, holding the post of secretary. Constantine was induced to refound, in a sort of manner, the university of Constantinople, and Psellos filled the chair of philosophy. Towards the end of this reign Leichudês was deposed, and Psellos, fearing, as he tells us, the weathercock nature of his master, determined to embrace the spiritual life and retired to a monastery, in spite of the Emperor's expressed wishes. Theodôra recalled him to court after Constantine's death, and he took part in the administration of Michael VI. He was one of the embassy sent by that monarch with proposals to Isaac Komnênos, under whose sovranty he succeeded Leichudês as Prime Minister. We need not touch on his political conduct in the following reigns, his education of Michael VII, and his relations to Rômanos Diogenês, as this paper will not go further than the accession of Isaac.

From this brief sketch we may see that the memoirs of Psellos as a distinguished contemporary who was initiated in the arcana (ἀπόρρητα) of political events are of the highest value. Through his artificial, often irritatingly artificial, rhetorical style,[1] his descriptions of the Emperors and Empresses whom he knew give an impression of reality and life. He presents us with pictures of men and women of the time more vivid than we could ever get from writers like Zônaras. He had seen Rômanos like a living corpse, when a boy of sixteen; he had seen George Maniakês, standing ten feet high, and looked up at him as at a pillar or a mountain; he had stood by the side of Constantine Monomachos when he witnessed the seafight with the Russians; he had stood by his side when an arrow narrowly missed him during the siege of Tornikios; he knew by personal experience that the queen Sklêraina was an excellent listener; he was an intimate friend of the first minister Leichudês and the great patriarch Michael Kêrularios; he was first minister himself.

In the rather pretentious preface to his chronography Joannês Skylitzês, whom George Kedrênos copies, enumerates some of his predecessors in the field of history. He remarks of Psellos and others that they do not give accurate details,, but "merely record a list of the Emperors, stating who succeeded whom, and nothing more".[2] In regard to Psellos this criticism is in one way

---

[1] As examples I may quote ὡς εὐθὺς τὸ κράτος διαδεξόμενον τοῦ κρατοῦντος τῷ κρατήσαντι πάθει καταναλωθέντος, where κρατήσαντι is chosen as a verbal antithesis to κράτος ἀκρατοῦντος (p. 61). Again (p. 131), ὁ βασιλεὺς Βασίλειος ἐν τοῖς βασιλείοις ἀπεθησαύρισε.

[2] καὶ ἄλλοι ἐπεχείρησαν οἷον ὁ Σικελιώτης καὶ ὁ ὑπέρτιμος Ψελλὸς καὶ ἕτεροι σὺν τούτοις· ἀλλὰ τῆς ἀκριβείας ἀποπεπτώκασιν ἀπαρίθμησιν μόνην

entirely false; in another way it expresses in exaggerated terms a certain truth. The events which Psellos does describe he describes in far more elaborate detail than Kedrênos himself, who gives us the dry bones; in this respect the criticism is false. But, on the other hand, many events of importance are not even mentioned by Psellos, as he tells us plainly himself; and so far the criticism has an element of truth. Skylitzês prides himself on giving us all, even the smallest, bones; Psellos gives us a selection of bones and flesh together. Psellos is quite aware of this, as we may see from a passage in which he states the scope and nature of his history. He does not attempt to describe, he says, all events in order and each in detail from its beginning to its conclusion, nor to enumerate every military engagement however trifling, and the other things which *accurate* historians describe.[1] He aims at a succinct relation, not at an ambitious history; and he therefore omits many things worthy of record, and, instead of dividing his history chronologically, simply dictates the most critical events and what most impressed itself on his recollection. "I do not note in detail every event, for it is my design to follow a middle course between the ancient historians of old Rome on the one hand, and our modern chronographers on the other, avoiding the roundabout flow of the former and not imitating the bald conciseness of the latter, so that my narration may neither weary the reader nor omit capital events".

ποιησάμενοι τῶν βασιλέων καὶ διδάξαντες τίς μετὰ τίνα γέγονεν ἐγκρατὴς καὶ πλέον οὐδέν (ed. Bonn, p. 2). The word ἀκρίβεια means accurate fulness of detail, not accuracy in our sense of trustworthiness. Both Skylitzês and Psellos might be called fond of detail, for "detail" is ambiguous. The remark already quoted from Thierry, *Les détails sont l'âme de l'histoire*, refers to details in the sense in which we should use the word of Psellos.

[1] See his history, pp. 135, 136. τοῖς ἀκριβέσι τῶν συγγραφέων would include Skylitzês.

Thus Psellos' intention was to compose readable memoirs in contrast to the prevailing style of Byzantine history, which he considered dry and wearisome. By his neglect of chronology he completely breaks through the stereotyped method. There was consequently a sort of opposition between Psellos and contemporary historians like Joannês Skylitzês, who held fast by the old method; there were, in fact, two historical schools—one instituted by Psellos, whose influence on historiography in method as well as in style was permanent, inasmuch as the best historians of the following centuries adopted a midway method.

While he often omits important facts, such as the Patzinak war in the reign of Constantine IX, he devotes pages to minor details of court life which he had personally observed, and he deems it necessary to apologise for such digressions.[1] He says he will not describe the grief exhibited by Constantine when his queen Sklêraina died, for such a description would be a descent to triviality ($\sigma\mu\iota\kappa\rho\omega\lambda\omega\gamma\epsilon\hat{\iota}\sigma\theta\alpha\iota$ $\kappa\alpha\grave{\iota}$ $o\hat{\iota}o\nu$ $\lambda\epsilon\pi\tau\omega\lambda\omega\gamma\epsilon\hat{\iota}\nu$). "But if I myself am sometimes guilty of that against which I warn writers of history to guard, it is no wonder, for the notion of history is not so absolutely bounded, so shaved off on every side, as not to leave some loopholes and passages for egress; but if anything take advantage of a loophole, the historian must quickly recall the waif, and must arrange his matter so as to bear on the general theme, considering all else as merely secondary".

His general view of history is, that it is directed by providence.[2] "I am wont to refer to the *pronoia* of the Deity the arrangement of the larger events of history, indeed to attach to his prevision all events that do not arise from the perversion of our human nature". Thus,

[1] P. 134.　　　　[2] P. 64.

as an orthodox member of the church, he believed in a combination of design and freewill.

Michael Attaleiatês was a younger contemporary of Psellos.[1] He dedicates his history to the Emperor Nikêphoros Botaneiatês, the predecessor of the great Alexios, and beginning with Michael IV gives a short eclectic sketch of the years 1034–1057, somewhat similar in compass, though different in style, to the sketch given by Psellos of the reigns of Basil, Constantine VIII, and Rômanos. His history becomes more complete with the revolt of Komnênos as that of Psellos with the accession of Michael IV. Although slight, the preliminary sketch is valuable, for Attaleiatês was a man superior in judgment and insight to the average Byzantine chronographer, and we shall have occasion to refer to it. He tells us in his introductory remarks that though he was distracted with official business which occupied him every hour of the day, it seemed good to him to undertake yet an additional labour and "digest a few things in a short and simple style—as is meet for historians, if the subject be not agonistic and therefore demanding an artificial method, but historical and superior to irrelevant prolixity—not concerning what I received from others by hearsay, but concerning what I myself witnessed and beheld, in order that things worthy of narrative may not be overwhelmed in the profundities of oblivion by the lapse of time". It seems to me evident that this pointed remark in regard to style is intended as a criticism on Psellos, whose florid and elaborate style Attaleiatês thought unsuitable for history, and himself followed the unadorned baldness of the older chronographers.

[1] Besides his history, published in the Bonn series of *Scriptores Byzantini*, there is also extant his διάταξις, or will, containing regulations for a charitable institution (πτωχοτροφεῖον) which he founded; it has been published in the first volume of Sathas' *Bibliotheca Græca Medii Ævi*.

Finlay did not know the history of Attaleiatês—there is not a single reference to it in his *History of Greece*; and it seems to have also escaped the notice of his learned editor.[1]

Joannês Skylitzês, also known as Thrakêsios,[2] was a contemporary of Attaleiatês and Psellos, and wrote a history of the Eastern Roman Empire from 811 to 1081. He held the offices of kuropalatês, drungarios of the guards, and protovestiarios, but we do not hear that he had any political influence. His history was plagiarised in a wholesale manner by George Kedrênos, who probably lived at the close of the century and wrote a universal history from the foundation of the world to the accession of Isaac Komnênos. The latter part of Skylitzês' history (1057–1081) is printed at the end of the Bonn edition of Kedrênos. A Latin translation of the whole work of Skylitzês, by J. B. Gabius, was published at Venice in 1570. Between Skylitzês and Attaleiatês there are very close resemblances, and I agree with Hertzberg that Skylitzês followed Attaleiatês. His criticism on Psellos was mentioned above.

Joannês Zônaras lived in the first half of the twelfth century, and probably finished his *Epitome of Histories* before 1150. He is so much superior in calibre to writers like Theophanês and Kedrênos that Hertzberg ranked him not among chronographers but among historians. From this judgment, however, Hirsch dissents.[3] Zônaras

---

[1] Mr Tozer mentions in his valuable notes almost every source of which Finlay was not aware. Besides Attaleiatês, I have noticed the omission of Kritobulos, the historian of the Ottoman conquest of Constantinople, who imitates Thukydidês. Whereas the other Greek historians, Phrantzês, Dukas, and Chalkokondylês, are patriots, Kritobulos is unique as writing in the Turkish interest; his hero is Mohammed.

[2] Called Thrakêsios by Kedrênos (I, 5) and Zônaras (IV, 196). He was probably a native of the Thrakêsian theme.

[3] F. Hirsch, *Byzantinische Studien*, p. 391: *Zonaras bemüht sich allerdings, wie wir gesehen, an einigen Stellen, verschiedenartige Berichte zu verarbeiten, aber*

complains at the beginning of his work of lack of books, and L. Dindorf, who examined carefully the sources of the earlier part of the work, concluded that his library was really very scanty. Whatever materials he lacked, he did not lack the history of Joannēs Skylitzēs, which he quotes, nor that of Psellos, which he also refers to and has utilised very largely, reproducing it even verbally, and constantly adopting from it expressions with a difference. It will not be amiss to give one or two examples, as Zōnaras, whose judiciousness was recognised by Gibbon, deserves attention, and the sources of the later portion of his history have not been adequately investigated.

Psellos.	*Zōnaras.*[1]
P. 36: ἐλπίσας τε ἀπὸ τῆς περὶ τὸν δημόσιον ἐπιμελείας τὰ ἀπολωλότα αὐτῷ ἐν ἴσῳ ἀνακτήσασθαι μέτρῳ πράκτωρ μᾶλλον ἢ βασιλεὺς ἐγεγόνει ...τοὺς παῖδας λογιστεύων πικρῶς.	P. 131: ἵνα γὰρ τῶν ἀπολωλότων ἰσοστάσια κτήσηται πράκτωρ ἀντὶ κρατοῦντος ἐγένετο καὶ πικρὸς λογιστής.
P. 12: ἐντεῦθεν ἕτερος ἀνθ' ἑτέρου ὁ βασιλεὺς γίνεται...ὕποπτος οὖν εἰς πάντας ὦπτο καὶ σοβαρὸς τὴν ὀφρὺν τάς τε φρένας ὑποκαθήμενος καὶ τοῖς ἁμαρτάνουσι δύσοργος καὶ βαρύμηνις.	P. 115: ὁ δὲ ἀλλοιότερος ἦν ἢ τὸ πρότερον· σοβαρός τε γὰρ ἐγεγόνει καὶ τὸ ἦθος ὑποκαθήμενος καὶ πάντας ὑπώπτευε καὶ τὴν ὀργὴν ἐτύγχανεν ἀπαραίτητος.

er verfährt dabei doch mit wenig Kritik. Hirsch gives a very good account of Skylitzēs. For the ninth and for the first half of the tenth century Hirsch's book is invaluable.

[1] The pages of Zōnaras referred to are those of the 4th vol. of L. Dindorf's ed. (1871).

P. 14: ἀθυμίας τε ἐνε-
πίμπλατο ... νέφους τὴν
κεφαλὴν πληρωθεὶς ... τὰ
μέλη παραλυθεὶς καὶ
νεκρὸς ἔμψυχος γεγονὼς
μετὰ βραχὺ καὶ αὐτὴν ἀπέρ-
ρηξε τὴν ψυχήν.

P. 115: ὅθεν ἐκεῖνος διὰ
ταῦτα νέφει περισχεθεὶς
ἀθυμίας παρεῖτο τὰ μέλη
καὶ ἔμπνους ὦπτο νεκρὸς
καὶ βραχύ τι διαλιπὼν
οἰκτρῶς τὸν βίον ἐξέλιπεν.

The later chroniclers, Glykas, Ephraem, Joel, and Constantine Manassês,[1] have no independent value. Events in "Italia"—by which Byzantine writers meant Calabria and Longibardia—and their Latin historians do not concern us here; but the chronicler, Lupus Protospata, it may be mentioned, is occasionally useful in supplying us with a date, and for the separation of the Greek and Latin churches, of which the Greek historians are silent, there is an important though short chapter in Leo of Ostia, the historian of Monte Casino.

2. *Basil II and Constantine VIII.** It is usual to say that Basil succeeded John Tzimiskês, and was succeeded by his brother Constantine. But, strictly speaking, Basil and Constantine were joint Emperors, although practically Basil was sole sovran, as his brother was a man of pleasure who, preferring horse-racing to State business, and a lady's chamber to the council-room, took no part in the administration. On their accession (976) Basil was twenty years old and Constantine seventeen, and it struck Psellos as a very remarkable and praiseworthy act of the latter to resign to his abler brother all claim to a share in the imperial power.

Basil was like Henry V of England. Wild and addicted to pleasure before and for some years after his accession, he suddenly exhibited a complete change of character,

[1] Manassês writes occasionally a good "political" verse.
[* John Tzimiskês, A.D. 969, Dec. 25, Basil II, A.D. 976, Jan. 10–1025, Dec. Constantine VIII (IX), A.D. 976, Jan. 10–1028, Nov.]

and proved an energetic and brilliant monarch. Psellos
was acquainted with men who had seen him. "Most of
our contemporaries", he says, "who saw the Emperor
Basil regarded him as a tart man, abrupt and rough in
character, prone to anger and obstinate, abstemious in
his mode of life, and abhorring all delicate living. But,
as I heard from historians of his time, he was not such at
first, but having been dissolute and luxurious in his
youth, he changed and became serious, for circumstances acted on his nature like an astringent; the loose
strings were stretched and the gaps closed in. At first he
was wont to indulge openly in wild revels, he used to en-
gage in amours, he loved conviviality; but after the two
revolts of Sklêros and the revolt of Phôkas and other
insurrections, he left the shores of luxury with full sail,
and devoted himself to the serious things of life".

The first overt act which manifested the inward
change in Basil's character was the deposition and
banishment of the eunuch Basileios, who was chamberlain and "President of the Senate", a title which had
been instituted for him by Nikêphoros Phôkas. Basileios
was a half-brother of the Emperor, who, feeling himself
incompetent and disinclined through youth and inex-
perience to undertake the administration, abandoned
the reins entirely to his namesake, who was personally
very much attached to him. The stature, form, and
bearing of the eunuch were imperial, and as John
Tzimiskês had vested the civil government altogether
in his hands, he was experienced in political affairs.
Basil gave him "voice and hand" over all, military as
well as civil, affairs; and thus the chamberlain was like
an athlete performing while the Emperor stood by as a
spectator, not intending, however, to place a crown on
his head, but in order to learn a lesson, and at some
future time perform in like manner himself. The act by

which he loosed the leading-strings and ceased to play a secondary part in the Empire took place, according to Psellos, soon after the suppression of the rebellion of Bardas Phôkas in 989. If this be correct, the power of Basileios had lasted for thirteen years. But Kedrênos (Skylitzês), the "accurate" historian, places his fall some years sooner—namely, after the subjugation of the first rising of Bardas Sklêros. Finlay, accepting the statement of Kedrênos, assigns the change in Basil's policy as the cause of the discontent and revolt of Phôkas. Psellos assigns no reason for it except that as the relation of the Emperor Nikêphoros he felt he had a claim to the throne, and he states clearly that the fall of the eunuch was subsequent to the revolt of Phôkas. Having narrated that pretender's strange death and how his head was brought to Basil, he writes, "From this time forward the Emperor becomes a different person . . . he became suspicious, haughty, reserved, and wrathful. Nor did he wish any longer to leave the administration to his chamberlain, but was ungracious to him", etc.[1] By the use of the pluperfect tense[2] Zônaras avoids committing himself to either opinion. He places his description of the change in Basil and the fall of the eunuch after the revolt of Phôkas, following herein the order of Psellos; but by his mode of expression, "he *had become* haughty", etc., he leaves it undetermined at what time the change took place.

Whatever the date may have been, Basil did not concern himself to smooth the way for the removal of his minister from office. He managed the matter with brutal simplicity, causing him to embark in a ship which carried him to exile. He then proceeded to examine all the acts of his ministry, and undid those which seemed aimed at personal display or private patronage, pro-

[1] P. 12. [2] ἐγεγόνει, p. 115.

fessing ignorance of them. He even dismantled the
splendid monastery which the president, who was im-
mensely wealthy, had built; and so, as he said, turned
the refectory into a reflectory, because the monks would
be obliged henceforward to reflect seriously how to obtain the necessaries of life.[1] Basileios was utterly overwhelmed with grief at this unkind treatment, and with
disappointment at having to say a long farewell to all his
greatness. His noble form became a living corpse, a
literal monument of the sudden change of fortune, and
he soon died. At the same time Basil began to apprehend
the difficulties that attend on an Emperor's office, and
the seriousness of his position so impressed him that he
became quite ascetic, abstaining from all good cheer,
wearing no ornaments on his person, not even a chain
on his neck, nor a diadem on his head, nor a chlamys
bordered with purple; superfluous rings he put away
from him, and eschewed many colours in his clothes.
He was completely preoccupied with the problem how
to make all the acts of his rule concur "to produce an
imperial harmony".[2]

The second revolt of Sklêros followed hard upon the
death of Phôkas, his old rival. In regard to this revolt
Psellos states a fact which Skylitzês[3] seems not to have
known or not to have believed, and Zônaras does not
record. From their narratives we should conclude that
the hostility of Sklêros was only momentary, and that

[1] P. 13: οὐκ ἀνῄει ἄχρις οὗ φροντιστήριον, ἰδεῖν χαριεντισάμενος
εἰπεῖν, τὸ μοναστήριον δέδρακε, διὰ φροντίδος τιθεμένων τῶν ἐν αὐτῷ,
ὅπως ἂν ἑαυτοῖς τὰ ἀναγκαῖα πορίσαιντο.
[2] ὅπως ἂν τὰ τῆς ἀρχῆς εἰς ἁρμονίαν βασιλικὴν συμβιβάσειε.
[3] Kedrênos, II, p. 446: ἄρτι δὲ τοῦ Φωκᾶ ἀποθανόντος κατὰ τὸν
Ἀπρίλλιον μῆνα τῆς δευτέρας ἰνδικτιῶνος τοῦ ͵ϛυϙζ΄ ἔτους καὶ τῆς κατ᾽
αὐτὸν ἀποστασίας διαλυθείσης ἀδείας λαβόμενος ὁ Σκληρὸς πάλιν
ἀνελάμβανεν ἑαυτὸν καὶ τὴν προτέραν ἐσωμάσκει ἀποστασίαν. ὅπερ
πυθόμενος ὁ βασιλεὺς γράμμασι παρῄνει, κ.τ.λ.... τούτοις δὲ τοῖς
γράμμασι μαλαχθείς... κατατίθεται τὰ ὅπλα.

his reconciliation with Basil took place almost immediately, certainly before the end of the year 989. But Psellos tells us that his rebellion, which began in the summer of that year, lasted many years longer. He did not venture on an engagement with the imperial troops, but strengthened and increased his army and cut off the traffic and means of communication with the capital, and intercepted supplies. His army was devoted to him —won by his kindness and good fellowship; he used to call each soldier by his name, eat at the same table with his men, and share the same wine-bowl. But he felt age with stealing steps creeping over his frame, and at the last listened to an embassy of Basil, who seems to have been at the end of his wit to disembarrass himself of the opposition of the able general.

Now the manner in which Psellos states the duration of the hostility of Skleros is peculiar.[1]* "This tyranny which began in summer did not cease in the autumn, nor was it circumscribed even by the limit of a year, but for many years the mischief surged". It is, I think, a legitimate conjecture that the negative clauses refer to, and are intended to refute, a prevailing view, which was shared by Skylitzes, and which Psellos considered an historical error. If this be so, the opposition between the historical schools was not confined to style and method.

Zônaras took from Psellos his account of the meeting between Basil and Skleros, but he omitted what is perhaps the most interesting point about it—the advice which the aged, now blind, commander gave to the young Emperor, who asked him as a general for his opinion as to the best policy for maintaining absolute power and avoiding rebellions. The advice which he

---

[1] *History*, p. 15...ἀλλ' ἐπὶ πολλοῖς ἔτεσι τουτὶ διεκυμαίνετο κακόν.
[* v. note 58, p. 216, vol. v, Bury's *Gibbon*, 1898 ed.]

gave, says Psellos, was not strategic, but unprincipled (πανοῦργος)—as we should say, Machiavellian. It was to do away with too exalted offices, to allow no military officer to be too rich, to wear them out with unjust exactions, so that their private affairs may claim all their attention, not to introduce a wife into the palace, to be to none easy to deal with, and to be chary of imparting to others his secret resolves.

This advice of a man who knew the condition of the Roman Empire well indicates clearly the danger which was threatening the Macedonian dynasty, and, staved off for a time by Basil's personal vigour, finally overthrew it—the power of the wealthy Asiatic aristocrats, who by their wealth could convert the imperial regiments which they commanded into private armies of their own.

Basil's subsequent policy was conceived fully in the spirit of his old opponent's advice. The law of *allêlengyon*, by which the rich taxpayers of a district were bound to make up the deficiencies of the poorer, is an instance of the "unjust exactions". The loyalty of terror, and not the loyalty of goodwill, was what he wished to secure. He managed the whole administration himself, and as he grew older experience made him quite independent of the wisdom of councillors. As Psellos expresses his policy of imperial absolutism, he steered the State not according to enacted laws, but according to the unwritten laws of his own well-constituted nature; and in this spirit he paid no attention to educated men, but utterly looked down on them. This was a feature of Basil's reign; culture was not patronised, but discouraged and scorned by the Emperor.[1] Nevertheless we

[1] This feature should doubtless be connected with the policy of depressing the nobility and higher classes who represented the culture of the Empire. The education of Basil's nieces Zôê and Theodôra was com-

are told that there was a large number of philosophers
and rhetoricians in those days. On which fact, which
strikes him as curious, Psellos makes the comment that to
these men culture was an end in itself, not a mere means
to favour or money, "whereas now money is the end".

Psellos does not enter on the subject of Basil's campaigns, but he has some interesting remarks on his
military system. One of his peculiarities was to pay no
attention to the traditional habit of limiting the season
of campaigns. It was usual to set forth in the middle of
spring and retire before the extreme heat began. Basil,
with "adamantine" indifference, despised heat and
defied cold when he had an object in view, and like
other great generals made season wait on occasion. His
great principle in tactics was to preserve the ranks un-
broken; he considered that this was the one secret which
would save the Greek phalanxes from rout, and he was
punctilious in punishing that too eager bravery which
led a man to step out before his fellows or leave his
column. When soldiers on one occasion openly grumbled
at his mode of battle, he calmly replied with a smile,
"There is no other means by which we can cease
waging war".

His personal appearance is minutely described by
Psellos. His stature was rather under-sized, but not dis-
proportionate; on horseback he looked incomparable,
like the statue of a master sculptor, presenting inflexibly
the same pose both uphill and downhill. His face was
an exact circle; his forehead neither retreated nor pro-
truded. His eyes were bright and flashing, and the brow,
avoiding the extremes of a feminine straight line and the
grim aspect lent by an overhanging shape, expressed his

pletely neglected. His secretaries were obscure men of little training, but
he wrote his despatches in so simple and unvarnished a style that no great
ability was required (p. 19).

innate pride. He wore a thick beard and whiskers which he was fond of twirling, particularly when he was angry or perplexed in thought; he had also the habit of sticking out his elbow and resting his fingers on his hips. He spoke in short abrupt sentences, more like a peasant than a gentleman, and when he indulged in laughter his whole frame assisted in the operation.

3. *Constantine VIII.** On Basil's death in 1025 his brother and sleeping colleague, if we may use the expression, at the advanced age of seventy became ruler of the Empire. His chief achievement was to spend the immense treasures which Basil had accumulated, and which were so large that he had to build subterranean treasure vaults. The money in the treasury amounted to 200,000 lb. of gold.[1] The arrears of two years' taxes were due when Basil died; these he rigorously collected. He was now an old voluptuary, utterly unfit to conduct the government, in which he had never taken any interest. He cared only for horse-racing, hunting, and dice-playing, or for tasting luxurious dishes. He had always been weak-minded, and his originally firm physique was so worn with age and indulgence and gout that, instead of meeting in the field the barbarians who were threatening the Empire, he preferred to buy them off. It was his custom to forestall conspiracies by depriving of sight those whom he suspected, and he inflicted the same penalty on any one who actually conspired. That the notion of justice was alien to him is further shown by his habit of overwhelming persons in his immediate environment with a bounty which he did not extend further. He was too capricious and flighty

[* Constantine VIII (IX), A.D. 976, Jan. 10–1028, Nov.]

[1] If Zônaras means *pounds* by the pedantic word *talents*, the sum exceeds nine million pounds sterling. (Finlay, II, p. 387.) I am afraid that Psellos (whom Finlay elsewhere calls a pedant) is originally responsible for the affected word *talents*.

to cherish resentment like Basil, and he often repented of his own severity.

Although his education was only superficial, he had a mother-wit and a remarkable fluency of speech—in this, too, contrasting with his brother—so that when he dictated business letters or despatches the fastest writer could not keep up with him.

It was Basil's custom to transact all business as far as possible himself. Constantine, on the other hand, transacted no business himself, except occasionally the dictation of letters. He entrusted the administration to six eunuchs of his household.[1]

His wife Helena, the daughter of Alypios, a man of distinction, bore him three daughters, of whom their childless uncle Basil had been extremely fond. The eldest, Eudokia, was unlike her family in being of equable and soft disposition; she was permitted at her own request to retire into a monastery. The other two, Zôê and Theodôra, who were of a prouder and more domineering temper, were destined to play a prominent part during the following years. When his death was approaching, the Emperor chose Rômanos Argyropôlos to be his successor as the husband of his second and fairest daughter Zôê, then forty-eight years old. The fact that he was already married was no impediment; his wife cut off her hair and sought the retreat of a convent.

Zônaras states that Constantine had originally destined Theodôra to be the wife of Rômanos, but that she refused.[2] Psellos makes a contrary statement—namely, that before the selection of Rômanos the Emperor's choice fell on his second daughter. Moreover, he omits to mention a circumstance recorded by Zô-

---

[1] Their names are recorded by Kedrênos.

[2] Vol. IV, p. 128: ἡ γὰρ τρίτη διὰ τὸ τὴν ἐκείνου εὐνέτειραν ἄκουσαν διαζυγῆναι αὐτοῦ παραιτήσασθαι τὴν μετ᾽ αὐτοῦ συμβίωσιν λέγεται.

naras and Kedrênos, that the first intention was to name Constantine Dalassênos as his successor.

4. *Rômanos III.** We are informed by Psellos that from the accession of Rômanos his narrative will become fuller; "for the Emperor Basil died when I was an infant, and Constantine when I was just beginning my lessons; I was never in their presence, nor did I ever hear them speaking, and I know not whether I saw either of them, as I was too young to remember. But Rômanos I saw and on one occasion met him. Thus my account of Basil and Constantine is derived from others, whereas I can describe Rômanos from personal knowledge".

Rômanos was well born and well educated, but Psellos expresses contempt for the amount and quality of his learning. "He thought that he knew far more than he did". He was ambitious to rival Marcus Antoninus and pose as a philosopher on the throne. It became the fashion to talk metaphysics at court, but it was mere pretence and show, due to no real concern for truth; and the learned of that time, says Psellos, had not reached further than the portals of Aristotle and only knew by rote a few catchwords of Platonism, never really penetrating into the secrets of metaphysics.

Another mania of Rômanos was warfare, of which he knew absolutely nothing. When he did not talk of the insoluble problems of parthenogenesis, his conversation was of greaves and corslets. He had high-flying schemes of subjugating all the eastern and all the western nations; he burned to rival the exploits of Alexander, Hadrian, or Trajan. His expedition against the Saracens in 1030 ended in a complete fiasco. Contrary to the advice of his officers he had rejected the proposals of the Caliph for peace, as he could not bring himself to give up the delightful prospect of cutting trenches, diverting the

[* Rômanos III, Argyros, A.D. 1028, Nov. 12–1034, Ap.]

courses of rivers, laying ambushes, and performing the military operations described in ancient history. The great Basil made war in order to be at peace; Rômanos made war for its own sake. Psellos says that he began the war without a pretext, but we read in Kedrênos that Spondylês, governor of Antioch, had suffered a serious defeat in the last month of 1029, which endangered the safety of Syria, so that Psellos is probably exaggerating for the sake of effect the sexagenarian Emperor's childish fancy to do what he read of.

Thus Rômanos "raught at mountains with outstretched arms, yet parted but the shadow with his hand". He had ascended the throne with high fantastical hopes of a brilliant and long reign, and perhaps the foundation of a new dynasty, and he held court with more splendour and practised a more profuse liberality than most sovrans. He had inaugurated his reign with popular measures, abolishing, for example, the *allêlengyon*. But the discomfiture at Azaz acted like cold water, and moreover placed his finances in a very unsatisfactory condition. Consequently, when he returned to Constantinople after his unlucky experiences, his domestic policy changed. He abandoned the idea of being a second Trajan or Hadrian, and set before himself the far more practical ideal of a Byzantine financier—"a less strange life". For his subjects this meant that he became a tyrant instead of a liberal if fantastic sovran. His object was to recruit the treasury for the money he had staked for the glory he had not won. He waked from their slumbers old and forgotten claims, dormant since the proverbial archonship of Eukleidês, and visited with bitter visitation the monetary deficiencies of the fathers upon the children. In these matters he did not sit as an impartial judge, but acted as an advocate of the exchequer.

The use to which he put the results of his financial abilities was such that not even the court, much less the mass of his subjects, derived any benefit from all the money that streamed into the treasury. For Rômanos had yet another mania. He desired not only to rival Basil I or Constantine the Great as the founder of a new dynasty, to imitate Alexander or Trajan as a general, to rank with Aurelius as a crowned philosopher; he wished also to emulate Solomon and Justinian as a builder. Justinian had built the immortal church of the Divine Wisdom; Rômanos determined to build a church to the mother of God on a grand scale. "A whole mountain was excavated" to supply the stones, and the art of excavation was reckoned a branch of philosophy; the workmen engaged in the edifice were ranked with the assistants of Pheidias and Polygnôtos. The work continued interminably, for the original design was not followed out, but modified and enlarged as it progressed. The sources of gold were being exhausted, and yet the church was not approaching completion.

Rômanos looked on this as a work of piety and undertook it professedly from pious motives, but Psellos says of course that they were only sham. It is interesting to read the philosopher's comments on the propriety of spending money on costly buildings for divine service. "It is good", he says, "to love the comeliness of the house of the Lord, as the psalmist says, and the habitation of his glory, and often to prefer throwing away money on it to winning happiness from other things. This is good, and who will gainsay those who are consumed with zeal for the Lord? But the principle holds good only when there is nothing to interfere with this pious end—when it does not involve injustice and harm to the public weal. Care that there should be nothing indecent in the.Lord's house does not imply that even walls, encircling pillars, and swinging drapery, or expensive sacrifices are necessary to serve God, the true requisite being a mind encircled with godliness, a soul hued with the intellectual purple, even actions, and the fair affection of heart which really consists in an unaffected manner. The Emperor understood syllogisms, and the puzzles of Sorites and Nobody, but he had no practical philosophy". He was not content with building the church; he added to it a monastery which he supplied with the greatest luxury.

While the Emperor's thoughts were occupied with building, intrigues were carried on at court of which he seems to have been intentionally ignorant. The Empress Zôê had cause for dissatisfaction and very good reason for laying plans for future contingencies. At the time of his accession, although he himself was sixty-five and Zôê almost fifty years old, Rômanos had cherished the hopes of founding a dynasty. But when charms and aphrodisiacs proved unavailing, and he found that there was no prospect of issue, he began to show a neglect to his wife, which she felt derogatory to her royal birth, and lived apart from her, an arrangement which, being a delicate liver, she could not endure. Moreover, as she had no child and as the Emperor's sister Pulcheria had great influence with her brother, and was not well disposed to herself, the prospect of what might happen on his death seemed precarious, and the state of his health indicated that he could not live long.

The most trusted counsellor of the Emperor was a eunuch named Joannês, a very clever man of low origin who held the post of *orphanotrophos*, or head of an institution for the support of orphans. We shall have occasion to learn more about his personal qualities when we come to the history of the next reign. He and Zôê were on very bad terms, and perhaps we may suppose that he influenced the Emperor in his behaviour towards her. But he had a very handsome brother named Michael, a youth of regular features, with bright eyes and a fair pink and white complexion. One day when the Emperor and Empress were sitting together, Joannês by imperial direction introduced his brother for inspection. The Emperor having addressed a few questions to him dismissed him, bidding him remain in attendance within the palace, but the Empress saw and loved. For a long time she kept her feelings a secret, but, unable longer to endure the pangs, she changed her behaviour to Joannês and became quite amicable, courting opportunities of conversation with him; and casually introducing the topic of his brother she desired him to convey to Michael a permission to enter her presence whenever he wished. Joannês, at first unsuspicious, soon ascertained the state of Zôê's affections, which were manifested clearly in her next interview with Michael. Grasping the situation and seeing the prospect of unlimited power by the devolution of the sovranty on his brother, he prepared Michael for the part he was to play.

The intrigue soon became an open scandal. Zôê, in the extravagance of her passionate admiration, used to array her lover in cloth of gold and rings; she was seen to place him on the throne with a sceptre and a crown. Pulcheria and her adherents indignantly informed the Emperor of what he could not, except intentionally, have avoided seeing. He felt no *tremor cordis* at Zôê's virginalling on Michael's palm. He merely for form's sake summoned the young man and questioned him on the matter, and when he denied the allegations on oath, professed to consider the informants calumniators and the alleged adulterer a most loyal servant. One point in Michael's favour was his liability to epileptic fits, which might be thought to unfit him for offices of gallantry; and it might be supposed that this circumstance really disarmed the suspicions of Rômanos. But Psellos learned from a well-informed person who moved in the court at that time, and was acquainted intimately with the course of the love-drama of the Empress and Michael, that Rômanos was perfectly aware that Zôê was madly in love with Michael, but was quite indifferent and determined to overlook it. And we can well understand that on the head of Rômanos, old and worn with disease, and devoid of affection for Zôê, the horns sat lightly. His sister Pulcheria, who led the party which disapproved of the intrigue, died soon afterwards, and then Joannês and Michael had a free field.

Psellos gives a description of the wasting disease which consumed the frame of Rômanos. He had himself seen him in a procession looking like a corpse; his hair had fallen off, and he used to stop and draw breath every few steps. It was generally believed that his death, which took place in a bath, was accelerated by poison administered by Zôê (1034).

The officials of the palace, both those attached to the Basilian family, and also the adherents of the late Emperor, advised Zôê to wait, nor in such weighty matters take a too hasty step. But her mind was quite made up, inasmuch as her affections were engaged, and she was incited to speedy action by Joannês. Michael the Paphlagonian was placed on the throne the same evening, and all the residents in the palace paid him the usual homage. Two commands were sent to the prefect of the city, that he should come early on the morrow with the members of the Senate to recognise the new Emperor, and that he should make arrangements for the obsequies of the deceased. The ceremony of homage consisted in the senators advancing one by one into the presence of the King and Queen, seated on thrones, and laying their heads on the ground before each; they then kissed the right hand of the Emperor, but not that of the Empress.

Psellos was in Constantinople at this time, a lad yet unbearded, and witnessed the funeral of Rômanos. The corpse, which was not, as with us, covered in a coffin, but carried in an open bier, was so changed that it was unrecognisable. The face was swollen, and the colour was not that of a dead body, but resembled persons who have been injured by drugs. Whether Rômanos was really poisoned was a question on which contemporaries could only entertain suspicions, but their suspicions seem to have been very strong.

5. *Michael IV.** Even from Zônaras it might be seen that Michael IV was by no means a bad Emperor. The energetic part he took in the Bulgarian expedition just before his death was really heroic, if heroism means the surrender of personal interests and endurance of pain for impersonal ends. But in Psellos we can see his judgment and ability far more clearly than in Zônaras, who gives us an abridgment of Psellos. He tells us plainly that he is combating against a prevailing opinion, detrimental to Michael; he has in fact made himself Michael's apologist. We may assume with tolerable certainty that he owed some of his information to Constantine Leichudês, who became a member of the Senate at this time, and through whose influence probably Psellos himself became judge at Philadelphia. "I am well aware", he says, "that many chroniclers in treating of his life will give an account diverging from ours; for the suspicion of the reverse of what was really the case was more prevalent in his times. But I, having partly had to do myself with the actual affairs, and having partly learned the secrets of state from persons who were

[* Michael IV, the Paphlagonian, A.D. 1034, April 11–1041, Dec.]

in close attendance on him, am a competent judge of the matter, except my eyes and ears be impugned".

As a contemporary, Psellos is the best authority we have, and his whole account of the reign of Michael IV gives us the impression of an impartiality which unfortunately we cannot always give him credit for. But his favourable representation of the Emperor's character is confirmed by the shortly expressed judgment of Michael Attaleiatês—"he left behind him many tokens of virtue".[1] "If we leave out of sight", says Psellos, "his conduct before his accession, he will rank among the few elect monarchs".

Michael is an instance of a man who suddenly became mature. For a short time at the beginning of his reign, he made the palace a sort of playground, gratifying the whims of the Empress and careless of everything serious, just like a boy. But he suddenly became conscious of the magnitude of supreme power and the responsibilities devolving on a true king, and, immediately rising to the situation, he put away childish things and proved that his nature was not superficial. It struck Psellos as notably admirable that he made no sudden change in the administration, but graduated all his alterations. He introduced no novelty in the ordinary practices, annulled no law, made no change in the Senate. To personal friends to whom he had pledged himself before his accession he kept his word, but did not immediately place them in high posts; he gave them subordinate positions as a preliminary training for advancement. His unwearying solicitude both provided that the provincial cities were well governed, and secured the Empire against invasion.[2]

[1] *History*, p. 10: πολλὰ τῆς ἀρετῆς καταλιπὼν εἰκονίσματα. Skylitzês' judgment is also favourable (Kedrênos, II, p. 534).

[2] παντοδαπὸς ἦν περὶ τὴν τῆς ἀρχῆς πρόνοιαν, οὐ μόνον τὰς ἐντὸς τῶν ἡμετέρων ὁρίων πόλεις εὐνομουμένας ποιῶν ἀλλὰ καὶ τοῖς πέριξ ἔθνεσι

He bestowed particular diligence on the efficiency and improvement of the army, "the sinews of Rômaioi". The administration of the finances he left entirely to his brother Joannês, who was experienced in that department.

Like Rômanos, his predecessor, Michael was very religious, but he was not like him a *dilettante*: he was really in earnest. He was not only a constant church-goer, but he cultivated the society of theosophists, whom Psellos calls philosophers and distinguishes from the metaphysicians, such as Rômanos used to patronise; they were the philosophers who despise the world, and live with beings that are above the world. Michael sent out to the highroads and hedges, searched high and low throughout the whole Empire to find such men, and when they arrived in his palace showed them the most extravagant veneration, rubbing their dirty feet with his own hands, and kissing them. He even went so far as to wrap secretly his imperial person in their rags. He used to set them on a couch, and lie at their feet on a stool. Those who had bodily sores or infirmities, and had thereby become disgusting to their fellowmen, were the objects of his special devotion; he used to wash them like a servant, and actually place his face on their sores.

Psellos speaks in tones of praise of this extravagant method of realising a spiritual life, which seems to us a sort of monomania. But Michael was really sincere, and we must remember that he had no "Hellenic culture" to preserve him from these aberrations of a self-annihilating gymnosophic asceticism, which seems so ludicrous in a sovran. He was not only ascetic himself, he also encouraged asceticism in others, and he laid out large sums in endowing monasteries for both male and

τὰς ἐφ᾽ ἡμᾶς ἀναστέλλων ἐφόδους τοῦτο μὲν πρεσβείαις τοῦτο δὲ δώροις τοῦτο δὲ μαχίμων ἐπετείοις ἀποστολαῖς. (*Hist.* p. 58.)

female recluses. He built a new hall at Constantinople,
called the Ptôchotropheion, a sort of refectory for poor
religious people. His zeal for saving lost souls extended
itself to unfortunate females, of whom there was a very
large number in the capital. As "such persons are apt
to be deaf to salutary advice", he did not think it
judicious to reclaim them by moral lectures, nor did he
think of using violence. He built a very large and fine
reformatory or penitentiary in the city, and then proclaimed to all women who made a trade of their persons,
:hat if any of them wished to live in plenty, she had only
to repair to this refuge and take the monastic habit.
A large swarm of the "ladies of the roof"[1] presented
themselves, and were enrolled as recruits in the army of
God. What the social effects of this step were, if "a large
swarm" is to be taken literally, we can only conjecture
from the well-known measure which was tried at
Venice. Such an effect, however, could only have been
momentary; for as Michael's object was not directly to
repress prostitution, but to save lost souls, and as he
passed no repressive measure, the curtailed supply
would, in a very short time, again equal the demand.

Persons ill disposed to the Emperor put a malicious
construction on his religious practices, asserting that before he ascended the throne he had had communication
with evil spirits with which he had made a compact to
deny God, and so lose his soul on condition of obtaining
the Empire. This is an interesting instance of the
medieval superstition of compacts with the devil.

It was Michael's close connection with his family that
prevented his good qualities from being appreciated;
his affectionate brothers proved his greatest misfortune,

---

[1] καὶ πολὺς ἐντεῦθεν ἑσμὸς τῶν ἐπὶ τοῦ τέγους ἐκεῖθεν συνέρρευσεν
(p. 67). Five hundred years before Theodôra and Justinian had made
efforts to reclaim prostitutes.

their vulgar grasping natures tarnishing the lustre of his. They were a sort of nemesis which attended his elevation. The eldest and chief of them, who possessed most political talent, was Joannês the orphanotrophos, of whom I must now give a more detailed account. Psellos, when old enough to be a capable observer, had seen him and heard him speaking, and been in his company while he was transacting business; and he had observed his character carefully. He sums up his good and bad qualities in a businesslike manner which reminds us of Ammianus Marcellinus. He was keen and ready of wit, as could be seen by the flash of his eye; in the transaction of business he was most diligent and hardworking, and very experienced; his keenness was manifested particularly in public finances. He did no evil to any one, but put on a sour face in order to frighten people, and often deterred men from bad actions by his threatening looks. Hence he was really a tower of defence for the Emperor, for night and day his thoughts were busy with the interests of the State, though this did not prevent him from attending banquets and public festivals. Nothing that went on escaped his many-eyed vigilance, which was so great that he used often in the dead hours of the night to walk through the whole city—"like lightning", says Psellos—easily escaping observation himself, for having been originally a monk he continued to wear a monastic dress. His excellent information on all that went on exercised a wholesome terror, which prevented gatherings and meetings that might look like illegal conspiracies.

Such were his laudable qualities, over against which Psellos places his profound dissimulation. He always adapted his words and looks to his company, and he had the habit of gazing at a person steadily when he was at some distance, and on his approach behaving as if he had not been aware of his presence before. If any one made a new suggestion which seemed likely to prove advantageous, he would pretend that he had himself decided on the course proposed long since, and rebuked the suggestor for his tardiness, who passed out crestfallen, while Joannês put the suggestion in practice and was under no obligation to its real author. He was ambitious to behave with princely grandeur and dignity, but the inner man continually exposed itself; he was not to the manner born. He used occasionally to indulge in potations, and it was then especially that his vulgarity came out in indecent behaviour. Yet even on such occasions he did not forget the absorbing cares of power. Psellos often met him at banquets, and wondered how a man unable to refrain from intoxication and laughter could draw the car of government. But when he was drunk he measured the behaviour of each of his fellows, and called them to account afterwards for what they said or did, so that men were more afraid of him drunk than sober. He was a strange compound, this man, dressed in his monastic gown. To the decency which such a dress might seem to demand he did not dream of paying any regard, though, in deference to some new imperial law which concerned the monastic orders, he might occasionally pretend some outward conformity. For dissolute livers he entertained a contempt, but to gentlemen of liberal culture and refined habits he felt a repugnance and tried to diminish their influence.

The shiftiness which he displayed towards the world in general was, in relation to his brothers, replaced by an unvarying affection. The other brothers are represented to have been a worthless lot. If Joannês was far inferior in virtue to Michael, he was far superior to the other three, Nikêtas, Constantine, and Geôrgios. They utilised their kinship to the Emperor as a cover for deeds of injustice of which Joannês did not approve; while Joannês was so fond of his brothers that he took care that the Emperor should not hear of them, and if anything did come to his ears used his influence to protect them from the imperial anger. Nikêtas was made duke (δούξ) of Antioch, where he signalised himself by an act of perfidy. The citizens, who before his arrival had wreaked summary vengeance on a tax collector who had behaved indecently towards them, shut the gates in fear lest Nikêtas should punish them. He bound himself by oaths to grant a plenary pardon, but when he was admitted put a great number to death and sent many of the chief men to the capital.[1] Some time after this Nikêtas died, and his brother Constantine, a eunuch like Joannês, succeeded him as duke of Antioch, and in that office relieved Edessa from a Saracen siege. He was soon raised to the rank of domestikos, or commander of the eastern armies. Geôrgios, of whom we hear least, was made protovestiarios; he too was probably a eunuch. The whole family was very unpopular:

> And what is Edward but a ruthless sea?
> What Clarence but a quicksand of deceit?
> And Richard but a ragged fatal rock?

And the Emperor Michael was involved in the unpopularity of the family with which he was identified.

Joannês was a man of boundless activity and resources. His object was to secure the succession for his own family—to found a Paphlagonian dynasty; and as Michael's health was very bad it was imperative to take precautions in good time. A scheme of personal ambition which he attempted to execute failed. This was his own

---

[1] Zônaras, IV, 138. The citizens of Antioch were suspected of a degree of goodwill towards Constantine Dalassênos which was inconsistent with their loyalty to the throne. Dalassênos was considered a dangerous person, and kept in strict confinement.

election to the patriarchal chair, which involved the deposition of the then patriarch Alexios, to compass which Joannês formed a cabal of clerical dignitaries who conspired to unseat Alexios on the ground that he had not been canonically elected. Alexios was equal to the occasion, and pointed out that if his election had not been canonical, the invalidity of all the appointments he had made during his tenure of office would follow of logical necessity. This manifesto caused the majority of the clergy to take the part of Alexios, and the scheme of Joannês fell through. If he had been successful—if Alexios had been a weaker man or had happened to die in the reign of Michael IV—Joannês would have been in so secure and influential a position that he might have saved his family dynasty from the catastrophe in which the conduct of Michael Kalaphatês involved it. Alexios was probably never well disposed to the Paphlagonian family, but he was a firm adherent of the Basilian house.

The epileptic fits to which the Emperor was subject became so constant that he was obliged to lead a life of great seclusion, and when his imperial duties made it necessary to hold an audience, purple curtains and curtain-pullers were so placed that if the least sign indicated that the disease was about to seize him his agony could in a moment be concealed from view, as it were in a separate room. And when he rode abroad he was accompanied by a guard which used to form a circle round him, so that if he were overtaken by a fit he should not be a public spectacle. In the intervals between the fits he was always actively engaged. But Joannês perceived that the sands of his life were running quickly down, and he framed a plan for securing the succession to his family, which consisted in the timely elevation of a nephew to the rank of Cæsar, and the adoption of him by the Empress Zôê as her son.

Besides his four brothers Joannês had a sister named Maria, who was the wife of a ship-tarrer (caulker) named Stephanos. The brother-in-law had taken his share in the successes of the family, and had been appointed to succeed George Maniakês in Sicily, where, as might be expected, he conducted affairs with such gross incompetency and corruption that the rich island was lost to the Saracens, with the exception of Messênê, which was preserved by the bravery of its commandant Kekaumenos Katakolôn. Psellos saw Stephanos after he had been transformed in the game of fortune from a pitch-smearer of ships to a military commander, and was highly amused with the figure he cut. He looked out of place on his steed, and his dress looked out of place on him; he was like a pygmy trying to act Hêraklês, but unable to manage the lionskin and wield a club bigger than himself. This man and Maria had a son named Michael, who was surnamed Kalaphatês after his father's profession. He had not been forgotten in the family preferments, and had been appointed captain of the bodyguard. On him the choice of Joannês fell to succeed his brother, for he seems to have been the nearest relative eligible,[1] and he decided to have him proclaimed Cæsar. It required some adroitness to suggest this to the Emperor and obtain his consent, as it is a matter of difficulty even for brothers to introduce to monarchs the subject of their own mortality.

Psellos professes to give a full account of the conversation which passed between Joannês and Michael. That some such conversation did take place we have no reason to doubt, though of course the actual words put into their mouths by Psellos are as fictitious as the dialogue of the Athenians and Mêlians in Thukydidês. It has a considerable value, however, as a dialogue

[1] Nikêtas was dead; Constantine and Geôrgios were eunuchs.

imagined as probable by a contemporary, and in this aspect claims our attention. Joannês begins by reminding the Emperor of his own unwavering loyalty and brotherly attachment. When the Emperor demands the aim of this prelude, he goes on to say: "Do not imagine that the ears of the majority of your subjects have not heard and their eyes seen that you suffer both from a secret and from an undisguised disease. That you are really in no danger on this account I know full well, but yet the tongues of men refrain not from discussing the possibility of your death; and this leads me to fear that, having got into their heads the idea that you are about to die immediately, they may combine against you and elect a new Emperor and place him in the palace. For myself and our family I feel less concern, but I am alarmed in your behalf lest such a good and excellent monarch should pay for want of prudence. He will escape the danger but not the reproach of not foreseeing the future". This punctiliously deferential speech is interesting as showing the tone in which Joannês would have spoken to his brother. He then proposed his plan, and Michael consented. As a greater security it was arranged that Zôê, who as an heiress of the old Basilian dynasty was very popular, should adopt him as her son. A public festival was proclaimed and the ceremony was performed.

Michael never loved Zôê, who was past fifty when their *liaison* began. For a time he acted the lover, but the part soon became tedious, and he not only grew cold, but, feeling suspicious that she might treat him as she is supposed to have treated Rômanos, he kept her in strict confinement in the women's apartments, cut down her income, and prevented access to her except by the special permission of a guard whom he appointed to superintend her. Zôê behaved under this treatment with the greatest self-control and patience, never even bestowing on her appointed keeper a hard word or look. The brothers did not trust this meek behaviour, which they viewed as consummate acting; they looked on Zôê as a caged lioness, and the meeker she seemed the greater precautions they took. The Emperor soon gave up living with her altogether. He suffered from dropsy, and was indisposed for conjugal life; and this indisposition was confirmed by the admonitions of his spiritual advisers.

The Bulgarian war which immediately preceded and hastened Michael's death—the rising of the false Dolianos, the double desertion of the genuine Alusianos, and the heroism of the Emperor—has been related fully by Zônaras, closely following Psellos, and by Finlay. We need not repeat it here. The Emperor after his exhausting labours returned in triumph, but nigh unto death, for which he prepared by assuming the monastic order. The ceremony was performed in the church of the Anargyroi which he had built himself, and when it was concluded the ex-Emperor was cheerful "like a man light and fleet for a journey", but his household and brothers, especially Joannês, were plunged in despondency. When the Empress heard the news, she immediately proceeded on foot to the monastery, but Michael refused to see her. Shortly afterwards the time for a hymnal service arrived, and Michael arose from his couch to attend it, but found that his imperial shoes had not been changed nor monastic foot-gear provided. He was obliged to totter barefoot to the chapel, and when he returned to repose he died. He was a man who, under more favourable circumstances, might have been an efficient ruler and have won the praise of historians; but he was sorely let and hindered, on the one hand by his ill health, and on the other hand by his kinsfolk.

PART II

6. *Michael V.** The irony of history forcibly impressed itself on the philosopher Psellos as manifested in
the elevation of Michael V. Joannês the orphanotrophos
had secured this elevation with the express purpose of
preserving his own power and the position of his family;
and destiny or providence made use of the same means
for the ruin of Joannês himself and his family's utter
catastrophe. *L'homme propose.*

Michael V is represented by historians to have been
a man of no principle and no conscience. He is said to
have been skilled in dissembling, hiding the fire of
hatred under the ashes of goodwill—*cineri doloso*;—he is
said to have been ungrateful to his benefactors. When
he was made Cæsar—an honour perhaps which he had
not dreamed of—he sketched out in his imagination (we
are informed by Psellos) plans of action to be followed
when his uncle Michael died. His chief feeling was detestation of his own family, and he determined to get
rid of his relations, especially Joannês, by death or
banishment—to stamp out his whole stock.

> And till I root out their accursed line
> And leave not one alive, I live in hell.

The more virulent his feelings, the more friendly to all
did he appear in the meantime, but the quicksighted-
ness of Joannês was not deceived by the dissimulation of
his most unnatural nephew, whose real sentiments he
suspected. But he decided to take no step at once.
Michael on his part became aware of Joannês' suspicions, and the dissembling friendliness deceived neither.
Michael IV did not like his nephew; he showed him no

[* The second article began here. Michael V, Kalaphatês, A.D. 1041,
Dec. 14–1042, Ap.]

consideration nor honour, except in the mere formal ceremonies in which he assisted as Cæsar, and kept him in a sort of banishment outside the city, not permitting him to appear in court, except in obedience to a command. But his uncle Constantine, who was jealous of the influence of Joannês, saw that it might be a profitable game to ingratiate himself with the apparent heir, and accordingly flattered him and lent him money.

On Michael's abdication of the throne, the family clique took their measures cautiously; and caution was necessary, as the city was excited and ready for a tumult. Psellos was a witness of the circumstances. They took no step without the countenance of the Empress, so that the elevation of Michael Kalaphatês should appear altogether due to her, and the adopted son made the most lavish protestations and took the most solemn oaths that she should be sole sovran and that he would merely act as a sort of hired minister to put her wishes into execution. Zôê was won, and, her attitude repressing the threatening populace, the new Emperor was consecrated and crowned. For the first day he was on his good behaviour towards both the Empress and his uncle Joannês, calling her, with emphatic repetition, "Empress", deferring to the opinion of "my lady", addressing Joannês as "my lord" and placing him next himself at table. All except Joannês were taken in by this conduct and thought him a most deserving and judicious young man. "His uncle", they said, "made a good choice".

This respectful deference was very soon dropped, and his uncle Constantine, who had been immediately created a *nobelissimos*, encouraged him to exhibit the coldness he felt towards Joannês. The latter did not say much, but concocted a plan, which came under the notice of Psellos but was not generally known, to replace the Emperor by one of his cousins, a certain Constantine. In order to provide against miscarriage he actually induced the Emperor, in a moment when he was indisposed to transact business, to sign a paper in which there was a clause that if any of his cousins were to attempt usurpation the matter should pass unpunished. But the plan came to nothing.

The smouldering envy between uncle and nephew soon burst into flame, the occasion being a difference of opinion between them, of which Constantine the nobelissimos availed himself to heap abuse and reproaches on Joannês for arrogance and disloyalty. Joannês immediately withdrew from the city accompanied by a personal retinue, expecting that his nephew would repent and besech him with importunity to return, and a large number of senators, not from love but from the same expectation, withdrew with him. Michael did not in the least regret his uncle's departure, but he was alarmed at the secession of the members of the *synkletôs*, and therefore wrote a letter to Joannês, in which he reproached him for his conduct and summoned him to a private interview in the palace. Joannês went, expecting reconciliatory overtures, but found that the Emperor had not kept his appointment, being absent at a horse-race. Considering this a sign that the breach was final, he left the city. Soon afterwards the Emperor sent a vessel to his place of retreat, with a mandate to present himself at the palace, which he obeyed. As the vessel was about to enter the great harbour, Michael, who was watching its approach from the palace windows, gave a preconcerted signal to the captain not to moor but to turn the vessel back. Then a second vessel came up which carried the orphanotrophos to a distant place of banishment.

In one point at least, Joannês and his nephew were of

diametrically opposite disposition. The uncle was remarkable for his unswerving attachment to his kindred; the nephew abhorred his relations with the most consistent detestation, making an exception in favour of Constantine. "The names of kinship, the common bond of kindred blood, appeared to him mere childishness, and it would have been nothing to him if one wave had engulfed all his relations". When he had disposed of Joannês he proceeded to gratify these disagreeable sentiments by emasculating most of the members of his family, many of whom were respectable men with wives and children.

This policy of exterminating his own family seems so obviously self-destructive for an Emperor in the precarious position of an upstart, that one might almost conclude that the young man must have been mad. Nobody had any reason to object to the banishment of the unpopular orphanotrophos, whose Argus-like supervision, oppressive taxation, and restless ambition had not conduced to making many friends. Once he was gone, the temerity of Michael hurried on the catastrophe; for "beggars mounted run their horse to death". His policy was to depress and show disfavour to the officials and persons of rank, removing or limiting their powers and privileges; and on the other hand to concede privileges to the populace and humour it, so as to rest his tenure of the throne on the many and not on the few. Tradesmen and retail dealers who profited by his *ad captandum* measures showed their goodwill by strewing silken carpets in the streets when he rode abroad; and this deluded him into the idea that he might with impunity try to set aside the old Basilian dynasty, by hanging on to which he had himself obtained power. This misconception of the popular mind led to his fall.

He had got rid of one political power which he disliked, his uncle. There was another political power which he disliked more, but whose position was more dangerous to assault. This was the Empress Zôê, on whom, as he found out too late, his position really depended. After the first days of his reign, during which he had lavished marks of deference towards her, he had "elbowed her aside" and kept her in confinement, withholding her income and not even permitting her to be attended by her own servants. But this was only preparatory. He hated her so much, we are told, that he was ready to bite his tongue out for having ever called her mistress. He determined to banish her, "that the beast might have the palace to house in all to himself".[1] He accused her of practising poisoning—it is said, with the most absurd details—and condemned her to exile. She was conveyed with only one maid to Prince's Island,[2]—the island where another Empress, Irene the Athenian, had been kept in confinement before she was removed to Lesbos. One of the persons who escorted her related to Psellos that, as the ship was starting, the Empress, looking up at the palace, apostrophised it with a rather theatrical lament. The Emperor ordered that her hair should be cut off, and thus she was sacrificed, "I know not if to the Lord", says Psellos, "but at least to the passion of the Emperor".

The next step was to give official publicity to this act. He first announced it to the Senate, and the Senate

[1] Psellos, *History*, p. 86: ἵν' ἔχοι μόνος ὁ θὴρ ἐν τοῖς βασιλείοις αὐλίζεσθαι. He consulted the astrologers as to his project; they forbade it: he laughed at them (*ib.* 87–88).

[2] Attaleiatês, p. 13: νῆσος δὲ αὕτη τῆς βασιλευούσης οὐ πόρρω is rendered in the Latin translation which accompanies the text in the Bonn edition by *insula hæc reginæ non longe abest*. Did the translator understand τῆς βασιλευούσης or not? If he did, he has not succeeded in expressing the meaning. In a passage in Kedrênos relating to the Chrysargyron tax which Anastasios abolished, I noticed that the word οὖρον was rendered *mulus* by the Bonn translator!

approved of the measure. He then caused a manifesto to be read aloud in the forum of Constantine in order to justify himself to the people.[1]

The great explosion that followed this ill-advised act of Michael made a deep impression on eye-witnesses. Psellos introduces his account of it with a solemn preparation as for a great scene in history—too great for human powers to narrate. He speaks of it in language that we might expect to be used about such an event as the French Revolution.[2]

The Emperor was congratulating himself on the success of his cherished scheme while the storm was gathering in the city. The usual routine of business and pleasure had been interrupted; all ages, sexes, and classes formed small groups and muttered their dissatisfaction. There was a threatening gloom over the whole city—grief at the Queen's misfortune and wrath with the audacity of the despot. On the second day the mutterings became distinct, and the half-formed wish to avenge the banished Empress assumed a definite shape. Officials of rank and public men joined with the populace, the classes with the masses, in the excitement; all were ready to lay down their lives for Zôê, and the Emperor's foreign guard could not allay the tumult. The women behaved like Mænads. Psellos says that he saw women, who had never been outside the female apartments in their lives before, coming forth in public, shouting and beating their breasts. The rioting inhabitants armed themselves with any implement they could lay hands on—axes, clubs, bows, or stones.

---

[1] This is recorded by Attaleiatês, p. 14: the Emperor in order to calm the anger of the Byzantines, when his act became known, ἔγγραφόν τι ποιεῖται τούτοις κατὰ τὸν ἐπισημότερον τόπον τοῦ φόρου ἐπαναγνωσθησόμενον, in which manifesto he threw all the blame on Zôê. The bill was called a πιττάκιον.

[2] P. 90: τὸ μέγα ἐκεῖνο καὶ δημοσιώτατον ἀπετελέσθη μυστήριον.

At this time Psellos was in the Emperor's ante-chamber. He was an under-secretary, and happened to be dictating some State document when the sound as of horses tramping struck his ears, and anon came a messenger with the news that the whole people had unanimously risen against the Emperor. To most persons in the palace it seemed incredible, but Psellos had observed the prognostics in the city, and understood that the spark had burst into a flame which it would require many rivers to quench. He immediately got to horse and rode to see the tumult himself, which he describes rhetorically. It is easy to read between the lines here that the philosopher had quite made up his mind beforehand to desert the Emperor, for whom he has no good word.

The mob first attacked the houses of all the relations of the Emperor, among them the house of Constantine the nobelissimos. The eunuch armed his household and at their head made a desperate rush through the crowds, and traversing the streets like fire reached the palace. There he found the Emperor sitting in dismay, utterly at a loss what to do, unable even to rely on his foreign guards, some of whom had deserted. He received his uncle with kisses of joy, and they decided to bring back Zôê from the adjacent island, to which she had been banished. Zôê sympathised, whether really or feignedly, with Michael's misfortune, and readily consented to show herself to the people. She appeared in purple robes on a balcony overlooking the hippodrome, but the device had not the desired effect; the mob was not imposed upon.

The life of Theodôra, Zôê's younger sister,[1] had been

---

[1] In the reign of Rômanos she had been compelled through Zôê's enmity to retire to a convent. From Kedrênos, II, 537, we learn that she lived at Petrion.

so recluse that Michael V was hardly even aware of her existence. A happy thought struck some of the leaders of the insurrection—to lead her forth from her retirement at Petrion and proclaim her Empress. This idea was carried out in a surprisingly orderly manner. One of her father's servants—a foreigner, *but* noble in form and spirit, according to Psellos—was appointed their guide, and they marched in regular order to her dwelling. At first the surprised princess, inured to her mode of life and perhaps afraid, would not listen to their proposals, and shut herself up in the sanctuary; they were obliged to force her by threats with drawn daggers. She was dragged from the altar, arrayed in royal attire, and borne on horseback to the church of St Sophia, where high and low acknowledged her as Empress. The participation of the patriarch Alexios in this movement is mentioned by Attaleiatês, not by Psellos.

The Emperor gave up all for lost, and exchanging his robes for the garb of a suppliant went by ship with his uncle to the famous monastery of Studion,[1] which presently became the place of a strange scene. When his flight became known, general exultation, displayed in songs and dances, prevailed, but also the desire of revenge.

Psellos rode with a friend, a captain of the guard, to the church at Studion, whither the greater part of the mob was thronging. There he saw the fugitive Emperor clinging to the altar and his uncle standing on the right side of it, both so disfigured and changed that Psellos could not feel any vestige of anger against them, but was so overwhelmed and aghast at the violent change that he could not refrain from weeping. The multitude, however, was not of as soft stuff as the philosopher; they stood around like wild beasts, eager to devour their prey.

[1] Situated in the south-west corner of Constantinople.

Psellos was standing hard by the altar, and the two hunted fugitives were quick enough to notice that he was affected, and catching at the chance they came to him for help. He "gently rebuked" Constantine for his evil counsels, and asked the Emperor what ill he had suffered at the hands of his mother Zôê. The nobelissimos denied any participation in the Emperor's acts, and remarked that if his advice had been followed his own kindred would not have been reduced to their present state. The Emperor could make no excuse.

In the afternoon a messenger, accompanied by a number of civil and military officials, arrived with orders from Theodôra to remove the fugitives elsewhere. But they were so much frightened by the threatening countenances of the crowd that they refused to leave the altar, and it was necessary to drag them from it. They were carried in mulecarts to a place called the Sigma, where their eyes were put out. The operation is described in Psellos: in undergoing it the Emperor behaved as a coward, his uncle with more fortitude. This punishment of the Emperor seemed a political necessity, as it was feared that Zôê, whose dislike of her sister was one of her strongest feelings, might restore the deposed monarch.

Michael V is generally looked upon as a sort of moral abortion, a monster without a virtue. Psellos and Zônaras, following Psellos, represent him as such, and in the preceding pages I have kept closely to Psellos' account.

But if we look merely at his actions and leave for a moment out of consideration a particular historian's view of his character—remembering that that historian was probably biassed, as he was an actor on the opposite side—we cannot pass a judgment of pure unmodified damnation. The two acts to which most prominence is given are the banishment of Joannês and the banishment of Zôê. The former of these seems to have been foolish for Michael's own interest, but can have been by no means unpopular, as Joannês was hated. During the long supremacy which he had enjoyed in the reign of Michael IV he had probably become overbearing and dictatorial, and may have made himself very offensive to the new Emperor if the latter had independent ideas and wished to act on them. The banishment of Zôê shows that Michael had not appreciated the conservative feeling which prevailed in the Empire, and attached itself to the Basilian dynasty as a sort of central rallying-point. In itself the exile of Zôê was hardly more or less flagitious than that of Joannês. She was probably a troublesome and meddlesome old woman, and of course we need not believe all that Psellos tells us of the deep-seated detestation, without any apparent ground, that Michael felt towards her.

Some other acts, reversing acts of the previous reign, deserve commendation. He delivered the able general George Maniakês from the confinement in which he had been placed by Michael IV, and made him magister and catapan of "Italy." He also released Constantine Dalassênos, who had been persecuted by Joannês. He made Psellos' own friend Constantine Leichudês, who afterwards won high repute as an able and upright statesman, his chief minister.[1]

Psellos is not by any means above the suspicion of partiality; his account of the reign of his pupil and pet Michael Parapinakês is a sufficient proof of this. In the present case it was not his interest to say a word for

[1] We learn this fact from Psellos' funeral oration on Leichudês, p. 398: εἶτα δὴ ὁ μετ᾽ ἐκεῖνον ἄρξας, εἰ καὶ μὴ ἐγνώκει τὴν ἐπιστήμην τοῦ κράτους, ἀλλ᾽ οὖν ἄρτι τοῦ ὀχήματος ἐπιβάς, καὶ δεδιὼς ὅπερ ἐπεπόνθει, πρὸς οὐδένα τῶν πάντων ἢ πρὸς τὸν ἄνδρα τοῦτον ἀπέβλεψεν· οὐκ ἔφθασε δὲ τοῦτον ἀναβιβάσας ἐπὶ τὸ ὄχημα, κ.τ.λ.

Michael V, as afterwards it was not his interest to speak good words of Rômanos Diogenês. He joined the general insurrection, as probably Leichudês also did, and he was a strong partisan of the next Emperor, Monomachos, whose power was founded on the ruins of Kalaphatês.

These considerations may lead us to conclude that Michael V, after all, was not so very diabolical; that the chief diabolical quality he possessed was perhaps that of not being so black as he was painted. But this view becomes stronger and less negative when we compare a neglected passage in the history of Michael Attaleiatês.[1] There we read that before his elevation this Emperor's views on politics were blamed and blameworthy, but that after his succession he was very highly praised for his honourable behaviour to the Senate and to his other subjects, in which respect he surpassed previous monarchs, conferring honours and dignities on many; moreover for his concern for the maintenance of order and his zeal for justice. This passage is sufficient to make us pause before accepting an extreme view unfavourable to Michael.[2]

It seems to me that Michael V conceived the bold idea of making a new start in the direction of reform, but

---

[1] ἦν δ' ἀνὴρ ἐπὶ μὲν τῆς προτέρας διαγωγῆς κακιζόμενος καὶ τοῖς ἐπαινετῶς πολιτευομένοις μὴ συναπτόμενος, ἐπὶ δὲ τῆς βασιλικῆς ἀναβάσεως καὶ λίαν ἐγκωμιαζόμενός τε καὶ σεμνυνόμενος οἷα φιλοτίμως ἄρτι πρῶτον ὑπὲρ τοὺς πρὸ αὐτοῦ βεβασιλευκότας τῇ συγκλήτῳ καὶ τοῖς ἄλλοις προσφερόμενος ὑπηκόοις καὶ τιμαῖς περιβλέπτοις καὶ ἀξιώμασι πλείστους ὅσους καταγεραίρων καὶ τὴν εὐνομίαν εἴπερ τις ἄλλος σπουδάζων ἀνεγερθῆναι καὶ τῶν ἀδικουμένων ἐκδικητὴς ἀναφαινόμενος ἀπαραίτητος καὶ δικαιοσύνην τῶν ἄλλων ἀπάντων ὑπεραίρων καὶ προτιμώμενος.— *Hist.* p. 17.

[2] Le Beau's words may be taken as typical of the general feeling of historians about this Emperor: *Plus indigne de régner par la bassesse de son cœur que par celle de sa naissance, il était fourbe, injuste, ingrate, ne reconnaissant ni les droits de la parenté ni ceux de l'amitié* ... etc. (XIV, 308, ed. Saint-Martin).

that the conservative elements—the *inertia*—were too strong for him. It had not escaped his observation that his predecessor was weighed down and impeded by his relations; and he consequently concluded that one condition of success was to make a clean clearance of his kinsmen. Joannês would never have fallen in with his new plans, but Constantine, who was merely a time-server, humoured him. The banishment of Zôê was also necessary to his designs, for she was a remnant of the old order of things.

The irrelevant consideration that his conduct to Zôê was ungrateful, combined with his unkind treatment of his relations, has obscured the attitude and the aims of Michael V, and perverted the judgment of historians in his regard. We have no reason to blame his political tendencies; it is his blunder in banishing the Empress that condemns him.

7. *Zôê and Theodôra.** The women's apartments in the palace were now changed into a council-chamber. There was some difficulty at first in the joint rule of two old sisters, between whom suspicion and dislike had prevailed for many years. Zôê was the eldest, but it was the proclamation of Theodôra that had overthrown Kalaphatês. The difficulty was solved by unexpected graciousness on Zôê's part; and Theodôra, in accordance with her retiring disposition, yielded precedence to her sister. State business was transacted and audiences were held just as usual, and the general loyalty was more pronounced than towards an Emperor.[1] Those who had

[* A.D. 1042, Ap.–June.]

[1] τό τε πολιτικὸν πλῆθος καὶ τὸ στρατιωτικὸν συμφωνοῦντας ὑπὸ δεσπότισι (Psellos, *Hist.* p. 104); cf. Zônaras, p. 155. Psellos adds an expression of wonder that no family seemed so favoured of Heaven as the Basilian, "though the root was fixed and planted not lawfully, but by bloodshed and slaughter"; the members of the family were all incomparable in both beauty and size.

held office under Kalaphatês were not disgraced nor deposed.

Zôê was quick in apprehension, but not fluent of speech; Theodôra, on the other hand, fluent and less swift-witted. Theodôra was fond of hoarding, Zôê extravagant in her liberality.

But the reign of the two women could not last, for the administration was neglected or mismanaged and the expenditure ruinous. Neither of them understood anything of finances or political affairs; they mixed up the trivialities of a lady's bower with the imperial business. The court was kept up with a degree of extravagant splendour and display that drained the treasury. The palace was full of flatterers, and Zôê spent the military funds in profusion to these nimble caperers.

This waste and height of brilliance were the beginnings, says Psellos, of the subsequent descent—the condition of state bankruptcy which ensued. A strong man's hand at the helm was imperatively required. Zôê's jealousy of her sister induced her to satisfy this requirement and choose a third husband. She fixed first on Constantine Dalassênos, a nobleman who had suffered from the ascendency of the Paphlagonian family, to which his birth, his position, and his high spirit had made him an object of alarm.[1] In the reign of Michael IV he had been confined in the island of Platy; Michael V released him, but made him become a monk. Zôê summoned him to the palace on some pretext, but his independent manner and his uncompromising spirit disappointed the Empress, who was used to smooth words, and she rejected him. Her choice then fell on a man, distinguished for beauty and sensual attractions, though not for rank or position,[2] Constantine Arto-

[1] Constantine VIII (IX) had thought of choosing him as his successor.
[2] οἷον πρὸς ἔρωτας ἐφελκύσασθαι καὶ μὴ μαχλοσύνῃ προσκειμένην ψυχήν (Zônaras, p. 155). This is not taken from Psellos, who merely says,

klinas, who had been a secretary of Rômanos III, and was then suspected of carrying on an intrigue with Zôê. The disposition of Rômanos was not jealous, but Michael IV found a pretext for removing him from Constantinople. It was fated, however, that Zôê should be obliged to make yet a third choice, for death suddenly carried off Artoklinas. This accident blew good to another Constantine, who had been banished by Michael IV to Mitylênê, Constantine Monomachos. Zôê recalled him from exile, married him, and raised him to the throne. The Monomachoi[1] were an old family, and Constantine had made a brilliant second marriage, which had joined him in affinity with the Emperor Rômanos. Pulcheria, the sister of Rômanos, was the wife of Basil Sklêros; Constantine married their only daughter. But this alliance did not procure him any appointment. His father Theodosios had conspired against Basil, and a cloud of suspicion continued to rest over the son.

8. *Constantine IX.** From Rômanos III to Michael VI the Basilian dynasty continued; for of the five Emperors three were husbands of Zôê, one was her adopted son, and one was the nominee of Theodôra. Thus the acci-

τὸ δὲ εἶδος ἀξιωματικὸς καὶ λαμπρός. Nor does Psellos mention the suspicion recorded by Zônaras that his death was caused by poison administered by his wife.

[1] ῥίζης ἀρχαίας τῶν Μονομάχων (Psellos, *Hist.* p. 110). In the *Epitaphios* on Leichudês, Psellos speaks of Constantine thus: ὁ καὶ τὴν κλῆσιν ὁμώνυμος τῷ τὴν οὐρανόπολιν ταύτην οἰκίσαντι καὶ τὴν προσηγορίαν φερώνυμος, μόνος τοῦ κράτους προκινδυνεύσας καὶ ὑπὲρ πάντας ἀξιόμαχος γεγονὼς καὶ ὑπὲρ τῆς κοινῆς τοῦ γένους μονομαχήσας εὐκλείας, κἀντεῦθεν τὴν ἐπωνυμίαν ὥσπερ ἀριστεῖον ἀνειληφώς (p. 398). Here of course there is only a play on the name Μονομάχος, which was a family name, not an ἐπωνυμία. One of the characteristics of Psellos' style is a love of speaking of people without mentioning their names, as though the names were something trivial, and it were more dignified to indicate by a periphrasis or indirection.

[* Constantine IX (X), Monomachos, A.D. 1042, June 11–1054, Nov.]

dent of the long lives of these women lends a sort of continuity to the history between Constantine VIII and Isaac Komnênos. But in the first part of this period the actual government of the Empire passed into the hands of a Paphlagonian family, and the attitude of Constantine IX was opposition to this administration,[1] an opposition which one of themselves, Michael V, had already initiated. This contrast is indicated by his choice of ministers. His first chief counsellor was Michael Kêrularios,[2] who had been concerned in a revolt against Michael IV, and when after a short time he became patriarch, he was replaced by Leichudês, who had held the same position under Michael V. Thus his ministers were trained and learned men. One of the most important events of his reign was the revival of letters, which had been on the wane since Constantine VII; influenced by Leichudês and the polymath Psellos, Monomachos patronised learning, in which respect he was the forerunner of the Komnênoi.

Psellos gives us a long account of this reign, which he compares to an ocean; for he had lived through so many very short reigns that the supremacy of Monomachos, which lasted thirteen years, seemed quite long. In describing the chief men and women at his court we may begin with the Emperor himself.

Love of pleasure and fickleness of disposition were the chief characteristics of Constantine; he was a thoroughly frivolous man. In a long banishment he had suffered many hardships, and when he ascended the throne his idea was to recompense himself for past pains by the greatest possible measure of enjoyment. He looked on

---

[1] The eyes of Joannês, the orphanotrophos, were put out in 1043, May 2.

[2] Psellos: ἐγκωμιαστικὸς εἰς τὸν μακαριώτατον πατριάρχην κῦρ Μιχαὴλ τὸν Κηρουλλάριον (p. 324).

the palace as a haven of rest which he had reached having endured the stress of the waves; and all he cared for was good cheer and the presence of smiling faces. He had no conception, says Psellos, that the function of a king is the performance of services beneficial to the *subjects* and demanding a mind constantly awake and alive. Consistently with this view he left the entire public administration to others, devoting very little time himself to business, and gave himself up to the life hedonistic; and as Zôê's inclinations were similar she was very well content. "He that must steer at the head of an Empire ought to be the mirror of the times for wisdom and for policy". Constantine did not even try to be wise or politic; his utter indifference reacted ruinously on the State, though his ministers seem to have been "indifferent honest".

He had a vulgar love of buffoonery and a childish love of triviality; any one who could make him laugh prepossessed him and was sure of promotion. Here we touch on a bad feature of his reign. There were fixed and definite conditions, and grades of promotion to rank; Constantine declined to be restricted by them and lavished titles and posts on the favourites of an hour. He filled the Senate with persons who had no right to be there. The consequence was that these honours became valueless, as they meant nothing. This profusion of titles was at least cheap, but unfortunately he was equally generous and unjust in spending the public money, following the example set by Zôê and Theodôra in their short reign before his accession. The State was really sound, says Psellos, before his accession; but his unprincipled principles as to the lack-duty privileges of the Emperor affected it with many germs of disease.

Nevertheless he had some good qualities; he was sharp-witted and very good-natured. Psellos, who en-

deavours to treat him impartially and does not scruple
to censure severely many of his acts and points out his
defects, had a high opinion of his personal character,
and comparing him with Alexander, "the two Cæsars",
and other great men of ancient ages, says that while inferior to these in bravery he excelled them in other good
qualities. Whenever he passed a sentence of imprison-
ment or banishment, he felt a pang of remorse for his
severity; and he was so afraid of his own clemency that
he used to bind himself secretly by oath not to commute
the sentence he had passed. He was beneficent and
compassionate in cases that came under his immediate
notice. For example, it happened that a rich man had
been accused and found guilty of peculating money
from certain military funds. The fine which was ad-
judged was larger than all he was worth, and he had the
prospect of not only present penury but a debt which
would be transmitted to his children. The claimant of
the fine being the public exchequer, it was impracticable
to supplicate an inexorable thing. The man gained an
audience of the Emperor, at which Psellos was present
as secretary; and professed his readiness to pay everything he possessed, if only the surplus should not be
handed down as an inherited obligation to his children.
He began to strip off his clothes in token that he would
surrender everything. The Emperor was moved to tears,
and ended by paying the whole debt for him.

We may be sure that Constantine was not really badly
intentioned. It was his fortune and not his fault that it
was an impossibility for him to be serious. He was a bad
Emperor, but a sufficiently amiable man. We can understand the leniency of an historian towards him, and are
not surprised at the favourable judgment of Attaleiatês,
who says that he was a good Emperor till the end of his
reign, when in a most unexpected manner he began a

system of exactions.[1] "He was generous in giving, and knew how to confer benefits in imperial style", solicitous for military successes, but addicted to luxury and lechery. The commendatory clause about his generosity reminds us of a remark of Psellos, that the unwise profusion which he himself censures will furnish to other historians a theme for praise. Attaleiatês goes on to mention his love of amusement and buffoonery, and notes especially that he provided an elephant and a camelopard, of which animals he gives long descriptions, for the delectation of the Byzantine populace. He gratified his love of magnificence and followed the fashion of preceding monarchs by building a monastery and church, dedicated to St George, with charming meadows attached to it. He also erected a hospital.

The Emperor and the Empress Zôê, who was now too old to be jealous, continued very good friends till her death in 1050. Theodôra fell back into her old secluded life, and her chief worldly pleasure consisted in hoarding money. Neither she nor Zôê cared for parks or gardens, or houses fitted with splendour and refinement. Zôê's taste was quite peculiar: she had a passion for perfumery. If you had entered her sleeping apartment, you might have thought you were in the workshop of a city mechanic. You would first be conscious of a very strong heat, which in winter might not be unwelcome, but in summer would drive the visitor away. The heat proceeded from an immense fire in the chamber, where you would have seen several maidservants engaged in the processes of brewing and mixing unguents and perfumes; one perhaps measuring the requisite quantities of the ingredients, another blending them, another boiling or

[1] *Hist.* p. 47: ἀνὴρ πολιτικὸς (which we may in the case of Constantine interpret by the negative of its antithesis, "not military") καὶ γένους ἐπισήμου γενόμενος δωρηματικός τε καὶ βασιλικῶς εὐεργετεῖν ἐπιστάμενος, κ.τ.λ. On his accession Constantine ἠγάθυνε τὸ ὑπήκοον (p. 18).

distilling them, and Zôê herself, impervious to the heat at midsummer, directing or assisting them. One who desired to win her favour had only to send her a rare spice or a precious perfume. She used her compounds for the purposes of divine worship, for she was very religious.

As the Empress was thus wholly devoted to the odours of sanctity, the Emperor was sufficiently free to prosecute his amours. He had been married twice, and when his second wife, who belonged to the family of the Sklêroi, died, he fell in love with her niece Sklêraina, but did not marry her from religious scruples, which however did not hinder him from becoming Zôê's husband. Sklêraina was his faithful companion during his exile, and in the day of his prosperity he did not forget her. As Psellos says, reminding us of a certain remark of Théophile Gautier, when he looked upon Zôê with the eyes of sense he saw Sklêraina with the eyes of the spirit, and when he held the Empress in his arms, his beloved was in the bosom of his soul. His first step was to recall Sklêraina to the capital, to which he obtained his wife's consent. He kept her at first in a private residence, and set building operations afoot in order to have an excuse for visiting her, without exciting suspicion, several times a month,[1] and he used to entertain his attendants there with such sumptuous repasts that it was their interest to smooth the way for these secret trysts. He used to lavish

---

[1] Psellos, *History*, p. 127: ἵνα δὲ πρόφασις εἴη τῷ βασιλεῖ ἐκεῖσε φοιτᾶν οἶκον ἑαυτοῦ πεποίηται τὴν σκηνὴν καὶ ἵνα δὴ μεγαλοπρεπὴς γένηται καὶ πρὸς βασιλικὴν ὑποδοχὴν ἐπιτήδειος θεμελίους τε ἔξωθεν μείζονας καταβάλλεται, κ.τ.λ....Προσεποιεῖτο γοῦν ἑκάστοτε ὅ,τι δήποτε τῶν οἰκονομουμένων καὶ τοῦ μηνὸς πολλάκις ἀπῄει, πρόφασιν μὲν ὀψόμενός τι τῶν γιγνομένων, κ.τ.λ. Zônaras (IV, p. 178) says that the Emperor began the building of the monastery of Mangana for the same reason, λέγεται δὲ τῆς οἰκοδομῆς ἄρξασθαι διὰ τὴν ἐρωμένην αὐτῷ, τὴν Σκλήραιναν λέγω, ἵν᾽ ἐκείνη προσφοιτᾷ συνεχῶς, ἐν τῷ οἴκῳ τοῦ Κυνηγίου ἐχούσῃ τότε δὴ τὴν κατοίκησιν. Thus the house of Kynêgios was the σκηνή.

the imperial treasures on his mistress, and as an example of his gifts Psellos mentions that, having found one day in the palace a bronze casket with carved work, he filled it with money and sent it to Sklêraina. But he soon became bolder, and finally introduced her to the palace, where Zôê treated her amicably and conferred on her the title of Sebastê. A contract of friendship between the mistress and wife was drawn up in a written form, and the blushing Senate, which was summoned to give its countenance to this measure of amity, praised the document as if it had fallen from heaven. On that day the two ladies sat together in the Emperor's company, and Zôê did not betray the least chagrin, whether her feelings were really indifferent or her long experience of Emperors and court life made her deem dissimulation advisable. But when the newcomer was once installed Zôê never visited her husband until she had assured herself that he was alone.

Sklêraina was not remarkable for beauty, but was sufficiently goodlooking to give no opening for malicious remarks. Her sympathetic disposition and graceful manners won the heart of Psellos; and the stylist goes so far as to say that her "speech was like nothing else, refined and flower-like, with a quite sophistic excellence in the rhythms; a sweet style ran along her tongue spontaneously, and when she described aught, indescribable charms hovered around". She was a very good listener, and was fond of Greek mythology, on which she used often to question Psellos. We can picture to ourselves the young philosopher of twenty-five entertaining the imperial lady with fluent accounts of old Greek stories, full of plays upon words, and not unseasoned with adroit compliments and elegant adulation.

He tells an anecdote that Zôê attended by her court, her sister Theodôra and the Sebastê, who had not been seen in public with the imperial sisters before, went in procession to a spectacle; and a bystander expert in flattery cried aloud οὐ νέμεσις, without finishing the quotation.[1] Sklêraina said nothing at the time, but afterwards received an explanation of the words, and rewarded the man who had pronounced them most richly. She conciliated the goodwill of Zôê and Theodôra by making them presents suitable to their whims—coins to Theodôra, to Zôê Indian perfumes and scented woods, very small-sized olives and very white laurel-berries. With the expenses of the three ladies the treasures which Basil accumulated "with toil and the sweat of his brow" were gaily and quickly spent on amusements. Psellos does not mention the tumult which Kedrênos alleges to have taken place in September 1044, owing to a general feeling of indignation against the influence of the mistress who seemed to be ousting the wife and sister-in-law. The multitude cried, "We will not have Sklêraina to reign over us, nor on her account shall our purple-born mothers (μάμαι) Zôê and Theodôra die". Zôê herself quieted this disturbance. Not long after, its cause was carried off prematurely by asthma, and the Emperor was inconsolable. Psellos declines to describe his puerile grief.

One of the personages at the Byzantine court in this reign was Boilas, a man who had a defect in his utterance and behaved as a sort of court jester. It was his defective speech and odd pronunciation that gained him the favour of Constantine, who delighted in nothing more than in personal oddity and silly conversation. He soon became so fond of this man—"this hypocrite", as

[1] See Homer, *Il.* III, 156—

οὐ νέμεσις Τρῶας καὶ ἐϋκνήμιδας Ἀχαιοὺς
τοιῇδ᾽ ἀμφὶ γυναικὶ πολὺν χρόνον ἄλγεα πάσχειν.

Homer was perhaps as familiar in educated Byzantine society as Shakespeare is in England nowadays.

Psellos calls him, for his real character was knavery—
that he could do nothing without him. He loaded him
with the highest titles and granted free access to himself
at all times, free use of all the private entrances and
rooms of the palace. Boilas had all the privileges of an
Emperor's fool. He managed even to gain access to the
women's apartments. He boldly asserted with oaths
that both Zôê and Theodôra had brought forth children,
and gave a detailed account of Theodôra's confinement,
repeating even the very words she uttered. These au-
dacious inventions made him so formidable that the
Empresses opened all the secret doors to him, and he
received innumerable gifts.[1]

"But he was not content with this good fortune", says
Zônaras; "he also coveted the Empire". Zônaras does
not tell us what put this idea into his head, but we learn
the reason from Psellos. After the death of Sklêraina the
Emperor loved a young Alan princess, whom he kept
as his concubine, and after the death of Zôê conferred
on her the title of Sebastê.[2] Boilas became enamoured

[1] Attaleiatês (p. 18) states that on the accession of Constantine IX [X]
Theodôra retired to her old solitary life. This seems to imply that she
left the palace, which is in accordance with the fact that before Constantine's death she was conveyed to the palace by ship (Kedrênos, II,
610). Moreover, when Sklêraina was installed in the palace, it is mentioned that she and Zôê resided on either side of the Emperor's apartments, μέσον δὲ σκηνοῦντος τοῦ βασιλέως ἑκατέρωθεν ᾤκουν παραλλὰξ
ἡ βασιλὶς καὶ ἡ Σεβαστή (Zônaras, p. 160); the residence of Theodôra is
not mentioned. Nevertheless the incident recorded above about Boilas
(see Psellos, *Hist.* pp. 172–3) implies that Theodôra resided in the palace,
and when we compare the passage of Psellos from which the statement
of Zônaras seems to be taken, we are led to the conclusion that Zônaras
mistranslated it. Διανειμάμενοι δὲ τὰς οἰκήσεις ὁ μὲν βασιλεὺς τὸ μέσον
ἔλαχε τῶν τριῶν αἱ δὲ πέριξ ἐσκήνουν τὸ δὲ ἄδυτον εἶχεν ἡ Σεβαστή.
Zônaras took τῶν τριῶν as meaning Constantine, Zôê, and Sklêraina;
whereas it really means Zôê, Theodôra, and Sklêraina, and αἱ δὲ refers
to Zôê and Theodôra. τὸ ἄδυτον means the innermost apartments, they
would correspond to the altar, πέριξ to the two aisles, τὸ μέσον to the
nave of a church.

[2] He did not marry her because he had been already married three
times, and from a feeling of respect for Theodôra.

of her, and, not being able to succeed in his suit while Constantine was alive, conceived the notion of slaying him and ascending the throne. The design seemed to present no difficulty, as the Emperor had complete confidence in him and was accustomed to sleep unguarded. But it was betrayed within less than an hour before its intended execution. One of the persons whom Boilas had taken into his counsels suddenly entered the Emperor's chamber out of breath, and, having told him that his dear friend Boilas was about to assassinate him, fled to the chapel altar and confessed the whole conspiracy. Constantine could hardly believe that it was a fact, and was half glad at escaping the danger, half angry at the chance of losing his indispensable favourite. When the conspirator was brought to trial in fetters, he could not bear the sight and cried, "Undo the fetters, for my heart is softened with pity for him". He then tried to put his defence into his mouth, and at last Boilas approached him, and, kissing his hands and placing his head on his knees, said all he wanted was to sit on the throne with a diadem of pearls. The Emperor leaped with joy, but his sister Euprepia and the Empress Theodôra were so vexed at his folly that for mere shame he sent the delinquent for a few days in mock banishment to an island hard by the capital. The attachment of Boilas to the Alan princess was not however extinguished, and the Emperor himself one day in the company of Psellos observed him making erotic signs to her, but looked on the matter as a joke.

Constantine Leichudês was invested with the administration of the Empire in 1043 when Kêrularios became patriarch. Leichudês was an able and cultured man who had made a study of rhetoric and had dipped deeper into the secrets of law than most of the Byzantine statesmen of the time, having sat at the feet of Joannês

Xiphilinos. He was an intimate friend of Psellos, who probably owed his advancement to him and honoured him with a panegyrical oration after his death. From it we learn that he was born at Constantinople of good family, and was very precocious as a boy. He carried the rhetorical powers with which he was naturally gifted to great perfection; and he made his rhetorical and legal studies react upon each other—a point on which Psellos strongly insists.[1] We must not, of course, give too much weight to the glowing terms of eulogy in which his friend, the philosopher, speaks of his administration. He says that when Leichudês came to the helm he showed himself at once fully equal to the very varied duties that demanded his attention, and displayed the most astonishing versatility;[2] he had the useful power of being all things to all men. Skylitzês also bears witness to the high reputation he bore as a minister;[3] but his capacity is best attested by the fact that he held the same office under Isaac Komnênos and was elected patriarch after the fall of Kêrularios. In everything, we are told by Psellos, he aimed at symmetry; his dress was neither very plain nor very rich, his table neither poorly furnished nor luxurious, his step measured, his speech at once dignified and fluent. In State documents his

---

[1] For his law studies see *Epitaphios*, p. 395; cf. *History*, p. 188. "He was a canon of orthography (correct writing), a manual of rhetoric, a chalk-line of legislation".

[2] *Epitaphios*, p. 401: οὗτός τε γὰρ πρὸς τοὺς διαφόρους τὰς γνώμας διάφορος ἦν.

[3] Skylitzês (Kedrênos, vol. II, Bonn ed.), p. 644, recording his election to the patriarchate, speaks of him as ἀνὴρ μέγιστον διαλάμψας τοῖς βασιλικοῖς καὶ πολιτικοῖς πράγμασιν ἀπό τε τοῦ Μονομάχου καὶ μέχρι τοῦ τηνικάδε καιροῦ καὶ μέγα κλέος ἐπὶ τῷ μεσασμῷ τῆς τῶν ὅλων διοικήσεως ἀνενεγκάμενος καὶ τῆς τῶν Μαγγάνων προνοίας καὶ τῶν δικαιωμάτων φύλαξ παρὰ τοῦ εἰρημένου βασιλέως καταλειφθείς. The expression by which the chief minister was denoted was ὁ παραδυναστεύων τῷ βασιλεῖ, but in the time of Constantine IX the phrase ὁ μεσάζων came into use; hence τῷ μεσασμῷ in this passage.

style was simple, pure, and ordinary; but he could write good "Attic".

It was probably by his suggestion that Constantine changed the constitution of the Senate and made the qualification merit instead of birth. He made an important reform in the administration of justice, by which the judges in the various themes were to commit their sentences to writing and deposit them in public registers. And there is no doubt that his influence contributed largely to the revival of the study of philosophy, rhetoric, and law, under the able guidance of Constantine, Psellos, and Joannês Xiphilinos.

The university of Constantinople which had been founded by Theodosios II lived for only three centuries. The study of letters declined in the seventh century, and the Emperor who founded the great dynasty of the iconoclasts, Leo III, abolished the university because the professors refused to support his religious doctrines. In the ninth century Theophilos licensed Leo, the famous scholar of his day, to give public lectures; and Constantine VII, himself a prolific author, encouraged the writing or compiling of books on an extensive scale. But there was no organised system of teaching in the Empire, no recognised body of men to whose judgments questions of learning might be deferred. Constantine IX had the honour of being the second founder of the university, though on a far more modest scale than the scheme of Theodosios. Two chairs were instituted, one for law and one for philosophy. The site of this new academy was a church of St Peter.

Psellos, who was the prime instigator of this revival of letters, gives an account of his first interview with Constantine, which is amusing from its naive self-conceit. He was well known at court, having been under-secretary in the preceding reign, and had a high repute for his learning and fluent speech. "My tongue", he writes, "has a certain flowery grace even in simple utterances, and without any intention or preparation certain natural qualities of sweetness distil from it"; he knew this from the manifest effect he produced on interlocutors. When he appeared before the Emperor, he informed him of his family, and of the nature and scope of his studies; and the impressionable monarch was so enthusiastic at the philosopher's speech and manner that he hung upon his lips and wellnigh kissed him.

Psellos was appointed to the chair of philosophy, and his friend Joannês Xiphilinos to the chair of law. Xiphilinos was a native of Trapezûs who came to study at Constantinople. These two students, with their friends Leichudês and Joannês Mauropûs,[1] formed a sort of new literary movement in Byzantium. In particular Psellos revived Platonism, which he valued above the ecclesiastical Aristotelianism in vogue, and he introduced a new atticising style, which was followed by Anna Komnênê, Zônaras, Nikêtas, etc. A tendency to purism—exclusion of colloquial and Latin words—may be traced even at the end of the tenth century in Leo Diakonos, who, in this respect, shows a particularity which is quite foreign to Constantine Porphyrogennêtos, Theophanês, or John Malalas. But Leo was not a stylist like Psellos; we may consider him the model of Attaleiatês and Skylitzês. These writers do not scruple to introduce a foreign or vulgar word when their meaning requires it—for example, τζουκανιστήριον or ἐξκούβιτα, words which Psellos would avoid, or, if he strained a point and admitted them, would apologise for. For the *Hellênismos* on which the Princess Anna prided her-

---

[1] This scholar was a relation of Leichudês. He was afterwards appointed archbishop of Euchaitoi. Letters of Psellos to him are extant, and he speaks of him and Xiphilinos as "the two Johns", τὼ Ἰωάννη.

self she was altogether indebted to the movement initiated by Psellos, and but for his influence in the revival of Platonic studies she could never have boasted that she had studied Plato's dialogues.[1] To this resurrection of the "divine" philosopher in the eleventh century is perhaps ultimately traceable also the Platonism of Gemistos Plêthôn, who wrote in the fifteenth century. We must note that Psellos considered the study of Greek philosophy necessary to the thorough comprehension of Christianity.[2]

Joannês Xiphilinos was appointed custodian of the laws, *nomophylax*, as well as professor of law. He was a man renowned for piety as well as for learning, and bore a high reputation. Modern writers on the *Jus Græco-romanum* have not been aware of his identity, knowing him only as he is cited in scholia on the Basilika by the name Joannês Nomophylax, and only conjecturing his date to be the middle of the eleventh century from the fact that in one scholion his opinion is opposed to that of Garidas, who was a distinguished lawyer of that age.[3]

[1] τὸ ἑλληνίζειν ἐς ἄκρον ἐσπουδακυῖα καὶ ῥητορικῆς οὐκ ἀμελετήτως ἔχουσα καὶ τὰς Ἀριστοτελικὰς τέχνας εὖ ἀναλεξαμένη καὶ τοὺς Πλάτωνος διαλόγους (Anna, Bonn ed. 1, 4). Compare an article by Mr Freeman on "Some Points in the later History of the Greek Language", in which the "Renaissance", as he calls it, is duly insisted on. "Go on to Leo the deacon, still more go on to Anna Komnênê and Nikêtas. . . . We are landed in a *Renaissance*" (*Journal for Hellenic Studies*, III, 377). Psellos intervenes between Leo and Anna, and explains the "still more".

[2] In an exhortation to his pupils (*Opuscula*, ed. Boissonade, pp. 151-3, quoted by Sathas, preface to vol. IV, p. li) he says: By studying Greek metaphysics, "ye will be drawing fresh water from salt water like mariners. For what do they? When in mid ocean they find themselves unprovided with fresh water, they hang sponges over the sea, and compressing the collected vapour into water have a perfectly sweet draught. So ye likewise, if ye suspend your souls above the brine of Hellenic doctrines and convert the heavy and terrestrial sound which is wafted up from them into a light and treble note, will perhaps hear the sweet melody of the highest string".

[3] Attaleiatês, *Hist.* p. 21: ἐκαίνισε δὲ (Constantine IX) καὶ δέκρετον δικῶν ἰδιωτικῶν ἐπὶ τῶν κρίσεων καλέσας τὸν τούτου προέχοντα—that

No one thought of identifying the scholiast on the Basilika with that Joannês Xiphilinos of whom Attaleiatês and Skylitzês give short notices.[1] This identification is demonstrated by the writings of Psellos.[2]

When Monomachos came to the throne, he sent a manifesto throughout the provinces to declare his accession and to promise to his subjects freedom of speech, the abolition of all abuses, and abundance of all blessings.[3] This was in fact a notification that his policy would be quite the reverse of that of the Paphlagonians. And until the last years of his reign he seems to have realised these promises, or allowed Leichudês to realise them, as far as the wars in which he was involved permitted him. But towards the end of his reign he became dissatisfied with the administration of his chancellor, because (says Psellos) he envied his power and felt uneasy under his restraint. It seemed as if Leichudês were the Emperor and Constantine the minister. But the true reason for this dissatisfaction was, we can have no doubt, that the Emperor wanted more money than Leichudês could provide, and Leichudês was not prepared to be

is Xiphilinos. Garidas flourished in the reign of Constantine Dûkas, and was the author of διαίρεσις περὶ φόνων (a tract which he dedicated to that Emperor) and a βιβλίον περὶ ἀγωγῶν. See Heimbach's notice of him in *Griechisch-römisches Recht*.

[1] Attaleiatês, p. 92: ἦν γὰρ τῆς συνόδου προεξάρχων καὶ τὴν πατριαρχίαν κοσμῶν Ἰωάννης ὁ ἐπικεκλημένος Ξιφιλῖνος ἐκ Τραπεζοῦντος μὲν ὡρμημένος ἀνὴρ δὲ σοφὸς καὶ παιδεύσεως εἰς ἄκρον ἐληλακὼς κἀν τοῖς πολιτικοῖς περίβλεπτος γεγονὼς καὶ ἀρετῆς εὐφρόνως ἐπιμελούμενος ὥστε τοῖς βασιλείοις ἔτι ἐμφιλοχωρῶν καὶ πρῶτα φέρων παρὰ τῷ βασιλεῖ τὴν μοναχικὴν πολιτείαν ἐν ἀκμῇ τῆς εὐημερίας καὶ τῆς ἡλικίας ἀσπάσασθαι καὶ τὸν ἀναχωρητικὸν βίον περὶ τὸ Ὀλύμπιον ὄρος ἑλόμενος χρόνον ἐπὶ συχνὸν ἦν διαλάμπων ἐπ᾽ ἀρετῇ καὶ φόβῳ θεοῦ. The corresponding passage in Skylitzês (p. 658) reproduces this, with some omissions, almost verbally.

[2] See especially his *Epitaphios* on Xiphilinos.

[3] Kedrênos, p. 542: παντὸς μὲν ἀγαθοῦ βλύσιν καὶ παρρησίαν πάσης δὲ κακίας ἀποτομήν. In the same place his promotions in the Senate and his largesses to the people are mentioned.

unscrupulous. Kedrênos refers this want of money to the expenses incurred in building the monastery of Mangana.[1] Psellos perceived a change in the sentiments of Monomachos towards Leichudês and told the matter to his friend, but he refused to make any alteration in his attitude. The Emperor deposed him—not suddenly, but gradually—and with this act we must connect the "great and unexpected change" for the worse which took place in the administration. "He attached himself to clever tax-collecting officers whom official language names *sekretikoi* [thus Attaleiatês apologises for using a non-Hellenic word]; with them he invented unforeseen fines and arrears, and, as it were, extracted the marrow of those who had any degree of wealth".[2] The prisons were filled with the bankrupt and ruined. Special dissatisfaction was given by seizing property destined for churches and supplies intended for monasteries. In another way too he injured the Empire. He disbanded the Iberian army in order that the treasury might receive in money the equivalent of the supplies which those provinces furnished in kind to the army. The chief of these unscrupulous financiers was a eunuch, the logothete Joannês.[3] He was a man of so little education that he could not speak or write grammatically correct Greek; his birth was base, and he was unfit for the higher branches of the administration; in fact, he was quite the reverse of Leichudês whom he succeeded. The new order of things was so oppressive that Constantine's death (January 1055) was universally felt to be a relief.

[1] Kedrênos, p. 602, where his new ministers are called δημοσίους... φροντιστὰς ἀσεβεῖς καὶ ἀλάστορας.

[2] Attaleiatês, p. 50: ἐκμυελίζων is the strong word used of this bleeding. The disbanding of the army of Iberia is recorded by Kedrênos.

[3] Our knowledge of Joannês is due to Zônaras (IV, 180), who says that he was the reverse in every respect of Leichudês. For some time before the deposition of the latter the two men were drawing the Emperor in different ways.

Yet before his end he seems to have repented his dismissal of Leichudês.[1]

The changes that had come over the spirit of the Emperor, who in small matters had always a character for instability and want of seriousness, produced a general feeling of uncertainty and want of confidence, which was shared by Psellos and his friends. He and Xiphilinos had always felt a leaning towards the spiritual life, and they considered that the time had come to take the step. So they took an oath together, which Xiphilinos at least kept with an equal mind until he was elected patriarch, to spend the rest of their lives in the seclusion of a monastery. They alleged bodily illnesses in order to obtain the Emperor's permission to retire; but with Psellos, "with whose tongue he was dreadfully in love", he was unwilling to part.[2] He first wrote most touching letters to him, which Psellos preserved, and when writing his history some years later was unable to read without weeping. When entreaties were of no avail, he used threats. But Psellos took the step of cutting his hair, and then Constantine, resigning himself gracefully, wrote an epistle of congratulation that he had chosen the better life and preferred the monk's gown to the soft raiment of a palace.

With Psellos and Xiphilinos vanished also the more refined tastes which their presence induced the Em-

---

[1] Skylitzês, p. 644: καὶ τῶν δικαιωμάτων φύλαξ παρὰ τοῦ εἰρημένου βασιλέως καταλειφθείς. For the deposition of Leichudês, cf. Psellos, *Epitaphios* on L., p. 405: καί γε θαυμάζων ἐπὶ πᾶσι τὸν αὐτοκράτορα ἐν τοῦτο ἐπαινεῖν οὐκ ἔχω ὅτι ὃν ἐπὶ πολλοῖς δοκιμάσας ἠκρίβωσε τοῦτον ὡς ἄρτι διαγινώσκων κατῃτιάσατο μεθιστᾷ τῆς ἀρχῆς οὐ τεταγὼς ἀπὸ βηλοῦ θεσπεσίοιο, τοῦτο δὴ τοῦ ἔπους· ᾐδεῖτο γὰρ τὴν τοῦ ἀνδρὸς ἀρετὴν καὶ ἀχθόμενος τούτῳ οὐδέ που παρακρημνίσας, ἀλλὰ βραχύ τι τοῦ ὀχήματος παρωσάμενος, ἵν᾽ αἰδέσιμος αὐτῷ καὶ ἡ μετάστασις γένοιτο.

[2] Psellos used to serve up his philosophy in a light and superficial dress to suit the light and superficial mind of the Emperor. When he was tired of philosophy, he used to treat him to rhetoric (*Hist.* p. 196).

peror to cultivate. On their retirement he had recourse
to amusements of the senses,[1] of which Psellos gives one
instance. He caused a large basin to be dug in the
middle of a park and to be filled with water up to the
brim, so that it was on a level with the surrounding land.
The Emperor used to lie in wait in order to observe and
laugh at the mishaps of unwary persons who, advancing
to pluck fruit from the trees with which the park was
stocked, would sometimes walk into the water. He afterwards made a summer-house in this park close to the
pond, in which he used constantly to bathe; and, perhaps from remaining in the water too long, he got an
attack of pleurisy which brought on his death.

The military history of Constantine's reign has been
given in full detail by Kedrênos. The chief events were
the revolt of Maniakês, the Russian war, the Servian
war, the Patzinak invasions, the Saracen war and loss of
Armenia, the revolt of Tornikios, the invasions of the
Seljuk Turks. Only three of these are described by
Psellos—the revolts of Maniakês and Tornikios and the
Russian war. Of the well-known circumstances of the
life of George Maniakês we learn nothing new, but receive a vivid impression of his personal appearance.
Psellos had seen and admired him standing nearly ten
feet high, like a mountain or a pillar.[2] The expression
of his countenance was not delicate nor pleasing, but
like a volcano; his voice was as the voice of thunder, his
hands were stalwart to shake walls to pieces or crush
bronze gates between them, his gait was as a lion's, and
his shadowy eyebrows gave him a grim look. In personal

[1] ἐπὶ τὰς ἐν αἰσθήσει πάλιν κατέφυγε χάριτας (p. 198).
[2] Cf. Constantine Manassês, 1. 6284:

ἀνὴρ γιγαντοπάλαμος ὀξύχειρ ἀνδροφόντης
θρασυσπλαγχνος εὐκάρδιος πνέων ὀργῆς ἐκθύμου.

The chosen men who fought with him in the battle of Ostrovos were also
γιγαντόσωμοι.

might and bravery he must have been equal to the bravest and mightiest western knight; and he was a worthy fellow of the adventurous Norseman Harald Haardrada, with whom he sailed in the Ægean and fought in Sicily, and, if we may believe the saga, sometimes quarrelled.[1] It was in the reign of Rômanos in Syria that Maniakês first gained reputation as a warrior and a general. At the beginning of the reign of Michael IV he was despatched to Sicily against the Saracens, and the castle of Maniakês still exists at Syracuse to attest his successes. On an absurd accusation of conspiracy he was recalled to Constantinople and imprisoned (1040), but was released by Michael V. Sicily had in the meantime been lost, but he was appointed commander in Calabria and Longibardia, and there he won a battle near Monopoli which was as fruitless in its results as the great victory of Remata had been in Sicily. A private wrong determined him to return to the East, and his conduct was interpreted as treasonable. Psellos blames Constantine for his want of tact in dealing with Maniakês. At the beginning he should have loaded him with honours, and at least subsequently, when he heard rumours that he intended to revolt, he should have feigned ignorance. Moreover, he sent the most unfit messengers—the men who were most likely to provoke the general. Maniakês was killed by a stray arrow in the battle near Ostrovos; otherwise he might have anticipated Isaac Komnênos.

Psellos was an eye-witness of the naval engagements

[1] The sources for the career of Harald Haardrada in southern Europe are: (1) Annalista Saxo (Pertz, VI, 695); (2) Adam of Bremen (Pertz, VII, 339, 31, and 341, 24); (3) Theodosius Monachus, *De regibus veteribus Norvagicis* (*Script. Rer. Dan.* v, 333, cap. 25); (4) the Saga of Harald in the Heimskringla of Snorro, for which see *Script. Hist. Island.* VI, 125, or Laing's translation of the Heimskringla; (5) the runic inscriptions on the lions formerly in the Peiræus, now in the arsenal of Venice, interpreted by Rafn.

with the Russians, which took place in the Bosphorus within sight of the palace in the summer of 1043. A tumult between some Greeks and the Russian traders resident in Constantinople, in which one distinguished Russian was killed, furnished the pretext of the expedition. This fact we learn from Zônaras, but it is completely ignored by Psellos, who informs us that this expedition had been designed and delayed for many years. Basil Bulgaroktonos had completely cowed the Russians, but after the death of his brother Constantine they began to revive their hostile projects. The reign of Rômanos, however, seemed to them too brilliant, and they were themselves too ill prepared to venture; but when Michael IV, a nobody, came to the throne, they decided to hesitate no longer. But before their preparations were completed Michael died, and in a few months afterwards Constantine IX became Emperor.[1] Though they had no reason for making war on him, they determined to do so, lest their preparations should go for nothing. It seems to me that the silence of Psellos as to the ostensible pretext of the war is not only intentional, but pointed; that he not only disregarded it as a mere pretext which had nothing to do with the real cause, but ignored it in pointed opposition to a contemporary historian who laid undue weight on it. During the engagements Psellos was standing beside the Emperor, and he gives a clear account of what happened, which Zônaras follows.

The revolt of Leon Tornikios took place several years later (1047). He was a sort of second cousin of the Emperor on the mother's side, and resided in Adrianople. He was very intimate with Euprepia, the Emperor's rich sister, who was a woman with a mind of her own,

---

[1] These observations are unsatisfactory, in that Psellos does not explain why the preparations of the Russians occupied so long a time.

on whom her brother consequently looked with suspicion and treated with caution as a strong-minded person cleverer than himself. She seldom visited him, and when she did so spoke out her sentiments with sisterly frankness.[1] The Emperor suspected her intimacy with Tornikios, and gave him an appointment in Iberia. His enemies accused him in his absence of treasonable intention, but it was not till Euprepia defended him (this point is omitted by Zônaras) that Constantine sent persons to cause him to become a monk. When he returned in monastic guise to the capital, the Emperor jeered at him, but Euprepia opened her house to him. The dissatisfied Macedonian faction, "men most ready to devise anything wild and most energetic in executing it", most punctilious in concealing and faithful in keeping their secret compacts, fixed on Leo as the most suitable leader, and conveyed him secretly to their headquarters, Adrianopolis, which Psellos is not guilty, like Zônaras, of calling Orestias.

The first important step was to win the troops stationed in the western provinces to their side, and in this they soon succeeded. The Emperor was not popular with the army, and Zônaras describes their desertion to the usurper as entirely due to this. Nevertheless it does not appear that they were quite so ready to take his part, for according to Psellos the leaders of the revolt were obliged to resort to a ruse in order to gain the support of the military captains. They sent round a number of agents to the different regiments with the news that the

---

[1] Psellos, *Hist.* p. 149: [τὴν δ' ἑτέραν] οὔτε τι λαμπρὸν ἐξ ἀρχῆς κομῶσαν καὶ εἰς περιφάνειαν τύχης ἐληλυθυῖαν, φρονήματός τε πλήρη τυγχάνουσαν καὶ γυναικῶν ἀπασῶν ὧν ἐγὼ τεθέαμαι σταθηροτάτην τε οὖσαν καὶ δυσπαράγωγον, κ.τ.λ. Zônaras, IV, 163: γυνὴ γενναία τε καὶ σταθηροτάτη τὸ φρόνημα καὶ εἰς τύχης ἐλάσασα περιφάνειαν καὶ εἰς πλούτου δαψίλειαν—which shows that the text of Psellos as it stands can hardly be correct. Something more than τὴν δ' ἑτέραν must have fallen out before οὔτε. The name of Constantine's other sister was Helena.

Emperor was dead, and that Theodôra had selected the Macedonian Leo Tornikios, in consideration of his good family, his mental ability, and energetic disposition, as the new Emperor. He adds that in addition to the effect of this artifice hatred of the sovran was operative. When the preparations were complete, they advanced to the siege of the capital.

One of the first measures of Constantine when he heard of the revolt was to banish his sister Euprepia. As the troops of the East could not arrive for several days, and all the forces he could muster did not fully amount to 1000, it was out of the question for him to take the field; his only chance was to defend Constantinople until succour arrived. He was very unwell at the time, suffering from gout and a severe attack of diarrhœa; and a rumour spread in the city that he was dead. The citizens collected to consider the advisability of joining the usurper, and the Emperor, ill though he was, had to dispel the false rumour by appearance in public. In the meantime Leo was acting as if he were already monarch; for as he had no money the only way in which he could reward or secure partisans was to remit taxes, distribute titles, and appoint ministers. One quality in his favour was his military experience; men wished to see a soldier on the throne who could in person defend the Empire against Turks or Patzinaks, like Basil or John Tzimiskês; for the only thing military about Monomachos was his name.

The army encamped round the whole city, and the first assault took place in the early morning. Both the Emperor and the tyrant were conspicuous, the latter riding on a white horse, the former sitting on a balcony that overlooked the field of action. Among the spectators of the teichomachy and the attendants of the Emperor was Psellos.

The siege lasted for three days, which Zônaras, though he follows Psellos, has not carefully distinguished and in some respects has confounded.[1] On the first morning the chief hostilities consisted of the buffooneries of the Macedonians, who danced and acted in a manner insulting to the Emperor. Constantine himself had a narrow escape; an arrow aimed at him passed very close and grazed the side of a court minion who was standing by. This incident forced the Emperor and his company, including Psellos, to retire. In the afternoon the forces of the besieged were increased by some civilians who volunteered and a few soldiers who were extracted from the prisons. The night was spent in digging a trench round the city, and the next morning the besiegers found a larger force drawn up in front of the gates than they had seen the day before. At first they were afraid that the army from the East had arrived; but soon, perceiving that it consisted of a town mob, they leaped over the narrow and shallow trench with loud cries and put the tumultuary band to flight. If this assault had been followed up, a change in the sovranty might have taken place on that day, but Leo restrained the pursuit, hoping perhaps to enter the city as an Emperor invited by citizens, not as a victorious general taking possession of a vanquished town. The policy of Leo throughout was to conciliate the inhabitants of the capital, and Constantine said he was more afraid of these kindly words than of anything else. On the third day a stone was thrown at the usurper, and though it missed him forced him and his party to flee. This created a panic and saved Constantine. The besiegers remained a few days inactive before the walls, and then, abandoning the siege, retired to Arkadiopolis. In the meantime the eastern troops arrived, and Tornikios was deserted

---

[1] He has thrown the first and second days into one.

by his followers. His eyes were put out, and the same punishment befell Joannês Vatatzês, a man celebrated for his strength and bravery, who was a sworn comrade of Tornikios and generously refused to desert him in his extremity.

Joannês, the eunuch, and others induced Constantine shortly before his death to select Nikêphoros Prôteuôn as his successor. But the design was frustrated by the promptness of Theodôra, who immediately appeared in the palace and was recognised as Empress.

9. *Theodôra.** It was expected that Theodôra would choose a partner to share the duties and prerogatives of imperial power, and there were some complaints uttered when it was found out that she had no such intention. Nevertheless her rule seems to have been popular and to have called forth no disloyalty, though some grumbled —for example, the patriarch Kêrularios[1]—that the government of a woman exercised an effeminate influence on the Empire. Yet Psellos says that she showed no weakness, on the contrary a degree of decision which might almost seem hardness.

Her chief minister was Leo Strabospondylês, and Attaleiatês speaks in most favourable terms of his administration.[2] He was a man of sense and experience, and most careful to maintain the law. Even Psellos, who speaks unfavourably of him, admits that he possessed ability and does not impugn his honesty. But he

---

[* Theodôra, A.D. 1054, Nov.–1056, Aug.]

[1] Psellos, *Hist.* p. 207.

[2] P. 52: εἶτ' ἀνενεγκοῦσα τῶν ἐλλογίμων ἀνδρί τινι ἱερωμένῳ τε (he was synkellos of the patriarch) καὶ συνέσεως γέμοντι καὶ πολυπειρίας οὐκ ἀποδέοντι (Λέων προσηγορία τῷ ἀνδρὶ) τὴν διοίκησιν τῶν πραγμάτων ἐπέτρεψεν. ἐπιεικῶς οὖν οὗτος ἐν ἅπασιν ἐνεργῶν καὶ κατὰ λόγον τοῖς παρεμπίπτουσι χρώμενος καὶ τὸν νόμον ποιούμενος βούλημα πᾶσαν εὐταξίαν καὶ εὐνομίαν πεποίηκε πολιτεύεσθαι. He refers the state of domestic peace (ἀστασίαστον) in Theodôra's reign to the fact that God was pleased with this ἀγαθοεργία.

had not, or did not choose to practise, the conciliatory manners of a courtier and the smooth arts of a diplomatist; he was not endowed with readiness and fluency of speech; he used to sit in silence and look at the ceiling, and was so careless or awkward in expressing himself that he often conveyed to his hearers exactly the opposite of what he intended. This want of a statesmanlike exterior—of political *éthos*, as Psellos says—created an unfavourable opinion; and his roughness made him unpopular. Yet he was free from all taint of bribery or avarice, and gave generous and magnificent entertainments.

The significance of the position of Leo in the reigns of Theodôra and Michael VI we can determine from two facts. He had been the minister of Michael IV,[1] and he was passed over by Constantine IX,[2] whose policy had been guided by opposition to the Paphlagonians. He seems to have been a rival of Constantine Leichudês, and the two men are contrasted by Psellos. I think I shall not be mistaken in conjecturing that Michael V, among his many reactionary acts, deposed Leo from office and appointed Leichudês in his place. Hence the administrations of Theodôra and Michael VI bear the character of a reaction against that of Constantine IX, just as that of Constantine was a reaction against the government of Michael IV, and as that of Isaac Komnênos was a reaction against the Macedonian Basilians.

Before her death[3] Theodôra placed the diadem on the head of a man already stricken in years, Michael VI,

---

[1] Zônaras, IV, 181: τὸ πάλαι τῷ βασιλεῖ Μιχαὴλ ὑπηρετήσαντι.

[2] Psellos, *Hist.* p. 206: ὁ γὰρ τὴν τῶν ὅλων πεπιστευμένος διοίκησιν ...ἐπειδὴ μὴ τῶν πρωτείων ἠξίωτο παρ' ἐκείνου (Constantine) μηδὲ παρὰ τῇ ἐκείνου εἰστήκει πλευρῷ, ὅπερ δὴ αὐτῷ ἔθος ἐν τοῖς προτοῦ βασιλεύειν ἐγίγνετο καὶ ζῶντι ἐμέμφετο καὶ ἀπεληλυθότι τῆς ἀτιμίας ἐμνησικάκησεν. These words express clearly enough Leo's position.

[3] August 30, 1056 (not 1057, as stated in Finlay's *Hist. of Greece*, II, 449).

whom Leo and his party selected as a man likely to be manageable and weak.

10. *Michael VI.** The position of the new Emperor rested on his nomination by Theodôra and on the support of a strong political party, headed by Leo the synkellos. By generosity and promotions he exerted himself to please the members of the Senate and the various civil functionaries; he also cultivated popularity with the people.[1]

But he was too old and too inexperienced to understand the political situation and the dangers which at that very moment were lurking around his throne; and so at the very outset he committed a radical mistake which produced the immediate operation of the very elements by which those dangers were threatened. While he showed marked kindness to the Senate and the people he pointedly and designedly ignored the army.

Now the army had been long discontented.[2] The soldiers were tired of Emperors ignorant of warfare, who devoted themselves to civil affairs and took little personal interest in the army, and the commanders felt keenly that their position was a very secondary one in the Empire; for the succession depended on the ministers, not on the generals.

And now that the Basilian line was extinct—connection with which had been a palladium for the preceding monarchs—it behoved the new sovran to deal most warily and delicately with the military power.

[* Michael VI, Stratiotikos, A.D. 1056, Aug. 22/30–1057, Aug.]

[1] Compare Psellos, *Hist.* p. 209 (Zônaras, IV, 182). He promotes too rapidly: οὐ γὰρ τῷ προσεχεῖ ἕκαστον συνίστα βαθμῷ, ἀλλὰ καὶ πρὸς τὸν ἐφεξῆς καὶ τὸν ἐπέκεινα ἀνεβίβαζεν.

[2] Psellos, *Hist.* p. 212: ἐβούλοντο μὲν καὶ πρότερον τὸ στρατιωτικὸν ξύμπαν τὸ κράτος Ῥωμαίων ὑποποιήσασθαι καὶ ὑπήκοοι γενέσθαι στρατηγῷ αὐτοκράτορι καὶ τὴν πολιτικὴν καταλῦσαι τῆς βασιλείας διαδοχήν.

But Michael was too old and stupid to see this.[1] He had the idea—a false generalisation derived from the reigns of his immediate predecessors—that his supremacy rested altogether on the civil power, and that the army, like a subordinate servant, was a *quantité négligeable*. He combined all the stubborn conservative tendencies of an old man with that love of making reforms in trivial matters which is perhaps also a characteristic of the old.[2]

He especially offended Katakalôn Kekaumenos, Duke of Antioch, whom he deprived of that post in favour of his own nephew Michael. Katakalôn and Isaac Komnênos, with a number of other distinguished officers, presented themselves before the Emperor to remonstrate with him on his injustice and imprudence; but he would not listen to them, and overwhelmed Katakalôn with reproaches. Psellos, who had been recalled to court by Theodôra, and was sometimes consulted by her and Michael, was present at this scene.

The insulted generals made another attempt to influence Michael through the medium of his counsellor Leo; but Leo did not attempt to mollify them and only exasperated them more. It is not necessary to suppose that they had any share in instigating the unsuccessful and unimportant insurrection of Theodosios Monomachos, which took place at about this time.[3]

---

[1] Manassês describes Michael as ἄνδρα τινὰ μακρόβιον πέμπελον τρομαλέον (l. 6331), and speaks of the military commanders as

καταφρονοῦντες Μιχαὴλ ἄντικρυς ὡς ἀνίκμου
κράμβης ἀφύλλου γηραιᾶς ἤδη διερρευκυίας.

See Kedrênos, II, p. 614. For example, he wished to enact that the heads of the citizens should no longer be covered δι' ἀγραμμάτων ὡς νῦν ἀλλὰ διὰ μεγαλογράμμων ὀθονίων ἐκ βυσσοῦ πορφυρᾶς ἐξυφασμένων.

[3] Zônaras, IV, 184. The Byzantine populace jeered at the feeble attempt of Monomachos in words that, if the text of Zônaras is correct,

They determined to overthrow Michael, and unanimously selected Isaac as his successor. Having made this arrangement, they withdrew from Constantinople to their estates in Asia Minor to mature their plans and collect their forces. Isaac took his measures with the utmost caution, and perfect order prevailed in his camp. Money was absolutely necessary for his success, and he raised it by regular and accurately defined impositions, and by intercepting all the wealth that happened to be on its way to the capital. Along with the rich and influential noblemen Katakalôn and Rômanos Sklêros, Isaac hoped to have the aid of Nikêphoros Bryennios, the commander of the Macedonian regiments and governor of Kappadokia, who had been also offended by the Emperor. But in the Anatolic theme, where he took up his quarters, he quarrelled with Opsaras, who was loyal to Michael, and his eyes were put out.[1] The rebels took up their quarters at Nikaia.

But in Constantinople itself there was not an undivided adherence to the Emperor. There was a large party which wished to dethrone him, and which was, we need not hesitate to assume, in direct communication with the leaders of the insurrection. What lent this party special weight was that the patriarch Kêrularios was hostile to the government and the Emperor; and Kêrularios, of whom I shall have more to say, was a man of unusual energy and importance. One can hardly avoid conjecturing that he and Isaac had arranged the whole matter between them before the latter left the capital.

are appropriately feeble: ὁ δημώδης ὄχλος ἐπεγγελῶντες ῥήματά τινα συνθέντες ἐπῆδον αὐτῷ· τὰ δ᾽ ἦσαν,

ὁ μωρὸς ὁ Μονομάχος, εἴ τι ἐφρόνει, ἐποίησε.

Let us hope that the words had at least the form of a "political" verse, and ran, by a slight transposition,

ὁ Μονομάχος, ὁ μωρός, ἐποίησ᾽ εἴ τι ᾽φρόνει.

[1] See Zônaras, IV, 185.

In this position of affairs Michael VI took counsel with men who had played a prominent part in the days of Monomachos, but whom he had hitherto gladly dispensed with.[1] In particular he asked the advice of Psellos. Psellos suggested three things: first, that he should become reconciled with the patriarch, as he might be able to give most powerful assistance to the usurper;[2] secondly, that he should send a conciliatory embassy to Isaac; thirdly, that he should collect all the military forces available (the western troops, some eastern troops that had been left in the capital, the foreign guards), obtain succour from neighbouring States, and appoint a competent general.

The first part of this advice was not followed, and the second part was set aside until the third had been tried. Michael appointed Theodôros, a eunuch of the Empress Theodôra,[3] and Aaron, a relative of the wife of Isaac Komnênos, to the command of his troops, and they encamped over against Nikaia. But neither soldiers nor commanders were loyal. "The commander of the forces", says Psellos—"his name I need not mention— was a waverer, or rather, as I fancy, a partisan".[4] Further on he tells us that the president Theodôros had a secret understanding with Komnênos. Hence we may conclude that the unnamed commander was

---

[1] Psellos, *Hist.* p. 214: ἄλλους τε πλείστους μετακαλεῖται τῶν γενναίων μὲν τὰς γνώμας τηνικαῦτα δὲ κατολιγωρηθέντων· καὶ δῆτα κἀμὲ εἰσποιεῖται καὶ ὅτι μὴ ἔχοι πάλαι ἐγκόλπιον ὡς ἄτοπόν τι πεποιηκὼς σχηματίζεται.

[2] *Ibid.*: ἐπεὶ γὰρ ἐγνώκειν ὅτι ἐκ διαφόρου γνώμης τῷ μεγάλῳ ἀντικαθεστήκοι ἀρχιερεῖ καὶ δυσόργως εἶχεν ἐκεῖνος αὐτῷ γνώμην αὐτῷ πρώτην ταύτην εἰσήνεγκα πᾶσαν αὐτῷ διαφορὰν διαλύσασθαι...ἐν τοῖς τοιούτοις μάλιστα δυναμένῳ καιροῖς καὶ συνεπιθησομένῳ τοῖς τυραννεύσασιν εἰ μὴ προλάβοι τοῦτον εἰς ἀκριβεστάτην οἰκείωσιν. It is quite possible that Psellos knew of the intentions of Kêrularios.

[3] Theodôra had created him *proedros*, and afterwards commander of the eastern army (Psellos, p. 216).

[4] ἀμφιρρεπὴς ἦν ὡς δ' ἐγῷμαι μονομερής.

Aaron. The result was that the Emperor's army was defeated.

After some days Michael resolved to send an embassy to Komnênos. He engaged on this commission three men of moderation and distinction, who were not identified with his own policy, and who would carry weight with the revolutionists. He first called Michael Psellos, on whose persuasive fluency he doubtless relied as a valuable auxiliary, and asked him to undertake the negotiation. Psellos says he was unwilling and yielded only to entreaties, making the condition that he might select a colleague. He chose Leo Alôpos, a distinguished member of the Senate,[1] and they chose a third, Constantine Leichudês. They helped the Emperor to compose a letter, of which the purport was to offer the rank of Cæsar to Komnênos.

The envoys sent a notice beforehand to Komnênos of their approach, and obtained a sworn promise of their personal safety in his camp. They were received with great cordiality and rejoicings; and in an interview with Isaac on the evening of their arrival nothing passed between them but commonplace civilities.[2]

The next morning Isaac, surrounded with imperial pomp, gave them a public audience. The doors of his tent were suddenly thrown open that the splendour might all at once burst on the amazed multitude, with whose cheers and shouts the ears of Psellos and his companions were dinned. When the noise ceased they saw Isaac in sumptuous raiment, sitting on a raised gilt throne, resting his feet on a footstool. His fixed eyes testified to the preoccupation of his mind, and his face

---

[1] κἀγὼ αἱροῦμαι τὸν κάλλιστόν τε καὶ συνετώτατον καὶ ὃν μάλιστα ᾔδειν τὴν σὺν ἐμοὶ θαρρήσοντα ἔξοδον. We learn his name from Zônaras.

[2] μηδέ τι πλέον παρ' ἡμῶν μαθεῖν ἠβουλήθη ἢ ὅσον τὰ περὶ τὴν πορείαν καὶ εἰ εὐκυμάντῳ τῷ πλῷ ἐχρησάμεθα.

bore marks of the recent conflict. The historian describes in full the successive circles of guards or attendants which stood around the throne, among whom the most striking were the foreign mercenaries, "the Italians and Tauroskythians". The ambassadors, at the sovran's sign, approached near the throne, and after an interchange of civilities a gentleman-in-waiting called upon them officially to state their commission. Psellos was put forward as spokesman, and he gives an elaborate account of his diplomatic speech. He began with an encomium on the rank of Cæsar and the dignities attached to it, and amid interruptions from the audience went on to speak of the adoption of the Cæsar by the Emperor. He finished with an appeal to Isaac to desist from his usurpation.

The speech was received with unfavourable clamours, which Komnênos was obliged to quiet by assuring the soldiers that the eloquence had produced no effect on him. He then dismissed the assembly and gave the envoys a private audience, at which he informed them that for the present he would be quite satisfied with the rank of Cæsar on condition that the Emperor named no other successor before his death, and deprived none of his companions of honours he had bestowed on them; he also required a certain measure of power, so far as to have the bestowal of some subordinate civil and military appointments. He also asked them to obtain the removal of the minister "of short stature", who was hostile to him and unpopular—Leo Strabospondylês we may presume. These proposals were not entrusted to writing; the letter which was openly sent did not contain them. Having breakfasted with Isaac they hastened to the shore, crossed the Bosphorus, and reached the imperial palace early in the day. The assembly and the negotiations had taken place in the early morning. The

Emperor agreed to all the demands, and after the space of a day the ambassadors recrossed the straits. Komnênos appeared perfectly satisfied with the reply of the Emperor, promised to disband his troops and proceed to Constantinople. Psellos, Leichudês, and Alôpos congratulated themselves that they had contributed a service to their sovran by their prudent conduct of the embassy, and prepared to return on the morrow; Isaac was to move to Scutari the day after.

But before eventide they were surprised by the news that the Emperor had been deposed by a conspiracy of senators. At first both the ambassadors and apparently the Cæsar looked upon the report as an invention, but messenger after messenger arrived confirming the tidings, and doubt could be no longer entertained. A more reliable and accurately informed person soon appeared, who explained that certain dissatisfied and seditious members of the Senate had excited the inhabitants of the city, and, compelling the patriarch to act as their leader, inveighed against Michael and extolled Isaac; so far nothing more had happened. Before sunset, as Isaac and the ambassadors were conversing outside his tent, one arrived out of breath with the news that Michael had been forced to become a monk, and that the city was awaiting the arrival of Isaac to take his place. Ere he had finished speaking another came with the same news.

"How my fellow-ambassadors passed that night", says Psellos, "I know not, but I despaired of life, and expected that I should without delay be led to the sacrifice". But before daybreak the camp was in motion, and the philosopher's terror was dispelled. The Emperor called him to his side and addressed him as a counsellor, asking his advice as to the best mode of administration, and by what policy he might rival the greatest sovrans.

He treated Alôpos and Leichudês with the same kindness.

The whole city streamed forth to meet the new Emperor, and he, turning to Psellos, said, "This extreme good fortune, philosopher, seems to me slippery, and I know not if the end will turn out favourable". The philosopher reassured the Emperor with smooth and flattering words, and took the opportunity of begging him not to bear a grudge against himself. The eyes of Komnênos filled with tears, and he said, "I liked your tongue better the other day when it reviled me than now when it speaks smooth words". He then appointed Psellos president of the Senate.

This important revolution, which transferred the crown from the Macedonian to the Komnênian dynasty, possesses considerable interest. It was accomplished by the coalition of a party within the city with the army without, and in this respect reminds us of the unsuccessful revolt of Vitalian in the reign of Anastasios. But our historians represent this coalition as undesigned; they represent Isaac Komnênos as completely surprised by the news of the part taken by the patriarch and certain members of the Senate. Of course we cannot believe this; we must seek for something a little more mystic, μυστικώτερον—to use a phrase of Byzantine diplomacy. It is clear that Komnênos had a party in the city, which he and his friends, Katakalôn and the others, had time to organise before they departed to Asia after their rebuff by Michael. We are told expressly that they remained for some time in the capital. The cabinet ministers of Theodôra and Michael were very unpopular with others as well as with the soldiers, and Isaac would not fail to take advantage of this.

This faction consisted of members of the Senate, and

of party organisations or clubs, *hetaireiai*.[1] These clubs, which Zônaras has fortunately mentioned, had politically somewhat the same signification in the eleventh century as the *dêmoi* or factions of the hippodrome in the sixth; though doubtless they were much smaller and possessed far less influence than the blues and greens. Whether the patriarch had an understanding with this party beforehand, or whether he was forced into the action he took on the day of the insurrection by the threats of the disaffected, was a question on which Byzantine historians differed. From the position of Kêrularios as opposed to and overlooked by the existing administration, and from his character as a man of strong will and great ambition, we might judge that he had throughout been a prime mover in the political revolution. The weight of the opinion of the historian Attaleiatês inclines in the same direction. And I think we cannot hesitate to suppose that Kêrularios and Komnênos had a distinct understanding with one another. The remarkable honours and privileges which Isaac, when he ascended the throne, conferred upon the patriarch, can be best explained by supposing a secret compact; and the negotiation would have been all the more easy, as Constantine Dukas was an intimate friend of both the Emperor and the patriarch.[2] In his *Epitaphios* on Kêrularios, Psellos gives an account of the

---

[1] Zônaras, IV, 190: στασιώδεις τινὲς τῶν τῆς συγκλήτου βουλῆς...οἷς καὶ οἱ τῶν ἑταιρειῶν συνῇεσαν ἄρχοντες. Attaleiatês merely mentions some of the persons ἐν τέλει as conspirators.

[2] Attaleiatês, *Hist.* p. 56: εἴτε δὲ καὶ ὁ τῆς ἀρχιερωσύνης ἔξαρχος καὶ πατριάρχης ὁ Κηρουλάριος κεκοινώκει τούτοις τῆς σκέψεως εἴτε καὶ μὴ, ἄδηλον καὶ προφανὲς οὐδέν. ὅμως δ' ἐκ προλήψεων καὶ τῶν μετὰ ταῦτα συνενεχθέντων τὰ τῆς ὑπονοίας εἰς ἀληθείας ἀμυδρὰν προκεχωρήκασι ἔμφασιν· καὶ γὰρ τῷ Κομνηνῷ τὰ πάντα συνδιαφέρων ἦν καὶ συμπράττων καὶ τῆς πρώτης βουλῆς γινωσκόμενος ὡς καὶ τῆς φιλίας καὶ τῆς ἀξίας καὶ τῆς ἀγχιστείας ἐγγύτατος ὁ βέσταρχος Κωνσταντῖνος ὁ Δούκας ἀδελφιδῆς τοῦ πατριάρχου σύνευνος καθιστάμενος καὶ πολλὴν εὔνοιαν διδοὺς καὶ λαμβάνων ἐκεῖθεν.

revolution, and represents the patriarch as acting the part of a conciliator between two foes, and attributes to his interference the fact that the revolution was effected with little violence or bloodshed.[1]

It took place in the following manner. On the fatal day the conspirators repaired to the church of St Sophia, and took oaths that bound them to carry out their purpose. The act was attended with commotion both within and without the sacred edifice, and the patriarch sent his nephews to discover the cause of the commotion. They were captured by the leaders of the insurrection and threatened with death if the patriarch did not consent to countenance the plot. "Moved with compassion for his nephews, who were as his sons, and deeming it necessary to prevent civil war", Kêrularios gave his consent. This was what apparently took place; but there can be little doubt that the whole affair was a preconcerted ruse.[2]

Some days before, Michael had induced all the senators and civil officers to sign a document, by which they engaged not to call Komnênos *Basileus*, nor to pay him imperial honour. The conspirators professed that their object was to cancel this document, which they had signed under compulsion, and the patriarch undertook to obtain it from Michael. But in a short time they waxed bolder, and openly proclaimed Komnênos Emperor. Kêrularios despatched one messenger to Isaac—one of those whose arrival in the camp we witnessed above—bidding him not tarry, and another to Michael

[1] P. 362 sqq.: δυεῖν τότε γεγονότων ἀντιπάλων τμημάτων μέσος ἐκεῖνος ἐφειστήκει καὶ ἄτμητος. He is compared to a pilot in the storm. He took the side of Komnênos because he saw Providence clearly leaning that way. Pp. 364–5: διαιτᾷ ὅπως ἂν τῷ μὲν περιλειφθείη τὸ ζῆν ἐκείνῳ δὲ ἀναιμωτὶ μνηστευθείη τὸ κράτος. Michael VI is praised for his ready compliance with the inevitable.

[2] Zônaras, IV, 190: λέγεται δὲ ταῦτα σκήψεις εἶναι καὶ προβουλεύματα ἵν᾽ ἄκων δοκοίη συνελθεῖν ὁ πατριάρχης τοῖς στασιάζουσι.

bidding him leave the palace. Michael asked the clerical messengers of the patriarch, "What will ye give me instead of the kingdom?" and they answered, "The kingdom of heaven".[1] He then put off his imperial robes and retired to a religious retreat, which was under the special care of the patriarch, who received him with a kind and smiling face, and kissed him and bade him farewell. And Michael said, "God requite thee thy kiss worthily, patriarch".[2]

11. *The Patriarch Michael Kêrularios.* The head of the Church who took such a prominent part in the revolution of 1057 was a striking and important figure in the middle part of the eleventh century. We have already come across him on several occasions; but I passed over his name lightly, preferring to give a short connected account of his career. He attempted, as far as was possible under the completely different circumstances, to do for the patriarchate in the eastern Church what his younger contemporary Hildebrand did for the pontificate in western Christendom.

He was a man remarkable for physical beauty as well as for learning and intellect. His first appearance on the scene of history is in the reign of Michael IV (1040); he was involved in a serious conspiracy against the Emperor, and was banished along with Joannês Makrembolitês—the father of the Empress Eudokia and spiritual brother of Psellos—and many others. In the notice of Kedrênos, Kêrularios is mentioned as a leader,[3] but Psellos in his *Epitaphios* gives a very curious account of the affair. A large number of noble and able men, dis-

---

[1] See Zônaras, IV, 191.

[2] Attaleiatês, p. 59: ἀντασπάσαιτο, "may he kiss in return". Although Psellos (*M. Kêrularios*, p. 365) describes the cordial reception given by the patriarch to the deposed monarch, I am sure that Michael's words were ironical, and that he looked on the patriarchal salute as the kiss of Judas.

[3] Kedrênos, II, 540.

gusted with the government of the Paphlagonian family, formed the design of electing a new Emperor. They determined to select the man on whom heaven had conferred in most abundance excellences of mind and body —the best man in the Empire; each excluded from his thoughts all wish to reign. They unanimously voted for Michael Kêrularios; and the unanimity seemed equivalent to oracular certainty that he was the best man. They did not, however, inform the object of their choice, feeling that he would be reluctant to yield to their wishes; Kêrularios remained in ignorance that a large assembly of men of light and leading had chosen him to reign over them. But some of the conspirators misdoubted the chance of success and turned informers; and Michael was punished even more severely than the others for the tribute which without his knowledge they had paid to his excellence.

He returned from exile in 1042, at the time of the accession of Monomachos, who showed him marked favour—although he had never met him before—and is reported to have exclaimed when he first saw him, "He is just the man for the patriarchate". In the meantime, as the patriarchal chair was not vacant, he made him his most confidential adviser;[1] but in less than a year (Feb. 1043) Alexios died, and Kêrularios was elected to the high and influential position of head of the eastern Church.

There were two limits on the ecclesiastical power of the patriarch. One of these was theoretical rather than practical; in the organisation of universal Christendom he held a subordinate position.[2] It had been defined in

[1] *Epitaph.* p. 324: καὶ συνοικίζει τοῦτον εὐθὺς ἑαυτῷ τοῖς ἀδύτοις καὶ τὰ πρῶτα τῶν περὶ ἐκεῖνον ποιεῖται, κ.τ.λ.
[2] The claim of the patriarch of Constantinople to the title of "ecumenical" was first raised in the reign of Maurice, and was then resisted

the council of Constantinople (381) that the See of Constantinople was second in dignity to the See of Rome. The other limit was practical rather than theoretical; the patriarch was dependent on the Emperor. The eastern Emperors, like Constantine and like Justinian, continued to interfere in ecclesiastical matters, as was indeed inevitable.

From such subordination and dependence Michael Kêrularios made an attempt to deliver the Byzantine pontificate, and was to a certain extent not unsuccessful.

To break with Rome was not difficult; the eastern and western Churches were practically severed. Into the details of the schism we need not enter here; we need merely indicate that a general account of it is given by Psellos in his *Epitaphios* on the patriarch. He notes the difference as to the "theology of the holy Trinity" as the main point of the dissension, and tells us that others thought the matter of no consequence, while the patriarch deemed the heresy intolerable and exerted himself in the matter with unusually ardent activity.[1] On July

by Gregory I. The claim was of practical value in so far as it was connected with the subordination of the sees of Alexandria and Antioch to Constantinople; and thus Leo IX (in his sixth epistle) writes that it is intolerable *quod nova ambitione Alexandrinum et Antiochenum patriarchas antiquis suæ dignitatis privilegiis privare contendens contra fas et jus suo dominio subjugare conaretur.* An attempt was made in 1024 to bribe the pope into conceding the coveted title to the Byzantine bishop (see Lequien, *Or. Christ.* i, 89).

[1] τῷ δὲ τῆς εὐσεβείας προμάχῳ καὶ προθύμῳ καὶ τοῦ θείου λόγου ἀγωνιστῇ οὐκ ἀνεκτὸν ἐλογίζετο· ὅθεν προὔκαμέ τε τῆς μητροπόλεως καὶ ὑπὲρ ἐκείνης πρὸς ἐκείνην πολλάκις ἠκριβολογήσατο καὶ θερμότερον ἢ περὶ τἆλλα διηγωνίσατο νουθετῶν ἐπιστέλλων παρακαλῶν γραφικαῖς χρώμενος ἀποδείξεσι...ὡς δ' οὐκ ἔπειθε πάντα πράττων ἀλλ' ἐγεγόνεισαν οἱ παιδαγωγούμενοι θρασύτεροι καὶ ἀναισχύντεροι τηνικαῦτα καὶ αὐτὸς ἀναρρήγνυται καὶ τῇ ἀναισχυντίᾳ τῆς ἀσεβείας τῆς εὐσεβείας ἀντιτίθησι τὴν ἀκρίβειαν. For the schism compare Leo Ostiensis, *Chronicle of Monte Casino*, bk. ii, chap. LXXXV. See Hefele, *Conciliengeschichte*, IV, 725 *sq.*, and the article on Cärularios by Gass in the *Realencyclopädie für protestantische Theologie*, edited by Herzog and Plitt (now by Hauck). Kêrularios threw down the gauntlet in a letter to the bishop of Trani.

16, 1054, the envoys of the pope deposited the act of excommunication on the altar of St Sophia.

That Kêrularios made some attempts to render his office independent of imperial interference during the reign of Constantine IX, I should infer from the incidental remark of Psellos that he owed many grudges to Monomachos.[1] He had a high ideal of the archieratic office. The patriarch was bound, he thought (for though Psellos speaks with his own words, he speaks in the spirit of Kêrularios), to speak "holy words" to secular powers, to resist *tyrannies*, to exalt the humble and pull down the self-willed, to superintend education:[2] it was the ideal of Ambrose and Chrysostom. The Emperor did not support Michael in his quarrel with the pope and did not approve of his unconciliatory attitude; he compelled Nikêtas Pectoratos, a partisan of Michael, to burn the book he had written against the false doctrines of the Latins.

We have seen how the patriarch was opposed to the governments of Theodôra and Michael VI, and how he assisted in the elevation of Isaac I. It seems extremely probable that he arranged beforehand with Isaac, as conditions of lending his support, those privileges which Isaac granted when he was seated on the throne. We are told that he honoured the patriarch as a father, and he granted to the Church a completer power in its own affairs than it had before possessed. The treasurer (σκευοφύλαξ) and the grand chancellor (ὁ μέγας οἰκο-νόμος) used to be appointed directly by the Emperor; Isaac transferred these appointments to the patriarch. He rendered the Church wholly independent of the

---

[1] *Epitaph.* p. 357: καίτοι πολλὰ μνησικακεῖν ἔχων τῷ ἀπελθόντι.

[2] *Ibid.* p. 354: τὸ πᾶσαν ἰδέαν παιδαγωγίας τοῖς πρὸς ἀρετὴν ἀπευθυνο-μένοις ἐπιδείκνυσθαι πρός τε δυναστείας παρρησιάζεσθαι καὶ τυραννίαις (usurpations) ἀνθίστασθαι καὶ τοὺς μὲν ταπεινοτέρους ὑψοῦν καθαιρεῖν δὲ τοὺς αὐθαδεστέρους καὶ θρασυτέρους.

palace; the entire ecclesiastical administration was to depend henceforward on the head of the Church.[1]

Kêrularios seems to have been popular with the clergy, and he tried to strengthen his position by the advancement of his nephews, who, as we saw, played a part in the revolt against Michael VI. Isaac conferred on them the highest honours and offices; and this is the nearest parallel to papal nepotism that we meet in Byzantine history—the advancement of the patriarch's nephews by the Emperor.

But Kêrularios presumed too far, and he fell. He took upon himself, in accordance with his idea of the duties or privileges of the patriarchal office, to admonish the Emperor like a father or censure him like a master, if he did or designed to do anything of which he did not approve. The ears of an Emperor are accustomed to praise, not to rebuke; and Isaac, however friendly his feelings to the patriarch were, could not long submit to the schooling of an ecclesiastic. Moreover, Kêrularios in mere external trivialities gave proof of a dangerously autocratic spirit; he wore red boots like the Emperor's, asserting that it was an ancient pontifical privilege. Things came to a crisis when on one occasion the Emperor exhibited his impatience and the indignant patriarch cried "It was I who gave you the Empire, I too can take it from you".[2] At the feast of the archangels it was necessary for the patriarch to officiate outside the city, and the Emperor seized the opportunity and caused Kêrularios to be arrested, as he feared that his arrest in the city might cause a disturbance. The Varangian soldiers who were employed for the purpose transported him to Prokonnêsos, where he died in a few days and relieved the Emperor from further trouble.

[1] See Attaleiatês, p. 60; Skylitzês, pp. 641–2; Zônaras, IV, 352.
[2] It is not easy to see the point of τὸ δημῶδες τοῦτο καὶ καθημαξωμένον, which Skylitzês (p. 643) puts into the mouth of the patriarch: ἐῶ σε ἔκτισα φοῦρνε· ἐῶ ἵνα σε χαλάσω.

THE PATRIARCHS
OF CONSTANTINOPLE

THE PATRIARCHS
OF CONSTANTINOPLE

BY

CLAUDE DELAVAL COBHAM, C.M.G.

WITH INTRODUCTIONS BY THE

REV. ADRIAN FORTESCUE, PH.D., D.D.

AND THE

REV. H. T. F. DUCKWORTH, M.A.

PROFESSOR OF DIVINITY, TRINITY COLLEGE, TORONTO CANADA

ARES   PUBLISHERS   INC.
CHICAGO   MCMLXXIV

Unchanged Reprint of the Edition:

London, 1911.

ARES   PUBLISHERS   INC.

150 E. Huron Street

Chicago, Illinois 60611

Printed in the United States of America

CONTENTS

PAGE

PREFATORY NOTE 7

INTRODUCTION I. By the Rev. Adrian Fortescue . 21
II. By the Rev. H. T. F. Duckworth 41

LIST OF THE PATRIARCHS OF CONSTANTINOPLE, with
dates, etc. 89

PREFATORY NOTE

The real Preface to this pamphlet is supplied by my learned and kind friends the Revs. Adrian Fortescue and H. T. F. Duckworth, but a few words from me are necessary to explain its origin and purport.

I do not claim an acquaintance with the original sources of the history of the Patriarchate of Constantinople. I do not know if the subject has received at later hands the treatment it deserves. But I lighted on a work entitled Πατριαρχικοὶ Πίνακες, by Manuel I. Gedeon, printed at Constantinople (without date of publication, but written between 1885 and 1890), containing short lives of the bishops of Constantinople from the Apostle St Andrew to Joakim III.[1] It is a useful book, but an index was wanting, and this I now supply in two forms, chronological and alphabetical, as well as a list of the Patriarchs who are numbered with the Saints. Besides this I have done little but summarise Gedeon's text.

It may be noted that ninety-five Patriarchs reigned for less than a year. Also that of 328 vacancies between A.D. 36 and 1884

---

[1] It received the *imprimatur* of the Imperial Ministry of Public Instruction 25 Rabi'al-awwal, 1304—Dec. 23, 1887.

                    140 were by deposition,
                     41 by resignation,
                      3 Patriarchs were poisoned,
                      2   murdered,
                      1   beheaded,
                      1   blinded,
                      1   drowned,
                      1   hanged,
                      1   strangled.

In all 191 : so that 137 only closed their term of office
by a natural death.

After the fall of Jerusalem the Jews had leaders, at
least in Alexandria and Tiberias, whom they called
Patriarchs, and this office was recognized from the reign
of Nerva to that of Theodosios II. (A.D. 420). Among
Christians the bishop of Antioch was the first to be
called Patriarch, but he probably shared the title with
other leading metropolitans. Later it was held that 'as
there are five senses,' so there should be five Patriarchs,
Rome, Constantinople, Alexandria, Antioch, Jerusalem.
From 1589 to 1700 the Patriarch of Moscow was
reckoned the fifth—Rome had fallen away in 1054—
but only in 1723 the Great Church recognized the
canonicity of the Russian Synod.

Patriarchs were elected by a synod of the bishops of
the province, acting under the consent, the counsel or
perhaps the orders, of the Emperor. Nor was the
practice changed after the Turkish conquest of Constantinople, and in 1741 a *firman* of Mahmud I. sanctioned
an orderly procedure, providing (*inter alia*) that the
candidate should first have the approval of the bishops
of Heracleia, Cyzicos, Nicomedeia, Nicaia and Chalcedon.

The laity took some part, not well defined, in the election. The expenses amounted in 1769 to 150,000 francs, in 1869 to less than 500.

The order of consecration of a bishop, following the Fourth Canon of Nicaia, and according to the form prepared by Metrophanes, bishop of Nyssa (Euchologion Mega, 176), is performed by the Ἀρχιερεὺς and δύο συλλειτουργοί, elsewhere in the rubric called οἱ τρεῖς ἀρχιερεῖς. The earliest Patriarchs were generally priests or monks, and rarely before the fall of Constantinople chosen from among the bishops of the province: the translation of bishops from one see to another being held at least irregular. Latterly it has been the rule that they should have for at least seven years filled a metropolitical see within the province. The Patriarch-elect should be consecrated or installed by the bishop of Heracleia, or, in his absence, by the bishop of Caisareia.

An interval of more than four years occurred between the retirement of Athanasios II. and the appointment of Gennadios II., and again between the patriarchates of Antonios III. and Nicolaos II. M. Gedeon cannot say who ought to administer the affairs of the œcumenical throne during a vacancy.

The Patriarch-elect was received by the Byzantine Emperors in great state, and, after the fall of Constantinople, by the earliest Ottoman Sultans. He is still presented to the sovereign, but with little pomp or ceremony.

Disputes arising in sees other than his own should be referred to him for decision: generally, he may pronounce judgment in all questions between the Orthodox—and woe betide him who appeals from such judgment to a secular court. He may give the rights of σταυροπήγια to churches not already consecrated, though they may be in another province. He only can receive clerics from another province without an ἀπολυ-τήριον (letters dimissory) from their own diocesan.

Upon taking up his duties the new Patriarch sends a letter, called ἐνθρονιστικὴ, to his brother Patriarchs, to which they reply in letters called εἰρηνικαί.

Homonymous Patriarchs are distinguished by the name of their birthplace, the see they had held, or by a nickname, never by numbers.

Probably no series of men, occupying through nearly eighteen centuries an exalted position, claim so little personal distinction as the Patriarchs of Constantinople. The early bishops are mere names :—

S. Andrew, Apostle and Martyr	Laurentios
Stachys	Alypios
Onesimos	Pertinax
Polycarpos I	Olympianos
Plutarchos	Marcos I
Sedekion	Philadelphos
Diogenes	Cyriacos I
Eleutherios	Castinos
Felix	Eugenios I
Polycarpos II	Titos
Athenodorus	Dometios
Euzoios	Ruphinos

Probos. The twenty-fifth in order of time.

Metrophanes I, A.D. 315–325, who saw the foundation of Constantinople, was too old to attend the first œcumenical council, and was represented in it by his successor,

Alexander, who was to have communicated with Arius on the very day of the heresiarch's appalling death.

Paulos, thrice expelled and twice restored, his place being first filled by

Eusebios, the Arian bishop of Nicomedeia, who consecrated
S. Sophia: secondly by another Arian

Macedonios. Paulos was at last exiled to Armenia, and there
strangled with his own pall by Arians.

Macedonios[2] deposed, anathematised by second œcumenical
council, 381.

Eudoxios, Arian, bishop of Antioch. Consecrated S. Sophia,
Feb. 15, 360.

Demophilos

Evagrios, banished by Valens.

Gregorios I, bishop of Nazianzum. Censured at second œcumenical
council and resigned.

Maximos I, deposed as a heretic by the same council.

Nectarios, a senator of Tarsus, chosen while yet unbaptized, and
installed by 150 bishops of the same council, at the bidding
apparently of the Emperor Theodosios.

Ioannes Chryostomos, born at Antioch, twice banished, died
Sept. 14, 407, at Komana in Pontus. S. Sophia burnt, 404.

Arsacios, brother of the Patriarch Nectarios.

Atticos, consecrated in 415 the restored church of S. Sophia.

Sisinios I

Nestorios, the heresiarch, condemned as a monophysite by the
third general council, of Ephesus, 431. Exiled to an oasis in
Egypt, where he died, 440.

Maximianos

Proclos, bishop of Cyzicos.

Flavianos, died of wounds received at the 'robber-synod' of
Ephesus.

Anatolios, installed by Dioscuros of Alexandria, fourth œcumenical
council, of Chalcedon, 431, condemned the heresy of Eutyches:
crowned the Emperor Leo I.

Gennadios I

Acacios. The first quarrel between the Church of the East and
Pope Felix III. The 'Henoticon' of the Emperor Zenon.
The finding of the body of S. Barnabas, and the independence
of the Church of Cyprus, 478.

Phravitas

Euphemios, deposed and banished.

Macedonios II, deposed and banished.

(**50**)   Timotheos I, Kelon.

Ioannes II, Cappadoces.

Epiphanios.   Pope John II visited Constantinople.

Anthimos I, bishop of Trapezus, promoted by the Empress Theodora, deposed by Pope Agapetus.

Menas.   Consecrated by Pope Agapetus.   Menas in turn consecrated Pope Agathon.   Controversy with Vigilius.

Eutychios[1].   Fifth œcumenical council, of Constantinople, 553. Second consecration of S. Sophia.

Ioannes IV, Nesteutes.   A synod at Constantinople, 587, declared the patriarch 'œcumenical.'

Cyriacos

Thomas I

Sergios, monotholete.   Incursion of the Avars, 626.

Pyrrhos[1], monothelete, deposed.

Pyrrhos[2]

Petros, monothelete.

Thomas II

Ioannes V

Constantinos I

Theodoros I[1], deposed by Constantine Pogonatus.

Gregorios I.   Sixth œcumenical council, of Constantinople, 680, counted Pope Honorius among the monothelete heretics.

Theodoros I[2]

Paulos III.   Council of Constantinople, 'Penthektes' or 'in Trullo II,' 692.

Callinicos I, blinded, and banished to Rome by Justinian II.

Cyros, deposed by Philippicus.

Ioannes VI, monothelete.

Germanos I, bishop of Cyzicos, a eunuch, resigned.

Anastasios.   The Patriarchate of Constantinople now conterminous with the Byzantine Empire.

Constantinos II, bishop of Sylaion, blinded, shaved and beheaded by Constantine Copronymus.

Nicetas I, a slave.

Paulos IV, a Cypriot, resigned.

Tarasios, a layman.   Seventh œcumenical council, of Nicaia, 787.

Nicephoros I, a layman, deposed and banished by Leo the Armenian.

Theodotos, illiterate. εἰκονομάχος.

Antonios I, Kasymatas ; a tanner, then bishop of Sylaion. εἰκονομάχος.

Ioannes VII, Pancration. εἰκονομάχος, deposed by Theodora.

Methodios I, bishop of Cyzicos, promoted by Theodora. First mention of M. Athos.

Ignatios[1], son of the Emperor Michael Rhangabe and Procopia, eunuch; deposed and banished by Baidas. Conversion of the Bulgarians.

Photios[1], a layman, deposed and banished by Basil the Macedonian. Conversion of the Russians.

Ignatios[2], canonised by Rome. Fourth council, of Constantinople, 869.

Photios[2], deposed and confined to a monastery by Leo the Wise. Synod of 879.

Stephanos I, son of Basil the Macedonian and Eudocia.

Antonios II, Kauleas.

Nicolaos I[1], mysticos ; deposed by Leo the Wise.

Euthymios I, deposed and banished by Alexander.

Nicolaos I[2], restored by Constantine Porphyrogennetos.

Stephanos II, bishop of Amaseia ; eunuch.

Tryphon

Theophylactos, a lad of sixteen, eunuch. Son of Romanus Lecapenus. Conversion of the Hungarians.

Polyeuctos, eunuch.

Basileios I, Scamandrenos. Deposed by John Tzimisces.

Antonios III, Studites

Nicolaos II, Chrysoberges

Sisinios II

Sergios II. The Patriarch of Alexandria declared κριτὴς τῆς οἰκουμένης.

Eustathios

(100) Alexios, appointed by Basil II.

Michael I, Cerularios, appointed by Constantine IX, deposed and banished by Isaac Comnenos. Excommunicated by Papal legates (the see of Rome was vacant), July 16, 1054.

Constantinos III, Leuchoudes : eunuch.

Ioannes VIII, Xiphilinos
Cosmas I, Hierosolymites
Eustratios, eunuch.
Nicolaos III, Grammaticos
Ioannes IX, Agapetos
Leon, Styppe
Michael II, Kurkuas
Cosmas II, deposed by a synod of bishops.
Nicolaos IV, Muzalon, archbishop of Cyprus.
Theodotos
Neophytos I
Constantinos IV, Chliarenos
Lucas
Michael III, bishop of Anchialos.
Chariton
Theodosios I
Basileios II, Camateros, deposed by Isaac Angelus.
Nicetas II, Muntanes
Leontios
Dositheos, Patriarch of Jerusalem. (In 1192 five ex-Patriarchs were alive.)
Georgios II, Xiphilinos
Ioannes IX, Camateros. Latin conquest of Constantinople, April 12, 1204.
Michael IV, Antoreianos
Theodoros II, Copas
Maximos II
Manuel, Sarantenos
Germanos II
Methodios II
Manuel II
Arsenios[1]
Nicephoros II
Arsenios[2]
Germanos III, present (after his deposition) at the second council of Lyons, 1274.
Ioseph I[1]
Ioannes XI, Beccos

Joseph I[2]
Gregorios II, a Cypriot.
Athanasios I[1]
Ioannes XII, Cosmas
Athanasios I[2]
Nephon I
Ioannes XIII, Glykys, a layman.
Gerasimos I
Hesaias
Ioannes XIV, Calekas
Isidoros
Callistos I[1]
Philotheos[1]
Callistos I[2]
Philotheos[2]
Macarios[1]
Neilos
Antonius IV[1], Macarios
Macarios[2]
(150) Antonios IV[2]
Callistos II
Matthaios I, sent the monk Joseph Bryennios to Cyprus, 1405.
Euthymios II
Joseph II, metropolitan of Ephesus: died at Florence, 1439, during
    the Council.
Metrophanes II, metropolitan of Cyzicos.
Gregorios III, died at Rome, 1459.
Athanasios II, resigned, 1450. Fall of Constantinople, May 29,
    1453. [The vestments and ornaments of the Patriarch,
    imitated from those of the Byzantine Court, could hardly
    have been assumed before the fall of the city.]
Gennadios II, Scholarios, resigned May, 1456.
Isidoros II
Sophronios I, Syropulos
Ioasaph I, Kokkas: thrust forth about 1466 because he would not
    sanction the marriage of a Christian girl to a Moslem courtier.
    The Sultan, Mohammed II, spat in his face, and mowed away
    his beard with his sword. The Patriarch threw himself down
    a well.

Marcos II, Xylocaraves.

Dionysios I[1]. [The Lazes for a thousand florins buy the Patriarchate for Symeon, a monk of Trebizond. He gave way to Dionysios, metropolitan of Philippopolis, for whom Maros, mother of Sultan Bayazid, bought the Patriarchate for 2000 sequins: after a reign of five years he was rejected as a eunuch. Symeon was recalled, and the synod paid 2000 sequins; but the Serb Raphael offered 2500. Symeon was deposed, and Raphael, an unlettered sot, succeeded; but as the money was not paid he was led chained hand and foot through the city to beg it from his flock: he failed, and died in prison.]

Symeon[1]

Raphael

Maximos III

Symeon[2]

Nephon II[1]

Dionysios I[2]

Maximos IV, paid 2500 florins.   Deposed and died at M. Athos.

Nephon II[2]

Ioakeim I[1]

Nephon II[3]

Pachomios I[1]

Ioakeim I[2]

Pachomios I[2], poisoned by a servant.

Theoleptos I, bishop of Ioannina.

Ieremias I[1], bishop of Sophia: visited Cyprus, 1520.

Ioannikios I

Hieremias I[2]

Dionysios II[1]

Hieremias I[3]

Dionysios II[2]

Ioasaph II, metropolitan of Adrianople.

Metrophanes III[1], metropolitan of Caisareia.

Hieremias II[1], Tranos, metropolitan of Larissa.

Metrophanes III[2]

Hieremias II[2], banished to Rhodes.

Pachomios II, Palestos: banished to Wallachia.

Theoleptos II

Hieremias II[3]

Matthaios II[1]
Gabriel I
Theophanes I, Carykes, metropolitan of Athens.
[*Meletios Pegas, Patriarch of Alexandria,* ἐπιτηρητὴς, *April,* 1597, *to early in* 1599.]
Matthaios II[2]
Neophytos II[1], metropolitan of Athens.
Raphael II, moved in 1603 his residence from S. Demetrios to S. George (the Phanar).
Neophytos II[2], deposed and banished to Rhodes.
Cyrillos I[1], Lucaris, Patriarch of Alexandria.
Timotheos II, poisoned.
Cyrillos I[2]
Gregorios IV, metropolitan of Amaseia, deposed and banished to Rhodes.
Anthimos II
Cyrillos I[3]
Isaac
Cyrillos I[4]
Cyrillos II[1], metropolitan of Berrhoia.
Athanasios III[1], Pantellarios, metropolitan of Thessalonica.
Cyrillos I[5]
Cyrillos II[2], Contares
Neophytos III
Cyrillos I[6]
Cyrillos II[3]
Parthenios I, Geron: deposed and banished to Cyprus; died of poison at Chios.
Parthenios II[1], metropolitan of Adrianople, deposed and banished.
Ioannikios II[1], metropolitan of Heracleia, Lindios.
Parthenios II[2], Oxys: murdered at the instigation of the Princes of Wallachia and Moldavia.
Ioannikios II[2]
Cyrillos III[1], Spanos: metropolitan of Tornovo.
Athanasios III[3], fifteen days, resigned and died in Russia.
Paisios I[1]
Ioannikios II[3]
Cyrillos III[2], deposed and banished to Cyprus.

Paisios I[2]

Ioannikios II[4]

Parthenios III

(**200**) Gabriel II, twelve days.

Theophanes II, three days.

Parthenios IV[1], Mogilalos

Dionysios III, Bardalis

Parthenios IV[2]

Clemes, a few days, deposed and banished.

Methodios III, Morones, resigned and died at Venice.

Parthenios IV[2], six months, deposed and banished to Cyprus.

Dionysios IV[1], Muselimes.   Synod of Jerusalem, 1672.

Gerasimos II

Parthenios IV[4]

Dionysios IV[2].   First Orthodox church built in London, 1677.

Athanasios IV, a week, deposed and banished.

Iacobos[1]

Dionysios IV[3]

Parthenios IV[5], seven months.

Iacobos[2]

Dionysios IV[4]

Iacobos[3], four months.

Callinicos II[1], Acarnan, nine months.

Neophytos IV, five months.

Callinicos II[2]

Dionysios IV[5], seven months, deposed and died at Bucarest.

Callinicos II[3]

Gabriel III

Neophytos IV, election not confirmed by the Porte.

Cyprianos[1], deposed and banished to M. Athos.

Athanasios V

Cyrillos IV

Cyprianos[2], three months.

Cosmas III

Hieremias III[1]

Callinicos III, died of joy on hearing of his election, Nov. 19, 1726.

Paisios II[1], Kynmurji-oghlu, deposed and banished to Cyprus.

Hieremias III[2], six months.

Serapheim I, a year, deposed and banished to Lemnos.

Neophytos VI[1]

Paisios II[2]

Neophytos VI[2], ten months, deposed and banished to Patmos.

Paisios II[3]

Cyrillos V[1], Caracalos

Paisios II[4]

Cyrillos V[2], deposed and banished to M. Sinai.

Callinicos IV, deposed and banished to M. Sinai.

Serapheim II, an Imperial Rescript of 1759 decreed that the expenses of the election, reckoned at 120,000 francs, should be met by the new Patriarch.

Ioannikios III, Carajas, deposed and banished to M. Athos.

Samuel[1], Khanjeris, deposed and banished to M. Athos.

Meletios II, six months, resigned and died in penury at Mitylene.

Theodosios II, Maridakes, deposed and banished to Chalcis.

Samuel[2], 13 months, deposed.

Sophronios II, Patriarch of Jerusalem.

Gabriel IV

Procopios, deposed and banished to M. Athos.

Neophytos VII[1], deposed and banished to Rhodes.

Gerasimos III, a Cypriot.

Gregorios V[1], deposed and banished to M. Athos.

Neophytos VII[2], deposed and banished to M. Athos.

Callinicos V[1]

Gregorios V[2], deposed and banished to M. Athos.

Callinicos V[2], eight months.

Hieremias IV

Cyrillos VI, Serbetoghlu

Gregorios V[3], on Easter Day, April 22, 1821, hanged over the gate of the Patriarchate.

Eugenios II

Anthimos III, deposed and banished to Caisareia.

Chrysanthos, deposed and banished to Caisareia.

Agathangelos, deposed and banished to Caisareia.

Constantios I, archbishop of Sinai.

Constantios II

Gregorios VI[1], Khatti-Sherif of Gülkhane, Nov. 2, 1839.

Anthimos IV[1], Bambakes
Anthimos V
Germanos IV[1]
Meletios III, seven months.
Anthimos VI[1], Ioannides
Anthimos IV[2]
Germanos IV[2], nine months.
(250) Anthimos VI[2]
Cyrillos VII, Khatti-Humayun, Feb. 18, 1856.
Ioakeim II[2], Kokkodes
Sophronios III, deposed 1866, elected 1870 Patriarch of Alexandria.
Gregorios VI[2]
Anthimos VI[3]
Ioakeim II[2]
Ioakeim III[1], born 1834, metropolitan of Thessalonica; resigned
    1884.
Neophytos VIII, deposed Oct. 1894.
Anthimos VII, deposed Feb. 1897.
(257) Constantinos V, deposed 1901.
Ioakeim III[2], re-elected June, 1901. εἰς πολλὰ ἔτη.

C. D. C.

INTRODUCTION I

THE rise of the see of Constantinople, the 'Great Church of Christ,' is the most curious development in the history of Eastern Christendom. For many centuries the patriarchs of New Rome have been the first bishops in the East. Though they never succeeded in the claim to universal jurisdiction over the whole Orthodox Church that they have at various times advanced, though, during the last century especially, the limits of their once enormous patriarchate have been ruthlessly driven back, nevertheless since the fifth century and still at the present time the Patriarch of New Rome fills a place in the great Christian body whose importance makes it second only to that of the Pope of Old Rome. To be an orthodox Christian one must accept the orthodox faith. That is the first criterion. And then as a second and visible bond of union all Greeks at any rate, and probably most Arabs and Slavs, would add that one must be in communion with the œcumenical patriarch. The Bulgars are entirely orthodox in faith, but are excommunicate from the see of Constantinople; a rather less acute form of the same state was until lately the misfortune of the Church of Antioch. And the great number of orthodox Christians would deny a share in their name to Bulgars and Antiochenes for this reason only. Since, then, these patriarchs are now and have so long been the centre of unity to the hundred millions of Christians who make up the great Orthodox Church, one might be tempted to think that their position is an essential element of its constitution, and to imagine that, since the days of the first general councils New Rome has been as much the leading Church of the East as Old Rome of the West. One might be tempted to conceive the Orthodox as the subjects of the œcumenical patriarch, just as Roman Catholics are the subjects of the pope. This would be a mistake. The advance of the see of Constantinople is the latest development in the history of the hierarchy. The Byzantine patriarch is the youngest of the five. His see evolved from the smallest of local dioceses at the end of the fourth and during the fifth centuries. And now his jurisdiction, that at one time grew into something like that of his old rival the pope, has steadily retreated till he finds himself back not very far from the point at which his predecessors began their career of gradual advance. And the overwhelming majority of the Orthodox, although they still insist on communion with him, indignantly deny that he has any rights over them. Though they still give him a place of honour as the first bishop of their Church, the other orthodox patriarchs and still more the synods of national churches show a steadily growing jealousy of his assumption and a defiant insistence on their equality with him. An outline of the story of what may perhaps be called the rise and fall of the see of Constantinople will form the natural introduction to the list of its bishops.

We first hear of a bishop of Byzantium at the time of the first General Council (Nicaea, 325). At that time Metrophanes (315—325) ruled what was only a small local see under the metropolitan of Thrace at Herakleia. Long afterwards his successors claimed St Andrew the Apostle as the founder of their see. This legend does not begin till about the ninth century, after Constantinople had become a mighty patriarchate. There was always a feeling that the chief sees should be those founded by apostles; the other patriarchates—Rome, Alexandria, Antioch and Jerusalem—were apostolic sees (Alexandria claimed St Peter as her founder too), and now that Constantinople was to be the equal of the others, indeed the second see of all, an apostolic founder had to be found for her too. The legend of St Andrew at Constantinople first occurs in a ninth century forgery attributed to one Dorotheos, bishop of Tyre and a martyr under Diocletian. St Andrew's successor is said to be the Stachys mentioned in Rom. xvi. 9; and then follow Onesimos and twenty-two other mythical bishops, till we come to a real person, Metrophanes I. The reason why St Andrew was chosen is the tradition that he went to the North and preached in Scythia, Epirus and Thrace. No one now takes this first line of Byzantine bishops seriously. Their names are interesting as one more example of an attempt to connect what afterwards became a great see with an apostle. Before the ninth century one of the commonest charges brought against the growing patriarchate was that it is not an apostolic see (e.g. Leo I. *Ep.* 104, *ad Marcianum*), and its defenders never think of denying the charge; they rather bring the question quite candidly to its real issue by answering that it is at any rate an imperial one. So the first historical predecessor of the œcumenical patriarch was Metrophanes I. And he was by no means an œcumenical patriarch. He was not even a metropolitan. His city at the time of the first Nicene synod was a place of no sort of importance, and he was the smallest of local bishops who obeyed the metropolitan of Herakleia. The council recognized as an 'ancient use' the rights of three chief sees only—*Rome, Alexandria* and *Antioch* (Can. 6). The title 'patriarch' (taken, of course, from the Old Testament as 'Levite' for deacon) only gradually became a technical one. It is the case of nearly all ecclesiastical titles. As late as the sixth century we still find any specially venerable bishop called a patriarch (Greg. Naz. *Orat.* 42, 43, *Acta SS.* Febr. III. 742, where Celidonius of Besançon is called 'the venerable patriarch'). But the thing itself was there, if not the special name. At the time of Nicæa I. there were three and only three bishops who stood above other metropolitans and ruled over vast provinces, the bishops first of Rome, then of Alexandria and thirdly of Antioch. It should be noticed that conservative people, and especially the Western Church, for centuries resented the addition of the two new patriarchates— *Jerusalem* and *Constantinople*—to these three, and still clung to the ideal of three chief Churches only. Constantinople eventually displaced Alexandria and Antioch to the third and fourth places: they both refused to accept that position for a long time. Alexandria constantly in the fifth and sixth centuries asserts her right as the 'second throne,' and Antioch demands to be recognized as third. The Roman Church especially maintained the older theory; she did not formally recognize Constantinople as a patriarchate at all till the ninth century, when she accepted the 21st Canon of Constantinople IV. (869) that establishes the order of five patriarchates, with Constantinople as the second and Jerusalem as the last. Dioscur of Alexandria (444—451) bitterly resented the lowered place given to his see. St Leo I. of Rome (440—461) writes: 'Let the great Churches keep their dignity according to the Canons, that is Alexandria and Antioch' (*Ep. ad Rufin. Thess.*, Le Quien, *Or. Christ.* I. 18), and he constantly appeals to the sixth Canon of Nicæa against later innovations (Ep. 104, *ad Marc.*). He says: 'The dignity of the Alexandrine see must not perish' and 'the Antiochene Church should remain in the order arranged by the Fathers, so that having been put in the third place it should never be reduced to a lower one' (Ep. 106, *ad Anatolium*). St Gregory I. (590—604) still cherished the older ideal of the three patriarchates, and as late as the eleventh century St Leo IX. (1045—1054) writes to Peter III. of Antioch that 'Antioch must keep the third place' (Will, *Acta et scripta de controversiis eccl. graecae et latinae*, Leipzig, 1861, p. 168). However, in spite of all opposition the bishops of Constantinople succeeded, first in being recognized as patriarchs and eventually as taking the second place, after Rome but before Alexandria. It was purely an accident of secular politics that made this possible. The first general council had not even mentioned the insignificant little diocese of Byzantium. But by the time the second council met (Constantinople I., 381) a great change had happened. Constantine in 330 dedicated his new capital 'amid the nakedness of almost all other cities'

(St Jerome, *Ckron.* A.D. 332). He moved the seat of his government thither, stripped Old Rome and ransacked the Empire to adorn it, and built up what became the most gorgeous city of the world. So the bishop of Byzantium found himself in a sense the special bishop of Cæsar. He at once obtained an honoured place at court, he had the ear of the emperor, he was always at hand to transact any business between other bishops and the government. Politically and civilly New Rome was to be in every way equal to Old Rome, and since the fourth century there was a strong tendency to imitate civil arrangements in ecclesiastical affairs. Could the prelate whose place had suddenly become so supremely important remain a small local ordinary under a metropolitan? And always the emperors favoured the ambition of their court bishops ; the greater the importance of their capital in the Church, as well as in the State, the more would the loyalty of their subjects be riveted to the central government. So we find that the advance of the Byzantine see is always as desirable an object to the emperor as to his bishop. The advance came quickly now. But we may notice that at every step there is no sort of concealment as to its motive. No one in those days thought of claiming any other reason for the high place given to the bishop except the fact that the imperial court sat in his city. There was no pretence of an apostolic foundation, no question of St Andrew, no claim to a glorious past, no record of martyrs, doctors nor saints who had adorned the see of this new city ; she had taken no part in spreading the faith, had been of no importance to anyone till Constantine noticed what a splendid site the Bosphorus and Golden Horn offer,

This little bishop was *parvenu* of the *parvenus* ; he knew it and everyone knew it. His one argument—and for four centuries he was never tired of repeating it—was that he was the emperor's bishop, his see was New Rome. New Rome was civilly equal to Old Rome, so why should he not be as great, or nearly as great, as that distant patriarch now left alone where the weeds choked ruined gates by the Tiber? Now that the splendour of Cæsar and his court have gone to that dim world where linger the ghosts of Pharaoh and Cyrus we realize how weak was the foundation of this claim from the beginning. The Turk has answered the new patriarch's arguments very effectively. And to-day he affects an attitude of conservatism, and in his endless quarrels with the independent Orthodox Churches he talks about ancient rights. He has no ancient rights. The ancient rights are those of his betters at Rome, Alexandria and Antioch. His high place is founded on an accident of politics, and if his argument were carried out consistently he would have had to step down in 1453 and the chief bishops of Christendom would now be those of Paris, London and New York. We must go back to 381 and trace the steps of his progress. The first Council of Constantinople was a small assembly of only 150 eastern bishops. No Latins were present, the Roman Church was not represented. Its third canon ordains that : 'The bishop of Constantinople shall have the primacy of honour ($\tau\grave{a}$ $\pi\rho\epsilon\sigma\beta\epsilon\hat{\iota}a$ $\tau\hat{\eta}\varsigma$ $\tau\iota\mu\hat{\eta}\varsigma$) after the bishop of Rome, because that city is New Rome.' This does not yet mean a patriarchate. There is no question of extra-diocesan jurisdiction. He is to have an honorary place after the pope because his city has become politically New Rome. The Churches of Rome and Alexandria definitely refused to accept this canon. The popes in accepting the Creed of Constantinople I. always rejected its canons and specially rejected this third canon. Two hundred years later Gregory I. says, 'The Roman Church neither acknowledges nor receives the canons of that synod, she accepts the said synod in what it defined against Macedonius' (the additions to the Nicene Creed, *Ep.* VII. 34); and when Gratian put the canon into the Roman canon law in the twelfth century the papal correctors added to it a note to the effect that the Roman Church did not acknowledge it. The canon and the note still stand in the *Corpus juris* (dist. XXII. c. 3), a memory of the opposition with which Old Rome met the first beginning of the advance of New Rome. The third general council did not affect this advance, although during the whole fourth century there are endless cases of bishops of Constantinople, defended by the emperor, usurping rights in other provinces—usurpations that are always indignantly opposed by the lawful primates. Such usurpations, and the indignant oppositions, fill up the history of the Eastern Church down to our own time. It was the fourth general council (Chalcedon in 451) that finally assured the position of the imperial bishops. Its 28th canon is the vital point in all this story. The canon—very long and confused in its form—defines that 'the most holy Church of Constantinople the New Rome' shall have a primacy next after Old Rome. Of course the invariable reason is given: 'the city honoured because of her rule and her Senate shall enjoy a like primacy to that of the elder Imperial Rome and shall be mighty in Church affairs just as she is and shall be second after her." The canon gives authority over Asia (the Roman province, of course— Asia Minor) and Thrace to Constantinople and so builds up a new patriarchate. Older and infinitely more vener- able sees, Herakleia, the ancient metropolis, Caesarea in Cappadocia, that had converted all Armenia, Ephesus where the apostle whom our Lord loved had sat—they must all step down, because Constantinople is honoured for her rule and her senate. The Roman legates (Lucen- tius, Paschasius and Boniface) were away at the fifteenth session when this canon was drawn up. When they arrive later and hear what has been done in their absence they are very angry, and a heated discussion takes place in which they appeal to the sixth canon of Nicæa. The council sent an exceptionally respectful letter to Pope Leo I. (440—461) asking him to confirm their acts (*Ep. Conc. Chal. ad Leonem,* among St Leo's letters, No. 98). He confirms the others, but rejects the twenty-eighth categorically. 'He who seeks undue honours,' he says, 'loses his real ones. Let it be enough for the said Bishop' (Anatolios of Constantinople) 'that by the help of your' (Marcian's) 'piety and by the consent of my favour he has got the bishopric of so great a city. Let him not despise a royal see because he can never make it an apostolic one' (no one had dreamed of the St Andrew legend then); 'nor should he by any means hope to become greater by offending others.' He also appeals to canon 6 of Nicaea against the proposed arrangement (*Ep.* 104). So the 28th canon of Chalcedon, too, was never admitted at Rome. The Illyrian and various other bishops had already refused to sign it. Notwithstanding this opposition the new patriarch con-

tinued to prosper. The Council of Chalcedon had made
the see of Jerusalem into a patriarchate as well, giving it
the fifth place. But all the eastern rivals go down in
importance at this time. Alexandria, Antioch and
Jerusalem were overrun with Monophysites; nearly all
Syria and Egypt fell away into that heresy, so that the
orthodox patriarchs had scarcely any flocks. Then came
Islam and swept away whatever power they still had.
Meanwhile Cæsar was always the friend of his own
bishop. Leo III., the Isaurian (717—741), filched his
own fatherland, Isauria, from Antioch and gave it to
Constantinople; from the seventh to the ninth centuries
the emperors continually affect to separate Illyricum
from the Roman patriarchate and to add it to that of
their own bishop. Since Justinian conquered back Italy
(554) they claim Greater Greece (Southern Italy, Calabria, Apulia, Sicily) for their patriarch too, till the
Norman Conquest (1060—1091) puts an end to any
hope of asserting such a claim. It is the patriarch of
Constantinople who has the right of crowning the
emperor; and the patriarch John IV., the Faster
(Νηστευτής, 582—595), assumes the vaguely splendid
title of 'Œcumenical Patriarch.' The new kingdom
of the Bulgars forms a source of angry dispute between
Rome and Constantinople, till just after the great schism
the œcumenical patriarch wins them all to his side,
little thinking how much trouble the children of these
same Bulgars will some day give to his successors.
Photios (857—867, 878—886) and Michael Kerularios
(Michael I., 1043—1058) saw the great schism between
East and West. Meanwhile the conversion of the
Russians (988) added an enormous territory to what

was already the greatest of the Eastern patriarchates.

The Turkish conquest of Constantinople (1453), strangely enough, added still more to the power of its patriarchs. True to their unchanging attitude the Mohammedans accepted each religious communion as a civil body. The Rayahs were grouped according to their Churches. The greatest of these bodies was, and is, the Orthodox Church, with the name 'Roman nation' (rum millet), strange survival of the dead empire. And the recognized civil head of this Roman nation is the œcumenical patriarch. So he now has civil jurisdiction over all orthodox Rayahs in the Turkisk empire, over the other patriarchs and their subjects and over the autocephalous Cypriotes as well as over the faithful of his own patriarchate. No orthodox Christian can approach the Porte except through his court at the Phanar. And the Phanar continually tries to use this civil jurisdiction for ecclesiastical purposes.

We have now come to the height of our patriarch's power. He rules over a vast territory second only to that of the Roman patriarchate. All Turkey in Europe, all Asia Minor, and Russia to the Polish frontier and the White Sea, obey the great lord who rules by the old lighthouse on the Golden Horn. And he is politically and civilly the overlord of Orthodox Egypt, Syria, Palestine and Cyprus as well. So for one short period, from 1453 to 1589, he was not a bad imitation of the real pope. But his glory did not last, and from this point to the present time his power has gone down almost as fast as it went up in the fourth and fifth centuries. The first blow was the independence of

Russia. In 1589 the czar, Feodor Ivanovich, made his Church into an autocephalous patriarchate (under Moscow), and in 1721 Peter the Great changed its government into that of a 'Holy directing Synod.' Both the independence and the synod have been imitated by most Orthodox Churches since. Jeremias II. of Constantinople (1572—1579, 1580—1584, 1586—1595) took money as the price of acknowledging the Russian Holy Synod as his 'sister in Christ.' It was all he could do. His protector the Sultan had no power in Russia, and if he had made difficulties he would not have prevented what happened and he would have lost the bribe. Since then the œcumenical patriarch has no kind of jurisdiction in Russia ; even the holy chrism is prepared at Petersburg. In two small cases the Phanar gained a point since it lost Russia. Through the unholy alliance with the Turkish government that had become its fixed policy, it succeeded in crushing the independent Servian Church of Ipek in 1765 and the Bulgarian Church of Achrida (Ochrida in Macedonia) in 1767. The little Roumanian Church of Tirnovo had been forced to submit to Constantinople as soon as the Turks conquered that city (1393). In these three cases, then, the Phanar again spread the boundaries of its jurisdiction. Otherwise it steadily retreats. In every case in which a Balkan State has thrown off the authority of the Porte, its Church has at once thrown off the authority of the Phanar. These two powers had been too closely allied for the new independent government to allow its subjects to obey either of them. The process is always the same. One of the first laws of the new constitution is to declare that the national

Church is entirely orthodox, that it accepts all canons, decrees and declarations of the Seven Holy Synods, that it remains in communion with the œcumenical throne and with all other Orthodox Churches of Christ; but that it is an entirely autocephalous Church, acknowledging no head but Christ. A Holy Synod is then set up on the Russian model, by which the theory 'no head but Christ' always works out as unmitigated Erastianism. The patriarch on the other hand is always filled with indignation; he always protests vehemently, generally begins by excommunicating the whole of the new Church, and (except in the Bulgarian case) Russia always makes him eventually withdraw his decree and recognize yet another sister in Christ.

In 1833 the first Greek parliament at Nauplion declared the Greek Church independent; Anthimos IV. of Constantinople first refused to acknowledge it at all and then in 1850 published his famous *Tomos*, allowing some measure of self-government. The Greek Church refused to take any notice of the *Tomos*, and eventually Anthimos had to give way altogether. In 1866 the cession of the Ionian Isles, and in 1881 the addition of Thessaly and part of Epirus to the kingdom of Greece, enlarged the territory of the Greek Church and further reduced the patriarchate. In 1870 the Bulgars founded an independent national Church. This is by far the worst trouble of all. They have set up an Exarch in Constantinople and he claims jurisdiction over all Bulgars, wherever they may live. The Bulgarian Church is recognized by Russia, excommunicate and most vehemently denounced by the patriarch. The inevitable moment in which the Phanar will have to give way

and welcome this sister too has not yet come. The
Serbs set up their Church in 1879, the Vlachs in 1885—
both establishments led to disputes that still distress the
Orthodox Church. The Austrian occupation of lands
inhabited by orthodox Christians has led to the establishment of independent Churches at Carlovitz in 1765,
at Hermannstadt (Nagy-Szeben) in 1864, at Czernovitz
in 1873 and of a practically independent one in Herce-
govina and Bosnia since 1880. The diminishing power
of the œcumenical patriarch is further shown by the
resistance, always more and more uncompromising,
shown when he tries to interfere in the affairs of the
other patriarchates and autocephalous Churches. In
1866 Sophronios III. of Constantinople wanted to judge
a case at the monastery of Mount Sinai. Immediately
the Patriarch of Jerusalem summoned a synod and
indignantly refused to acknowledge his 'anti-canonical
interference and his foreign and unknown authority.'
The Church of Greece since its establishment has had
many opportunities of resisting the patriarch's foreign
authority. She has not failed to use each of them.
The see of Antioch still bears the excommunication
proclaimed against her late Patriarch Meletios (†Feb. 8,
1906) rather than allow the Phanar to interfere in her
affairs. The patriarch of Alexandria (Photios) has sent
away the legate whom the Phanar wished to keep at
his court. The Church of Cyprus, now for nearly nine
years in the throes of a quarrel that disturbs and scan-
dalizes the whole orthodox world, has appealed to
every sort of person—including the British Colonial
Office—to come and help her out of her trouble. From
only one will she hear of no interference. Every time

the Phanar volunteers a little well-meant advice it is told sharply that it has no authority in Cyprus; the Council of Ephesus in 431 settled all that, and, in short, will his All-Holiness of Constantinople mind his own business?

The diminished authority of the œcumenical throne now covers Turkey in Europe (that is, Thrace, Macedonia and part of Epirus) and Asia Minor only. And in Macedonia its rights are denied by the Bulgars; and both Serbs and Vlachs are on the point of setting up independent Churches here too.

The patriarch however takes precedence of all other orthodox bishops. His title is 'Archbishop of Constantinople, New Rome and Œcumenical Patriarch' ('Ο παναγιώτατος, ὁ θειότατος, ὁ σοφώτατος κύριος, ὁ Ἀρχιεπίσκοπος Κωνσταντινουπόλεως, Νέας Ῥώμης καὶ οἰκουμενικός Πατριάρχης). He is addressed as 'Your most divine All-Holiness' ('Η Ὑμετέρα Θειοτάτη Παναγιότης). To assist him in his rule he has two tribunals, a synod for purely ecclesiastical affairs and a 'mixed national council (μικτὸν ἐθνικὸν συμβούλιον)' for affairs that are partly ecclesiastical and partly secular.

Since 1860 the patriarchs are elected—nominally for life—in this way: a committee of the metropolitan bishops present in Constantinople, with certain laymen and representatives of twenty-six provincial bishops, meets not less than forty days after the vacancy and submits to the Porte the names of all for whom their votes have been recorded. From this list the Sultan may strike out not more than three names. Out of the corrected list the mixed council chooses three; and the synod finally elects one of the three. But the candidate who has steered his way through all these trials is not yet appointed. He must be confirmed by the Sultan, who may even now reject him. The patriarch-elect at last receives a *berat*, that is a form of appointment by the Sultan, in which his civil and ecclesiastical rights are exactly defined, is solemnly invested by the Great Wazīr in the Sultan's name, pays certain visits of ceremony to various Turkish officials and is finally enthroned in the Church of St George in the Phanar. The enthronement is performed by the metropolitan of Herakleia (last shadow of his old jurisdiction over Byzantium) after the Turkish officer has read out the berat. The patriarchs are still obliged to pay heavy bribes for their berat. Their dress is the same as that of other orthodox bishops, except that the veil of the patriarch's *Kalemaukion* is often violet. As arms on their seal they bear a spread eagle imperially crowned.

The first glance at the list will reveal what is the greatest abuse of the œcumenical throne, namely the enormous number of its occupants and the short length of their reigns. Even before 1453, and very much more since the Turk has reigned here, the patriarchs are deposed incessantly. Sometimes it is the government, more often the endless strife of parties in the Church, that brings about this everlasting course of deposition, resignation and reappointment. The thing has reached incredible proportions. Scarcely any patriarch has reigned for more than two or three years before he has been forced to resign. Between 1625 and 1700, for instance, there were fifty patriarchs, an average of eighteen months' reign for each. But when a patriarch is deposed he does not take final leave of the œcumenical throne. He always has a party on his side and that party immediately begins intriguing for his restoration. Generally there are three or four candidates who go backwards and forwards at short intervals; each is deposed and one of his rivals reappointed. All the Phanariote Greeks then naturally swerve round to the opposition and move heaven and earth to have the present occupier removed and one of the ex-patriarchs re-elected. They quarrel and criticize all the reigning patriarch's actions, the metropolitans refuse to work with him; everyone besieges the Turkish Minister of Police with petitions till he is made to resign. Then one of his old rivals is appointed again and everyone begins trying to oust him. So the proceeding goes on round and round. And the Porte gets its bribe for each new berat. Some patriarchs have had as many as five tenures at intervals (Cyril Lukaris had six). There are always three or four ex-patriarchs waiting in angry retirement at Athos or Chalki for a chance of reappointment; so unless one has just seen the current number of the Ἐκκλησιαστικὴ Ἀλήθεια it is never safe to say certainly which is the patriarch and which an ex-patriarch.

The reigning patriarch, Joakim III., had already occupied the see from 1878 to 1884. When Constantine V. fell in 1901 he was re-elected and has reigned for nearly seven years—an almost unique record. There are now three ex-patriarchs, each with a party angrily demanding its favourite's reappointment, Neophytos VIII., Anthimos VII. and Constantine V. Anthimos VII. has made himself specially conspicuous as a critic of his successor's actions. He constantly writes to point out how much better he managed things during his reign (1884—1897) and how much better he would manage them again if he had the chance.   In 1905 nine metropolitans (led by Joakim of Ephesus and Prokopios of Durazzo) proceeded to depose Joakim III. They telegraphed to Petersburg, Athens, Belgrade and Bucharest that the patriarchal see was again vacant. Joakim of Ephesus was the popular candidate for the succession.   This was all natural and right, and would have four ex-patriarchs instead of three—till they had ousted the Ephesian.   Only this time they counted without their host.   The Porte means—or meant then—to keep Joakim III.; and the only thing that really ever matters in the Byzantine patriarchate is what the Sultan decides.   So these metropolitans were severely lectured by Abdurrahmān Pasha, the Minister of Police; Joakim was lectured too and his duty as patriarch was plainly explained to him, but he kept his place, and for once the Porte threw away a chance of selling another berat.   Abdurrahmān seems to be the normally appointed person to point out the laws of the Orthodox Church to its metropolitan, and there is an inimitable touch of irony in the date, ' 18 Rabi'al-awwal, 1323,' for instance, that he puts at the end of his canonical epistles to the patriarch.

The list that follows contains an astonishingly small number of great names.   One is always reminded that but for the protection of the emperor and then of the Sultan the see of Constantinople has no claim to dignity. Alexandria, Antioch and Jerusalem have all incomparably more honourable memories.   At Constantinople only two really great patriarchs have brought honour

to their see—St John Chrysostom (398—404) and
Photios (857—867, 878—886). Nestorios (428—431),
the Monotheletes Sergios I. (610—638), Pyrrhos I.
(638—641) and Paul II. (641—652), and especially
poor Cyril Lukaris (1621 at six intervals to 1638),
made a certain name for themselves, but their successors would hardly glory in their memory. On the other
hand, in a long list that tells of little but time-serving,
grovelling subjection to the Turk and ludicrous intrigue,
there are some names that stand out as those of men
who stood boldly for the cause of Christ against the
unbaptized tyrant to whom they owed their place; and
there are even martyrs who have left to this see a more
real glory than that of the mythical apostle-patriarch,
St Andrew. Isidore II. (1456—1463) was murdered
for refusing to allow a Christian woman to become the
second wife of a Mohammedan, Maximos III. (1476—
1482) was mutilated for the same cause and Gregory V.
(1797 at three intervals to 1822) was barbarously hanged
on Easter-day 1821 as a revenge because his countrymen
were defeating his master.

And lastly, of the reigning patriarch, Joakim III.,
there is nothing to say but what is very good. He
began his second reign by sending an Encyclical to the
other Orthodox Churches in which he proposed certain
very excellent reforms (for instance that of their Calen-
dar), wished to arrange a better understanding between
the sixteen independent bodies that make up their communion and expressed his pious hope for the re-union of
Christendom. Pity that their never-ending jealousies
made those of these Churches that answered at all do
so in the most unfriendly way. But of Joakim himself

one hears everything that is edifying. He is evidently really concerned about the scandals that disgrace the Orthodox name—the affairs of Bulgaria, Antioch, Cyprus and so on—and he has shown himself in every way a wise, temperate and godly bishop. So one may end this note by expressing a very sincere hope that he may be allowed to go on ruling the Great Church of Christ for many years still before the inevitable deposition comes.

And for the sake of removing the crying scandal of these constant changes in the patriarchate, as well as for the sympathy we all feel for his character, the Western outsider will join very heartily in the greeting with which he was received at his enthronement : Ἰωακεὶμ ἄξιος—εἰς πολλὰ ἔτη.

ADRIAN FORTESCUE.

INTRODUCTION II

The population of the Roman Empire was divided into groups by the system of provinces, and to this grouping the Churches of Christendom seem to have accommodated themselves almost, if not quite, from the very beginning. Thus, for instance, the Churches of Syria, from very early days indeed, formed one group, the head of which was the Church of Antioch, the chief city of the province. The Church of Antioch was indeed the 'metropolis,' of which the other Syrian churches, for the most part at any rate, were 'colonies'; but Antioch had been selected as the missionary centre, we may be sure, on account of its being the provincial capital. Again, the Churches of Asia formed a group, in which the lead belonged to the Church of Ephesus, the Churches of Macedonia (Eastern Illyricum) another group, in which the chief place was taken by the Church of Thessalonica, and yet another group was that of the Achaian Churches, centreing about the Church of Corinth. Other examples of Churches whose grouping corresponded with provincial divisions of the Empire were those of Cyprus, Egypt, and Africa.

This correspondence of grouping between the Church and the Empire is more easily exemplified from the regions to the east of the Adriatic than from those to the west of it. One reason, no doubt, is the fact that, even down to Bishop Jewel's famous limit of 'Catholic Antiquity,' viz. the end of the sixth century, the history of Christendom is the history of the Eastern, much more than of the Western, Churches. Still, the correspondence does not cease when we pass from Greece and the East to Italy and the West. Carthage and Africa have been already mentioned, and in connection with that region of the Roman Empire it should be noticed that just as Carthage and the African provinces were, if anything, more Latin than Rome and Latium itself, in the earliest period of Christian history, so it was in Carthage and Africa, not in Rome, that the forefathers of Latin Christianity arose—Tertullian, Cyprian, Augustine[1]. Again, in the Eastern half of the Empire, great and famous cities were numerous—Alexandria, Antioch, Tarsus, the Cappadocian Cæsarea, Ephesus, Thessalonica, Corinth—and so were notable Christian bishoprics. In the Western half, Rome, Milan and Carthage for a considerable time threw all the rest very much into the shade. Lyon, of course, was a considerable city—and we find one of the most ancient Churches of the West founded there, and undergoing persecution in the year 177. But Lyon was a new creation. The Roman Empire had called it into being, whereas the great cities of the East had a history reaching back to times long before the Roman Empire had begun to be. Very naturally, then, in the grouping of Christendom, the

---

[1] The 'Old Latin' version of the New Testament was produced in the province of Africa, in the second century. See Westcott, *Canon of the New Testament*, I. iii. 3.

whole West, speaking generally, was regarded as one group, with Rome as its head and centre. Even those who made a separate group or province of the African Churches would hardly assign anything less extensive than Italy and the Italian islands, Spain and Gaul, and Britain, as the province of the Roman See. The care of all the churches in those countries would be regarded by all as properly coming upon and assumed by the bishop of Rome.

Among the cities of the East, two stood far out and above the rest, for size, and wealth, and all that goes to make urban greatness—Alexandria, to wit, and Antioch. Speaking generally with regard to the first 300 years of the Christian era, one would say that next in the scale of greatness and importance came the following three—Cæsarea in Cappadocia, Ephesus and Thessalonica; three most important points, one may observe, on the chief line of communication between Rome and the Euphrates frontier of the Empire. In the West, Rome shone with absolutely unique glory. Lyon, Milan, Ravenna, even Carthage itself, which after all had been resuscitated by the grace of her quondam rival—these were nothing accounted of in comparison with Rome.

The Emperor Diocletian (A.D. 284—305) made considerable modifications in the provincial system of the Roman Empire, distributing all the provinces into 12 'dioceses' or groups of provinces. During the fourth century other changes were made, and in A.D. 400 the number of dioceses had been increased from 12 to 13[1]. A profoundly important change in the structure of the

[1] See Professor Bury's edition of Gibbon, *Decline and Fall*, vol. II. p. 541 f.

Empire was effected by the foundation of a new imperial capital, Constantinople, the 'Encænia' of which were celebrated on the 11th of May, A.D. 330[1].

At the time of the great Council of Nicæa, the building of 'the city of Constantine, New Rome,' had only just been begun. The greatest cities of Christendom, in A.D. 325, are also the greatest cities of the Empire—Rome, Alexandria, Antioch. The Nicene Council, representative of all Christendom, ordered in the sixth of the twenty canons which it passed, that the ancient customs should prevail, whereby the bishop of Alexandria exercised authority over the churches in Egypt, Libya, and Pentapolis ('the parts of Libya about Cyrene'), and similar authority over a wide area was exercised, in the West by the bishop of Rome, in the East by the bishop of Antioch[2]. The limits of authority and jurisdiction are not specified in the case either of Rome or of Antioch, so that the canon, taken by itself, is evidence for no more than the fact that the bishop, in each of these cities, had a 'province' in which he was the chief pastor. Other churches, besides those of Rome, Alexandria and Antioch, had prerogatives and privileges—πρεσβεῖα—which were to be maintained. The Canon goes on to speak of the necessity incumbent

---

[1] Gibbon, *Decline and Fall*, II. p. 157, note 65 (Bury's edition). Ὡρολόγιον τὸ Μέγα, p. 310, where the 11th of May is called τὰ γενέθλια ἤτοι τὰ ἐγκαίνια τῆς Κωσταντινουπόλεως. The Orthodox Church placed the city under the especial favour and protection of the Blessed Virgin Mary.

[2] Concil. Nicæn. Can. VI. τὰ ἀρχαῖα ἔθη κρατείτω, τὰ ἐν Αἰγύπτῳ καὶ Λιβύῃ καὶ Πενταπόλει, ὥστε τὸν ἐν Ἀλεξανδρείᾳ ἐπίσκοπον πάντων τούτων ἔχειν τὴν ἐξουσίαν, ἐπειδὴ καὶ τῷ ἐν Ῥώμῃ ἐπισκόπῳ τοῦτο σύνηθές ἐστιν. ὁμοίως δὲ καὶ κατὰ τὴν Ἀντιόχειαν, καὶ ἐν ταῖς ἄλλαις ἐπαρχίαις, τὰ πρεσβεῖα σώζεσθαι ταῖς ἐκκλησίαις.

on every bishop of obtaining his metropolitan's consent to his election and consecration. 'If any be made a bishop, without consent of his metropolitan, this great Synod has determined that such person ought not to be bishop[1].' This ruling finds illustration in the ninth Canon of the Council of Antioch, A.D. 341, according to which 'the bishop presiding in the metropolis ought to know the bishops of his province, and undertake the care of the whole province, because all, who have any business, congregate in the metropolis[2].' Without the metropolitan's cognizance, the bishops of a province ought not to take any action. This, it is asserted, was 'the rule of our fathers, established of old.' Each bishop had his distinct rights and duties, within the limits of his παροικία, or district; beyond those limits he could only act in concert with his metropolitan, and the metropolitan, in turn, must not act without the co-operation of his comprovincials.

The words 'metropolis' and 'province' were taken over by the Church from the official vocabulary of the Empire. 'Metropolis' in the sense of a 'capital' city or

---

[1] *Ibid.*, καθόλου δὲ πρόδηλον ἐκεῖνο, ὅτι εἴ τις χωρὶς γνώμης τοῦ μητρο-πολίτου γένοιτο ἐπίσκοπος, τὸν τοιοῦτον ἡ μεγάλη σύνοδος ὥρισε μὴ δεῖν εἶναι ἐπίσκοπον. ἐὰν μέντοι τῇ κοινῇ πάντων ψήφῳ, εὐλόγῳ οὔσῃ, καὶ κατὰ κανόνα ἐκκλησιαστικόν, δύο ἢ τρεῖς δι' οἰκείαν φιλονεικίαν ἀντιλέγωσι, κρατείτω ἡ τῶν πλειόνων ψῆφος.

[2] Concil. Antioch. Can. IX. τοὺς καθ' ἑκάστην ἐπισκόπους εἰδέναι χρὴ τὸν ἐν τῇ μητροπόλει προεστῶτα ἐπίσκοπον καὶ τὴν φροντίδα ἀναδέχεσθαι πάσης τῆς ἐπαρχίας, διὰ τὸ ἐν μητροπόλει πανταχόθεν συντρέχειν πάντας τοὺς πράγματα ἔχοντας, ὅθεν ἔδοξε καὶ τῇ τιμῇ προηγεῖσθαι αὐτόν, κατὰ τὸν ἀρχαῖον κρατήσαντα τῶν πατέρων ἡμῶν κανόνα, ἢ ταῦτα μόνα, ὅσα τῇ ἑκάστου ἐπιβάλλει παροικίᾳ καὶ ταῖς ὑπ' αὐτὴν χώραις. ἕκαστον γὰρ ἐπίσκοπον ἐξουσίαν ἔχειν τῆς ἑαυτοῦ παροικίας, διοικεῖν τε κατὰ τὴν ἑκάστῳ ἐπιβάλλουσαν εὐλάβειαν, καὶ πρόνοιαν ποιεῖσθαι πάσης τῆς χώρας τῆς ὑπὸ τὴν ἑαυτοῦ πόλιν, ὡς καὶ χειροτονεῖν πρεσβυτέρους καὶ διακόνους, καὶ μετὰ κρίσεως ἕκαστα διαλαμβάνειν,

town is met with as far back as the days of Xenophon[1]. In the Roman epoch it was a title of honour much sought after, and disputed over, by the cities of the province of Asia. The proper metropolis of Asia was Pergamus, the seat and centre of the government and of the κοινὸν or confederation of the provincial cities, but the title was claimed by, and allowed to, Ephesus, Smyrna, Sardis, and others besides[2]. As it happened, Ephesus was, in ecclesiastical relations, a true metropolis, the Churches of Asia being subordinate to it. There St Paul and St John had dwelt and laboured, and thence had the sound of the Gospel gone forth into all the province[3].

περαιτέρω δὲ μηδὲν πράττειν ἐπιχειρεῖν, δίχα τοῦ τῆς μητροπόλεως ἐπισκόπου, μηδὲ αὐτὸν ἄνευ τῆς τῶν λοιπῶν γνώμης. Compare the thirty-fourth of the so-called *Canons of the Holy Apostles*—τοὺς ἐπισκόπους ἑκάστου ἔθνους εἰδέναι χρὴ τὸν ἐν αὐτοῖς πρῶτον, καὶ ἡγεῖσθαι αὐτὸν ὡς κεφαλήν, καὶ μηδέν τι πράττειν περιττὸν ἄνευ τῆς ἐκείνου γνώμης, μόνα δὲ πράττειν ἕκαστον, ὅσα τῇ αὐτοῦ παροικίᾳ ἐπιβάλλει, καὶ ταῖς ὑπ᾽ αὐτὴν χώραις. ἀλλὰ μηδὲ ἐκεῖνος ἄνευ τῆς πάντων γνώμης ποιείτω τι. οὕτω γὰρ ὁμόνοια ἔσται, καὶ δοξασθήσεται ὁ Θεός, διὰ Κυρίου, ἐν Ἁγίῳ Πνεύματι, ὁ Πατὴρ καὶ ὁ Υἱὸς καὶ τὸ Ἅγιον Πνεῦμα. Also Concil. Nicæn. Can. IV. ἐπίσκοπον προσήκει μάλιστα μὲν ὑπὸ πάντων τῶν ἐν τῇ ἐπαρχίᾳ καθίστασθαι, εἰ δὲ δυσχερὲς εἴη τὸ τοιοῦτον... ἐξάπαντος τρεῖς ἐπὶ τὸ αὐτὸ συναγομένους, συμψήφων γενομένων καὶ τῶν ἀπόντων, καὶ συντιθεμένων διὰ γραμμάτων, τότε τὴν χειροτονίαν ποιεῖσθαι. τὸ δὲ κῦρος τῶν γινομένων δίδοσθαι καθ᾽ ἑκάστην ἐπαρχίαν τῷ μητροπολίτῃ.—Ἔθνος in the Apostolic Canon = provincia. See Ramsay, *Letters to the Seven Churches*, p. 229.

[1] Xenophon, *Anabasis* V. ii. 3, iv. 15.
[2] Mommsen, *The Provinces of the Roman Empire*, vol. I. pp. 329—330 (Eng. Transl.), Ramsay, *Letters to the Seven Churches*, pp. 227—230,289—290.
[3] Acts xix., Rev. i. 9—11, Eusebius, *Hist. Eccl.* III. i. 23 (with citations from Irenæus and Clement) and v. 24 (letter of Polycrates, bishop of Ephesus, to Victor, bishop of Rome). In the last-mentioned passage Eusebius speaks of Polycrates as follows—τῶν δὲ ἐπὶ τῆς Ἀσίας ἐπισκόπων... ἡγεῖτο Πολυκράτης.

The bishops of Christendom, then, were grouped round metropolitans. In their turn, the metropolitans were subordinate to the bishops of the first-rate cities of the Empire. Thus the metropolitans in Spain, Gaul and Britain, and Italy, were subordinate to the bishop of Rome, who also claimed primacy over the bishops of Africa—a claim injurious to the prerogative of Carthage[1]. In Egypt, and the adjoining Libya and Pentapolis, the bishop of Alexandria was, at the time of the Nicene and Antiochene Councils, probably the only metropolitan. In Syria, the metropolitan of Cæsarea (Palæstina) was among the bishops subordinate to the see of Antioch. When we come to Asia Minor and the region known nowadays as the Balkan Peninsula we find three great dioceses, of which express mention is made in the second canon of the Council of Constantinople (A.D. 381). This word 'diocese,' like 'province' and 'metropolis,' came into the vocabulary of the Church from that of the Empire. The three dioceses mentioned in the Constantinopolitan Canon just referred to are (1) Asiana, (2) Pontica, (3) Thracia[2]. In the Asian diocese, the

---

[1] The pretensions of the bishop of Rome, however, encountered sturdy resistance in Africa. See Salmon, *Infallibility of the Church*, pp. 407, 414, 415, Robertson, *History of the Christian Church*, II. pp. 149—151, 236, 237.

[2] Concil. Const. Can. II. τοὺς ὑπὲρ διοίκησιν ἐπισκόπους ταῖς ὑπερορίοις ἐκκλησίαις μὴ ἐπιέναι μηδὲ συγχέειν τὰς ἐκκλησίας, ἀλλὰ κατὰ τοὺς κανόνας τὸν μὲν 'Αλεξανδρείας ἐπίσκοπον τὰ ἐν Αἰγύπτῳ μόνον οἰκονομεῖν, τοὺς δὲ τῆς 'Ανατολῆς ἐπισκόπους τὴν 'Ανατολικὴν μόνην διοικεῖν, φυλαττομένων τῶν ἐν τοῖς κανόσι τοῖς κατὰ Νίκαιαν πρεσβείων τῇ 'Αντιοχέων ἐκκλησίᾳ, καὶ τοὺς τῆς 'Ασιανῆς διοικήσεως ἐπισκόπους τὰ κατὰ τὴν 'Ασιανὴν μόνον διοικεῖν, καὶ τοὺς τῆς Ποντικῆς τὰ τῆς Ποντικῆς μόνα, καὶ τοὺς τῆς Θρακικῆς τὰ τῆς Θρακικῆς μόνον διοικεῖν......τὰ καθ' ἑκάστην ἐπαρχίαν ἡ τῆς ἐπαρχίας σύνοδος διοικήσει, κατὰ τὰ ἐν Νικαίᾳ ὡρισμένα. In the fifth Canon of Nicæa, another phrase

leading see was that of Ephesus, though at the time of
the Canon Iconium also, and the Pisidian Antioch, were
prominent and important. In the Pontic diocese, the
lead was taken by the Cappadocian Cæsarea, and in
the Thracian the metropolis was Heracleia. Before
the foundation of Constantinople, Thessalonica was the
most important city in all the countries between the
Danube and Cape Malea, and the Church of Thessalonica, founded by St Paul, and connected with a city
of such pre-eminence, was naturally the 'metropolitan'
Church of Thrace, Macedonia and Illyricum. But
Thessalonica appears already to have been reckoned,
along with sees subordinate to it in Macedonia and
Illyricum, as belonging to the jurisdiction of Rome—
and the same is to be said of Corinth with Achæa
(or Greece) and even Crete[1]. These regions remained

of secular origin should be noticed—τὸ κοινὸν τῶν ἐπισκόπων, meaning the
episcopate of the province (ἐπαρχία). Compare the phrase Κοινὸν Κυπρίων
on coins of Cyprus belonging to the first three centuries of the Christian
era, and the use of τὸ κοινὸν in Thucyd. IV. 78; also 'commune Siciliæ' in
Cicero, *Verr.* Act. II. Lib. ii. 114 and 145. For the κοινὸν of Asia, the
κοινὸν of Bithynia, etc., see Mommsen, *Provinces of the Roman Empire*, I.
pp. 344—350.—'Diœcesis' occurs in Cicero, *ad Fam.* III. viii. 4, XIII. lxvii.,
in the sense of a district within a province. Three 'dioceses' of Asia, he
says, were attached to his Cilician province. See Lightfoot, *Colossians*,
pp. 7—8 for further illustrations. In *C.I.G.* 4693 Egypt is called a
διοίκησις. The use of the word to denote a group of provinces appears to
have come in with the reorganization of the Empire by Diocletian. The
ecclesiastical 'dioceses' mentioned in Conc. Const. Can. II. appear to have
generally coincided in extent with the civil dioceses, Aegyptus, Oriens,
Pontica, Asiana, Thracia. For provinces included in these dioceses, see
Bury's *Gibbon*, II. 550—552.

[1] In the civil divisions of the Empire, Crete was included in the diocese
of Macedonia, after the breaking-up of the diocese of the Mœsias into the
two dioceses of Dacia and Macedonia. The Macedonian diocese included
donia, Thessaly, Epirus, Achaia (i.e. Greece), and Crete. Jurisdiction

within the ecclesiastical jurisdiction of Rome down to the age of the Iconoclast controversy (A.D. 733)[1]. The predominant position of Constantinople led to the extension of the bishop's authority over the Asian and Pontic dioceses or 'exarchates,' as we learn from the 28th Canon of the Council of Chalcedon. The Constantinopolitan Council (Canon 3) had decreed that the Bishop of Constantinople should ' have the prerogative of honour next after the Bishop of Rome ' on the express ground of reason that ' Constantinople is New Rome[2].' At Chalcedon the assembled Fathers re-enacted the ruling of their predecessors, and on the same ground. ' For the Fathers reasonably allowed primacy to the throne of the elder Rome, because it was the imperial city, and for the same reason the 150 most godly bishops,' i.e. the Council of Constantinople in A.D. 381, ' assigned equal honours to the most holy throne of the New Rome, judging soundly that the city honoured with the presence of the Imperial Majesty and the Senate should enjoy the same honours and prerogatives as the elder imperial city of Rome, and be made pre-

---

over 'eastern Illyricum,' i.e. Macedonia, Thessaly, Greece, Epirus, was assumed by Innocent I. in pursuance of a policy initiated by Siricius, at the beginning of the fifth century. The pope constituted the bishop of Thessalonica his vicar for the administration of these regions. In 421, Theodosius II. ordered that Macedonia, etc. should form part of the Constantinopolitan 'diocese,' so that the bishops in those provinces should recognize the prelate of the eastern capital as their chief, but within a year or two, at the request of Honorius, he allowed the Roman jurisdiction to be restored.

[1] Paparregopoulos, Ἰστορία τοῦ Ἑλληνικοῦ Ἔθνους, III. 396, 411.

[2] Concil. Const. Can. III. τὸν μέντοι Κωνσταντινουπόλεως ἐπίσκοπον ἔχειν τὰ πρεσβεῖα τῆς τιμῆς μετὰ τὸν τῆς Ῥώμης ἐπίσκοπον, διὰ τὸ εἶναι αὐτὴν Νέαν Ῥώμην.

eminent in the same manner, in ecclesiastical relations, taking the next place[1].' The Chalcedonian Council further ordained that the metropolitans of the Pontic, Asian and Thracian dioceses or exarchates[2], *but these*

---

[1] Concil. Chal. Can. XXVIII. πανταχοῦ τοῖς τῶν ἁγίων πατέρων ὅροις ἑπόμενοι, καὶ τὸν ἀρτίως ἀναγνωσθέντα κανόνα τῶν ἑκατὸν πεντήκοντα θεοφιλεστάτων ἐπισκόπων τῶν συναχθέντων ἐπὶ τοῦ τῆς εὐσεβοῦς μνήμης μεγάλου Θεοδοσίου τοῦ γενομένου βασιλέως ἐν τῇ βασιλίδι Κωνσταντίνου πόλει Νέᾳ Ῥώμῃ, γνωρίζοντες τὰ αὐτὰ καὶ ἡμεῖς ὁρίζομεν καὶ ψηφιζόμεθα περὶ τῶν πρεσβείων τῆς ἁγιωτάτης ἐκκλησίας τῆς αὐτῆς Κωνσταντίνου πόλεως Νέας Ῥώμης. καὶ γὰρ τῷ θρόνῳ τῆς πρεσβυτέρας Ῥώμης, διὰ τὸ βασιλεύειν τὴν πόλιν ἐκείνην, οἱ πατέρες εἰκότως ἀποδεδώκασι τὰ πρεσβεῖα, καὶ τῷ αὐτῷ σκοπῷ κινούμενοι οἱ ἑκατὸν πεντήκοντα θεοφιλέστατοι ἐπίσκοποι τὰ ἴσα πρεσβεῖα ἀπένειμαν τῷ τῆς Νέας Ῥώμης ἁγιωτάτῳ θρόνῳ, εὐλόγως κρίναντες τὴν βασιλείᾳ καὶ συγκλήτῳ τιμηθεῖσαν πόλιν καὶ τῶν ἴσων ἀπολαύουσαν πρεσβείων τῇ πρεσβυτέρᾳ βασιλίδι Ῥώμῃ, καὶ ἐν τοῖς ἐκκλησιαστικοῖς ὡς ἐκείνην μεγαλύνεσθαι πράγμασι, δευτέραν μετ᾽ ἐκείνην ὑπάρχουσαν. καὶ ὥστε τοὺς τῆς Ποντικῆς καὶ τῆς Ἀσιανῆς καὶ τῆς Θρακικῆς διοικήσεως μητροπολίτας μόνους, ἔτι δὲ καὶ τοὺς ἐν τοῖς βαρβαρικοῖς ἐπισκόπους τῶν προειρημένων διοικήσεων, χειροτονεῖσθαι ὑπὸ τοῦ προειρημένου ἁγιωτάτου θρόνου τῆς κατὰ Κωνσταντινούπολιν ἁγιωτάτης ἐκκλησίας, δηλαδὴ ἑκάστου μητροπολίτου τῶν προειρημένων διοικήσεων, μετὰ τῶν τῆς ἐπαρχίας ἐπισκόπων χειροτονοῦντος τοὺς τῆς ἐπαρχίας ἐπισκόπους, καθὼς τοῖς θείοις κανόσι διηγόρευται. χειροτονεῖσθαι δέ, καθὼς εἴρηται, τοὺς μητροπολίτας τῶν προειρημένων διοικήσεων παρὰ τοῦ Κωνσταντινουπόλεως ἀρχιεπισκόπου, ψηφισμάτων συμφώνων κατὰ τὸ ἔθος γινομένων καὶ ἐπ᾽ αὐτὸν ἀναφερομένων.

[2] Ἔξαρχος τῶν ἱερέων (pontifex maximus) is found in Plutarch, *Numa* 10. On the 34th 'Apostolic' Canon (see above, p. 45, n. 2) the *Pedalion* has a note, pointing out that the first bishop of a 'nation' (ἔθνος) or province is called, in the sixth Canon of the Council of Sardica, 'bishop of the metropolis' and 'exarch of the province'—ἐπίσκοπος τῆς μητροπόλεως, ἔξαρχος τῆς ἐπαρχίας. The same note also refers to the Greek version of the records of the Council of Carthage (A.D. 418), in which the chief bishop of a province is called ὁ πρωτεύων or ὁ ἐπίσκοπος τῆς πρώτης καθέδρας (episcopus primæ cathedræ). 'But in the general usage of the majority of canons he is called the metropolitan (μητροπολίτης).' The ninth and seventeenth Canons of the Council of Chalcedon ruled that any bishop or cleric who had a cause to plead against the metropolitan of his province should go to '*the exarch of the diocese*' *or* 'the throne of the imperial City

only, together with bishops in barbarian lands on the frontier of those dioceses, should receive consecration from the see of Constantinople.

Thus four great groups of ecclesiastical provinces were formed, each presided over and directed by a bishop residing in one of the four greatest cities of the Empire. These four patriarchates, as they came to be called, corresponded in number only to the four great prefectures of the Empire—in boundaries they were

of Constantine.'—In a long note upon the former of these two Canons the *Pedalion* points out that the Patriarchs of Constantinople never claimed universal jurisdiction on the strength of the ruling thus worded, from which it is to be inferred that the fathers assembled at Chalcedon never intended to confer such authority upon the see of New Rome. By the 'exarch of the diocese' is meant, not the metropolitan of the province, for the diocese is a group of provinces, but the metropolitan of the diocese, i.e. the metropolitan who is first among the metropolitans associated in one diocesan group. At the present day, proceeds the author of the note in the *Pedalion* (p. 193), though some metropolitans are called 'exarchs' they have no effective superiority over other metropolitans. The 'exarchs of dioceses' at the time of the Council of Chalcedon, then, occupied a position superior to that of other metropolitans, without being equal to that of patriarchs. According to Zonaras, the metropolitan bishops of Cæsarea (in Cappadocia), Ephesus, Thessalonica, and Corinth were 'exarchs,' distinguished by wearing πολυσταύρια (a sort of chasuble embroidered with crosses) when they officiated in church. The exarchate, however, appears to have ceased to exist, save as a title of honour, soon after the Council of Chalcedon. So far as the evidence of conciliar canons goes, the only exarchs then existing were those of the Pontic, Asian, and Thracian dioceses, which were all included in the patriarchate of Constantinople. The ninth Canon of Chalcedon, therefore, really gave the archbishop of the New Rome appellate jurisdiction over the dioceses just named, the practical consequence being that the exarchic jurisdiction came to an end. No mention, apparently, of exarchs is made in the laws of Justinian relating to clerical litigation. Again, the Council of Chalcedon, in its ninth and seventeenth Canons, had in view only the patriarch of Constantinople and the metropolitans recognized as subject to his primacy.

quite different from them, Rome, for instance, being the headquarters of an ecclesiastical jurisdiction extending over regions included in no less than three out of the four prefectures, while the bishop of Antioch, if not the bishop of Alexandria also, exercised spiritual authority in lands outside the boundaries of the Roman Emperor's dominions[1]. The language of the 20th Canon of Chalcedon, however, proves that the Fathers of Christendom had, as a rule, tended to adapt the territorial organization of the Church to that of the civil state. This appears again in the history of the see of Jerusalem or Ælia Capitolina. Jerusalem was, and is, the mother-city of the Christian religion. The city was destroyed by Titus in A.D. 70, but a town of some sort formed itself after a time on the ruins of the city. It was not in Jerusalem, however, but in Cæsarea, the provincial capital, that Palestinian Christianity had the headquarters of its government, even after the foundation of Ælia Capitolina as a Roman colony. The Christian community in Jerusalem naturally cherished a desire to take precedence of Cæsarea, but this ambition was not satisfied till the fifth century, when Jerusalem was constituted a ·patriarchal' see, the bishop of Jerusalem thenceforth having metropolitans under him, and recognizing only a 'precedence of honour' in his brethren of Rome, Constantinople, Alexandria and Antioch, the sphere of the new patriarchal jurisdiction consisting of territories hitherto included in that of Antioch, viz. the three regions into which Palestine was then divided. This settlement was arrived at in the Council of Chalcedon, A.D. 451. It was a compromise, for Juvenal, the

[1] The jurisdiction of Alexandria extended into Abyssinia.

bishop of Jerusalem, who had been scheming for twenty years past to free himself from subordination to the Antiochene prelate, had claimed the region of Arabia, and part at least of Phœnicia, as his diocese[1].

The title 'patriarch' is not found in the Canons of the first four Œcumenical Synods, but it appears, from the quotations given by M. Gedeon in the preface to his 'Πατριαρχικοὶ πίνακες,' to have been in use before the date of the Council of Constantinople. According to M. Gedeon, it was taken over by the Church from the Old Testament (i.e. the Greek version), II. Chron. xxvi. 12, πᾶς ὁ ἀριθμὸς τῶν πατριαρχῶν τῶν δυνατῶν εἰς πόλεμον δισχίλιοι ἑξακόσιοι—'the whole number of the chief of the fathers of the mighty men of valour was two thousand and six hundred.' M. Gedeon might have added Acts ii. 29, 'the patriarch David,' and vii. 8, 'Jacob begat the twelve patriarchs'; and Hebrews vii. 4, where Abraham is called 'the patriarch.' But the ecclesiastical use of the title resembles not so much the Scriptural as the use established for nearly three centuries in Jewry after the suppression of Bar-Khokba's insurrection and the foundation of Ælia Capitolina on the site of Jerusalem. The Jews dispersed throughout the Roman Empire found a new bond of union in common acknowledgment of the authority of a 'patriarch' who resided in Tiberias. This patriarch appointed subordinate ministers, among them being his envoys to the children of Israel scattered abroad in the lands of the heathen; these envoys were called 'apostles.' 'It is a singular spectacle,' wrote Dean Milman, 'to behold a nation dispersed in every region of the world, without

---

[1] Robertson, *History of the Christian Church*, II. pp. 227—229.

murmur or repugnance, submitting to the regulations, and taxing themselves to support the greatness, of a supremacy which rested solely on public opinion, and had no temporal power whatever to enforce its decrees.' The Jewish Patriarchate of Tiberias is curiously like the mediæval Papacy, and the resemblance is heightened by the fact that the Jews inhabiting the lands to the east of the Roman Empire observed allegiance to a spiritual sovereign, the 'Prince of the Captivity,' resident in Babylon, who stood over against the Western prelate very much as the Patriarch of Constantinople over against the Pope[1].

The Patriarchate of Tiberias was abolished by an edict of the younger Theodosius, about A.D. 420[2]. By that time the title patriarch had come into accepted use among Christians, though that use was as yet not quite fixed. In the passages quoted or referred to by M. Gedeon, we find it applied by Gregory Nazianzene to his father, the bishop of Nazianzus, by Gregory Nyssene to the bishops assembled at Constantinople in the Second Œcumenical Council, by Theodosius II. to John Chrysostom and Leo of Rome. Leo is also designated 'patriarch' in the 'Acta' of the Council of Chalcedon. A passage of considerable importance in the history of the title is given at length by M. Gedeon, from the eighth chapter of the fifth book of Socrates' *Ecclesiastical History*. The passage runs as follows: 'They,' i.e. the Council of Constantinople, 'established

[1] Milman, *History of the Jews*, ch. xix. Gibbon, *Decline and Fall*, II. 73, 74 (Bury's ed.).

[2] Bingham, *Antiquities*, bk II. ch. xvii. § 4 (vol. I. p. 197. Oxford edition of 1855). Bingham seems to think that the Jewish patriarchate dated from the first century, C.E.

patriarchs, among whom they distributed the provinces, so that diocesan bishops should not interfere with churches outside the limits of their jurisdiction—a matter in which irregularity had set in by reason of the persecutions. Nectarius obtained the capital (Constantinople) and Thrace as his portion. The patriarchate (πατριαρχεία) of the Pontic diocese fell to Helladius, successor of Basil in the bishopric of Cæsarea in Cappadocia, Gregory of Nyssa, Basil's brother, and Otreius, bishop of Melitene in Armenia. The Asian diocese was assigned to Amphilochius of Iconium and Optimus of the Pisidian Antioch, while the affairs of Egypt became the charge of Timothy, bishop of Alexandria. The diocese of the East was given to the same bishops as before—Pelagius of Laodicea and Diodorus of Tarsus—under reservation of the privileges of the Church of Antioch. These were given to Meletius, who was then present[1].'

---

[1] Socrates *H. E.* v. 8. The 150 bishops assembled at Constantinople in 381 πατριάρχας κατέστησαν διανειμάμενοι τὰς ἐπαρχίας, ὥστε τοὺς ὑπὲρ διοίκησιν ἐπισκόπους ταῖς ὑπερορίοις ἐκκλησίαις μὴ ἐπιβαίνειν, τοῦτο γὰρ πρότερον διὰ τοὺς διωγμοὺς ἐγίνετο ἀδιαφόρως. καὶ κληροῦται Νεκτάριος μὲν τὴν μεγαλόπολιν καὶ τὴν Θρᾴκην· τῆς δὲ Ποντικῆς διοικήσεως Ἑλλάδιος ὁ μετὰ Βασίλειον Καισαρείας τῆς Καππαδοκῶν ἐπίσκοπος, Γρηγόριος ὁ Νύσσης ὁ Βασιλείου ἀδελφός (Καππαδοκίας δὲ καὶ ἥδε πόλις), καὶ Ὀτρήϊος ὁ τῆς ἐν Ἀρμενίᾳ Μελιτηνῆς τὴν πατριαρχίαν ἐκληρώσατο. Τὴν Ἀσιανὴν δὲ λαγχάνουσιν Ἀμφιλόχιος ὁ Ἰκονίου καὶ Ὄπτιμος ὁ Ἀντιοχείας τῆς Πισιδίας. τὸ δὲ κατὰ τὴν Αἴγυπτον Τιμοθέῳ τῷ Ἀλεξανδρείας προσενεμήθη. τῶν δὲ κατὰ τὴν Ἀνατολὴν ἐκκλησιῶν τὴν διοίκησιν τοῖς αὐτῆς (αὐτοῖς?) ἐπισκόποις ἐπέτρεψαν, Πελαγίῳ τε τῷ Λαοδικείας καὶ Διοδώρῳ τῷ Ταρσοῦ, φυλάξαντες τὰ πρεσβεῖα τῇ Ἀντιοχέων ἐκκλησίᾳ, ἅπερ τότε παρόντι Μελετίῳ ἔδοσαν. According to this arrangement, the exarchic powers were given to commissions, of three metropolitans in the Pontic diocese, and two each in the Asian and Oriental. In the Oriental diocese, however, the bishop (patriarch) of Antioch had

The phraseology of the Canons of the first four Œcumenical Councils shows that, even as late as the middle of the fifth century, the usage of ecclesiastical titles was still somewhat fluctuating. Of this we have manifest proofs in the 30th Canon of the Chalcedonian Council. In this document we find it recorded that the *bishops* of Egypt deprecated signing 'the letter of the most pious archbishop Leo,' it being the custom 'in the Egyptian diocese' not to take such a step without the cognizance and authorization of 'the *archbishop*' (sc. of Alexandria). They therefore requested dispensation from subscription 'until the consecration of him who should be *bishop* of the great city of Alexandria. It seemed good to the Council that they should be allowed to wait until the "*archbishop* of the great city of Alexandria" should have been ordained.' In the third Canon, again, of the Council of Constantinople, it is decreed that the *bishop* of Constantinople should have the πρεσβεῖα τῆς τιμῆς after the *bishop* of Rome. Similarly, the first four Councils in their Canons speak of the Antiochene prelate as 'bishop,' though the

---

πρεσβεῖα, the nature of which may be inferred from the sixth of the Nicene Canons (*supra*, n. 2, p. 44). The old Roman province of Syria included Cilicia, which again was subsequently included, along with Syria, in the civil diocese 'Oriens.' In Cilicia the chief city was Tarsus, which nevertheless, just as much as Laodicea, yielded precedence to Antioch. Here we note a close correspondence between the civil and the ecclesiastical arrangements, which John of Antioch, half a century later, would have been glad to see rounded off by the subordination of Cyprus to his see. Cyprus, however, though a province of the diocese 'Oriens,' remained independent in matters ecclesiastical. See Hackett, *Church of Cyprus*, pp. 13—21. It is curious that the bishop of Ephesus was not made one of the exarchs of the diocese Asiana.'

patriarchal title must have already been applied to him as well as to his brethren of Rome and Alexandria. In the Quinisext or Trullan Council, Theophilus of Antioch was saluted as 'patriarch,' while in the second Canon of that Council Dionysius, Peter, Athanasius, Cyril and other prelates of Alexandria are entitled 'archbishop,' an honour bestowed in the same document upon Cyprian of Carthage and Basil of Cæsarea. The only 'patriarch' mentioned in the Canon by that title is Gennadius of Constantinople.

The distribution of the Churches of Christendom into five main groups, having their respective headquarters in Rome, Constantinople, Alexandria, Antioch and Jerusalem, was an established and recognized fact from the time of the Fourth General Council (Chalcedon) onwards. It also came to be felt that the patriarchal title ought to be reserved for the bishops of the five cities just named. But while the occupants of the four Eastern centres of primacy were thenceforth constantly spoken of as patriarchs, till this became their regular designation, the bishops of Rome seem not to have greatly cared to avail themselves of their privilege in this respect. One reason, if not *the* reason, of this was probably the conception they held of their lawful precedence among all the chief pastors of Christendom—a conception which included much more than the Eastern prelates were willing to allow. Thus the title 'Patriarch of Rome' was never established in permanent use, like the titles 'Patriarch of Constantinople,' 'Patriarch of Alexandria,' etc., and it is quite in agreement with this fact that we find the Popes, in later ages, claiming not merely titular or honorary precedence, but actual power of jurisdiction, over the Patriarchates[1].

With regard to the title 'Patriarch of Constantinople' it is important to note that it is an abbreviation. The full form is 'Archbishop of the City of Constantine, New Rome, and Œcumenical Patriarch' (Ἀρχιεπίσκοπος Κωνσταντινουπόλεως, Νέας Ῥώμης, καὶ Οἰκουμενικὸς Πατριάρχης). The first part of the title must obviously be traced back to the very earliest period in the history of 'New Rome,' to a time when the name 'patriarch' had hardly obtained a place in the official and legal vocabulary of the Church. The second part sounds as though it were an assumption of world-wide jurisdiction, and a counterblast to the Papal claim of sovereignty over the Church Catholic. Its actual origin, however, is probably to be found in the estimate not unnaturally formed, by Christians in the eastern regions of the Roman Empire, of the importance and authority of the 'Great Church of Constantinople'—especially after the Empire in the West had crumbled into ruins, and Constantinople was indisputably the head of the οἰκουμένη, the 'orbis terrarum' of the Roman Empire.

[1] The title of *patriarch* was assumed in the West by the metropolitans of Aquileia, in the latter part of the sixth century, but by no means with the consent of the Pope, or on any authority except their own. Their assumption of the title, in fact, emphasized their renunciation of the papal primacy as nullified by acceptance of the 'Three Capitula' propounded by Justinian to the Council convened at Constantinople in A.D. 553. The schism between Rome and Aquileia was not finally healed till the end of the seventh century. Another western patriarchate, that of Grado (Venice), was subsequently created by the Papacy. Robertson, *History of the Christian Church*, II. p. 306, note g. At the present day, the Pope numbers several *patriarchs* in the host of bishops subordinate to him.

Such an estimate the 'Great Church' of Constantinople would hardly be disposed to call in question.

M. Gedeon observes that Theodosius II., in A.D. 438, spoke of St John Chrysostom as οἰκουμενικὸς διδάσκαλος. The imperial compliment, however, in all probability had reference, not to the extent of St John Chrysostom's episcopal jurisdiction, but to the character of his doctrine, and the general esteem in which it was held. At the time of the Council of Chalcedon, certain opponents of Dioscorus referred to Pope Leo as 'the most holy and blessed œcumenical archbishop and patriarch.' This could only have meant that it was the duty and the right of the bishops of Rome to render assistance to any Christian Church 'by heresies distressed.' The same persuasion will best account for the salutation of John the Cappadocian, archbishop of the New Rome, in 518, in the letters received from certain clergy and monks of Syria, denouncing the wickedness of Severus, who then occupied the See of Antioch, but was a fautor of the Monophysite heresy. At the beginning of the sixth century, Constantinople was indubitably the head and metropolis of the οἰκουμένη, i.e. the dominions of the Roman Emperor, the 'circle of lands' Roman, Christian civilized—in those days the epithets were interchangeable—and by that time the οἰκουμένη was identified to a far greater extent with Eastern or Greek than with Western, Latin, Christendom. Nothing could have been more natural than the appeal for aid from the vexed orthodox clergy and monks of Syria to the archbishop of the imperial city. The defence of the οἰκουμένη in its political aspect—i.e. the Empire—devolved upon the monarch; similarly, the defence of the οἰκουμένη in its

spiritual or religious aspect, the Church, might be regarded as part at least of the ' daily charge¹' of the chief
pastor in ' the house of the kingdom².'

¹ II. Cor. xi. 28, ἡ ἐπισύστασίς μοι ἡ καθ᾽ ἡμέραν, ἡ μέριμνα πασῶν τῶν
ἐκκλησιῶν.

² In order to arrive at a proper estimate of the title οἰκουμενικὸς
πατριάρχης, one has to ascertain as nearly as possible what meaning it
was likely to convey at the time when it first came into use. It must be
remembered that its local origin was the Hellenic East, and that those by
whom and among whom it originated had a very different conception of
' the world' from ours. The imperial system occupied their mental outlook
to an extent which is difficult for us to appreciate. Some light is thrown
on the subject by the language of Polybius, who may be taken as a representative of Hellenism in other ages besides his own. In Polybius' view,
the Romans were already masters of the world (ἡ οἰκουμένη) when they had
annihilated the power of Macedon and established their hegemony over
the Hellenic commonwealths and the Hellenized kingdoms occupying the
western part of Asia Minor.

'Η οἰκουμένη is a phrase that needs to be interpreted in accordance
with its context. There are passages in which it is intended to mean the
whole world, the whole earth—e.g. Ps. xviii. (xix.) 4, S. Matth. xxiv. 14,
Rev. iii. 10, xii. 9, xvi. 14, S. Luke iv. 5. In other passages it has to be
understood with limitations—e.g. Demosthenes, *De Corona*, 242, Polybius,
iii. 1, vi. 1 and 50, viii. 4, Acts xi. 28, xvii. 6, xix. 27, S. Luke ii. 1.

The patriarchs of Constantinople could hardly have intended to claim
an exclusive right to the use of the title ' œcumenical.' It was a title that
any or all of the four other patriarchs could have assumed. The patriarch
of Alexandria, in fact, was distinguished by the title κριτὴς τῆς οἰκουμένης.
According to one account, the origin of this title was the assumption by
Cyril of Alexandria, at the request of Celestine, of the function of papal
delegate or deputy at the Council of Ephesus in 431. This explanation,
however, can hardly be reconciled with the fact that Celestine sent three
representatives to that Council. Another account connects the title with
the duty assigned by the Council of Nicæa to the bishop of Alexandria
with reference to the observation of Easter. The bishop of Alexandria
was to notify to the bishop of Rome, year by year, the day, as ascertained
by astronomical investigation, on which the next Easter festival was to be
held, and the bishop of Rome was to communicate this information to the
world at large. However that may be, we find no patriarch of Alexandria

Nothing, probably, was heard in Rome in 518 of the high-sounding title bestowed upon John the Cappadocian in the letter from the Syrian clergy and monastics. At any rate, no objections appear to have been made by Pope Hormisdas. Even if any had been made, very little account of them would have been taken by Justinian, who had a high-handed fashion of dealing with papal opposition. In edicts and 'novellæ' Justinian gave a legal character to the title 'œcumenical bishop,' which he bestowed upon John the Cappadocian's successors, Epiphanius, Anthimus, Theunas and Eutychius. It was no innovation, therefore, when the patriarch John the Faster, in A.D. 587, assumed the title, but his action provoked the severe displeasure of his contemporaries in the Roman See, Pelagius II. and Gregory the Great, who declared that such pride and self-exaltation marked a man out as a forerunner of the Antichrist. Jealousy of the pre-eminence of Constantinople can hardly be left out of the account in explaining the attitude taken up by Pelagius and Gregory. But in fairness to Gregory, if not to his predecessor also, it must be pointed out that he understood the title 'œcumenical bishop' to mean 'sole bishop,' implying a claim to be the fountain of episcopal authority for the whole Church, and when Eulogius of Alexandria addressed him in a letter as 'universal Pope,' Gregory refused the title, as enriching him unlawfully at his brother's expense. 'If,' he said, 'you style me universal Pope, you deny that you are *at all* that which you own me to be universally[1].'

setting up a literal claim to 'judge the world' by representing his see as the supreme court of Christendom.

[1] Robertson, *History of the Christian Church*, II. 376—379.

In defence of the Constantinopolitan prelates it is urged that they never thought of claiming to be 'œcumenical' in the sense ascribed to the word by Pope Gregory. The claim involved in its assumption, however, cannot have been less than a claim to primacy in the Roman Empire, within the pale of which, they might argue, the old imperial metropolis was no longer included, or, if it was included, its rank was that of a provincial town, of less consequence than Ravenna, where the imperial Exarch resided. One cannot help suspecting a covert design to reverse the relations of Rome and Constantinople on the strength of the political situation, and so effecting a development of the principle underlying the third Canon of Constantinople and the twenty-eighth of Chalcedon, in resisting which the Popes had a good deal of right and reason on their side. Gregory's remonstrances and censures, however, were of no avail to the end for which they were uttered, the persuasion of the archbishop of the New Rome to discard the title 'œcumenical.' The persistency of their eastern brethren in this matter may have been an inducement to Leo II. to acquiesce in the ascription of the much-disputed title of honour to him by the Emperor Constantine Pogonatus in A.D. 682, and the compliment was returned a little over a century later, when the papal legate addressed Tarasius as 'œcumenical patriarch' in the Second Council of Nicæa, A.D. 787[1]. This concession, however, on the part of the Pope can hardly have been made without some counterbalancing reservation, possibly an *a fortiori* argument based on the second Canon of the Council of Constantinople in A.D. 381, which would have run as follows—

[1] *Pedalion*, p. 209 n.

the See of Constantinople is recognized by the Canon as being next in honour and exaltation to the See of Rome; the Patriarch of Constantinople claims the title of οἰκουμενικός; much more, then, may the Pope claim that title.

The explanation given by the Greeks at the present day, as set forth in the *Pedalion*, is the same as the explanation elicited by the criticisms of Anastasius, the Librarian of the Papal See, in the ninth century. 'While I was residing at Constantinople,' says Anastasius, 'I often used to take the Greeks to task over this title, censuring it as a sign of contempt or arrogance. Their reply was that they called the patriarch "œcumenical" (which many render by "universal") not in the sense of his being invested with authority over the whole world, but in virtue of his presiding over a certain region thereof, which is inhabited by Christians. What the Greeks call *œcumene* is not only what the Latins call *orbis*, and from its comprehensiveness, orbis *universalis*, but also answers to "habitatio" or "locus habitabilis."' In like manner the author of the long note on the 28th Canon of Chalcedon in the *Pedalion*, pp. 207—209. 'The word οἰκουμενικὸς means either of two things. First, it may be understood comprehensively in relation to the whole Church, in the sense that the œcumenical bishop is one who possesses peculiar and monarchical authority over the whole Church. Or, secondly, it means a large part of the inhabited earth. Many kings, though not lords over the whole earth, are thus entitled "masters of the world" (so, for instance, Evagrius speaks of Zeno) in so far as they have dominion over a large part of it. In the first significance of the title, the patriarch of Constantinople is never styled "œcumenical," nor is the patriarch of Rome, nor anyone else, save Christ alone, the true Patriarch of all the world, to whom hath been given all power in heaven and upon earth. It is in the second sense that the patriarch of Constantinople is styled "œcumenical" as having subject to his authority a great part of the world, and furthermore as being a zealous defender of the faith and the traditions of the Councils and the Fathers, not only in his own province (διοίκησις), but in the others as well.'

The meaning thus attached to the title is not very closely defined, but this lack of definiteness leaves room for considerable latitude in practical application. It enables a patriarch of Constantinople to intervene in ecclesiastical affairs outside the limits of his ordinary jurisdiction just so far as the occasion allows him to do so safely, without exposing himself to the charge either of stretching himself beyond his measure or of failing to come up to it.

In the course of more than fifteen centuries since the foundation of Constantinople, the territorial limits of the patriarch's jurisdiction have frequently been changed. They were enlarged by Leo the Iconoclast, who withdrew Crete, Greece and Macedonia from the Roman 'diocese' and assigned them to that of Constantinople. From 923 to 972 Bulgaria was a separate patriarchate, in virtue of the treaty made between Romanus I. and Simeon, the king of Bulgaria. The conquest of Bulgaria by John Zimiskes in 972 deprived the Bulgarian primate of his patriarchal dignity and title, but left him 'autocephalous,' i.e. independent of any patriarch. About ten years later the headquarters of the Bulgarian kingdom were transferred to Achrida in Illyria, and with them the primatial see, the occupant of which bore the title of Archbishop of Prima Justiniana, Achrida and All Bulgaria. The measure of independence claimed for the See of Achrida was no small one, as the coronation of Theodore Angelos showed, this ceremony being performed by the Bulgarian primate at Thessalonica (A.D. 1222). From the early part of the thirteenth century to the time of the capture of Constantinople by the Turks there were two other independent archbishoprics in the Balkan Peninsula, viz. Pekion in Servia and Tirnova in Bulgaria. These independent jurisdictions were recognized by the œcumenical patriarchate as useful checks and restraints upon the archbishopric of Achrida, the attitude of which was generally one of hostility to the East-Roman Empire. They were both reincorporated in the patriarchate after the fall of Constantinople, though Pekion regained its independence for a time towards the close of the seventeenth century, only to surrender it again in 1766. In the following year the archbishop of Achrida surrendered his autonomy, and together with the bishops subordinate to him took his place under the jurisdiction of Constantinople[1].

At one time the patriarch of Constantinople claimed authority over the Church of Russia, which was first founded by Greek missionaries in the tenth century.

---

[1] Hackett, *Church of Cyprus*, pp. 250—283. Finlay, *History of Greece*, II. 311. 'The Arch-Bishop of Epikion in Servia, who hath 16 Bishops under him, and of Ocrida which hath 18, are not subject to the Patriarch of Constantinople'—Paul Ricaut, *The present State of the Greek and Armenian Churches, Anno Christi* 1678. Smith, *Greek Church* (London, 1680), pp. 73, 74.

Towards the close of the sixteenth century, when the Principality of Muscovy had become a large and powerful empire, a new patriarchate was created, having its local habitation in Moscow. The new line of patriarchs, however, did not continue for more than 111 years, the place of the patriarch, as the chief ecclesiastical authority, being taken in the eighteenth century, in the last years of Peter the Great, by the 'Spiritual College,' or, as it was subsequently named, the 'Most Holy Governing Synod,' consisting at first of ten, subsequently of eight members[1].

[1] The Russian patriarchate was first established by the patriarch of Constantinople, Jeremias II., on his own initiative, in January, A.D. 1589. Jeremias was then making a tour in Muscovy, collecting the alms of the orthodox faithful for the support of the œcumenical patriarchate. A curious account of the event, written in decapentesyllabic metre, was drawn up by Arsenios, Metropolitan of Elassona, who accompanied Jeremias II. on his tour. See K. N. Satha's biography of Jeremias II. (Athens, 1870). The last patriarch of Moscow, Adrian, died A.D. 1700. In A.D. 1721 the 'Spiritual College' or 'Most Holy Governing Synod' was instituted. The metropolitans of Kiev, Moscow, and S. Petersburg, and the 'Exarch' of Georgia, are ex-officio members. See *The Russian Church and Russian Dissent*, by A. F. Heard (New York, 1887), pp. 118, 124—5, 156—7.

The Princes of Moscow assumed the title of Tsar in A.D. 1547. Their dominions at that time covered an area of about 500,000 square miles. This had been increased to $1\frac{1}{2}$ million square miles in 1584 (the last year of Ivan the Terrible) by conquests to the east and north, reaching beyond the Urals. In 1584, then, Moscow had become the capital of a very considerable realm, and this appears to have suggested the creation of a patriarchate for the befitting exaltation of the Church in the new Christian empire. At any rate, it was avowedly on the principle expressed in the twenty-eighth Canon of Chalcedon, and the third of Constantinople (A.D. 381), that the synod assembled in Constantinople in A.D. 1593 decreed that 'the throne of the most pious and orthodox city of Moscow should be, and be called, a patriarchate (πατριαρχεῖον).' See K. N. Satha, *op. cit.*, pp. 86 and 88. This synod, however, would not allow the new patriarchate to rank third, as had been originally proposed, but appointed it to the fifth place, in order

At the beginning of the nineteenth century the jurisdiction of the œcumenical patriarch extended over the greater part of the Balkan Peninsula, and on the Asiatic side of the Bosphorus and Hellespont as far as the Taurus range in the one direction and the country round Trebizond in the other. Since that time the boundaries of the patriarch's jurisdiction have been greatly contracted by reason of the political changes which have taken place in South-eastern Europe. In Greece, Roumania, Servia and Bulgaria new states have come into existence, and so many provinces have been withdrawn from the œcumenical patriarchate. On the other hand, the Asiatic provinces remain unchanged. Crete also is still included in the patriarchate[1].

not to innovate upon the ruling of the Quinisext Council in its thirty-sixth Canon. 'The Muscovites and Russians,' wrote Ricaut in 1678, 'have their own Patriarch of late years, yet they acknowledge a particular respect and reverence unto the See of Constantinople, to which they have recourse for counsel and direction in all difficult points controverted in Religion.' Ricaut, *op. cit.*, p. 83.

[1] Not only in the extent and boundaries of the patriarchal jurisdiction, but also in the number and location of metropolitan and episcopal sees included within it, have there been changes. The Ἔκθεσις νέα Ἀνδρονίκου βασιλέως, drawn up by or by order of the Emperor Andronicus I., about A.D. 1320, contains the names of 109 metropolitan sees subordinate to the throne of Constantinople. Of the see-cities mentioned in this catalogue, some have ceased to exist, and had even ceased to exist at the time when the catalogue was drawn up. The rest, for the most part, are places of no great importance. Many of the sees, again, are no longer in existence, and no less than twelve are in the kingdom of Greece and therefore no longer subject to the œcumenical throne. It should be remembered that in A.D. 1320 the boundaries of the Eastern Empire, both in Asia and in Europe, had undergone a great deal of shrinking. A catalogue of metropolitan sees existing in the patriarchate about A.D. 1640, drawn up by Philippus Cyprius, would indicate about 40 as the number of such sees at that date. The catalogue, however, is defective. It appears to have

In the East-Roman or 'Byzantine' Empire the patriarch of Constantinople was the 'first subject of the realm.' The exalted nature of his position was shown by the privileges which the court-etiquette conceded to him. He was the only person in the Empire to greet whom the sovereign rose from his seat. At the ἀποκοπτή, the table set apart for the Emperor in a State banquet, the patriarch was the guest most honoured and distinguished. The two most important constituents of the State, according to the theory of the mediæval Empire, were the Emperor and the Patriarch (τῆς πολιτείας τὰ μέγιστα καὶ ἀναγκαιότατα μέρη βασιλεύς ἐστι καὶ πατριάρχης)[1]. But just because the patriarchate was so exalted an office in the Church, and consequently in the State, the personality of its occupant could not be a matter of indifference to the temporal sovereign. To make use of the hierarchy as agents of the imperial power was one of the principles of government in the Roman Empire after it became Christian. Both the vicinity of the patriarchal residence and the imperial palace in Constantinople, and the loss of Egypt, Syria,

been originally drawn up ages before the time of Philippus Cyprius, by whom certain notes were added here and there. In it Calabria and Sicily appear as regions subject to the jurisdiction of Constantinople—a state of affairs past and over long before the seventeenth century. Thomas Smith, in his *Account of the Greek Church* (A.D. 1680), gives a list of 79 sees, metropolitan and diocesan taken together. There are now 74 metropolitan and 20 diocesan sees in the patriarchate. The following bishoprics, after the liberation of Greece, and in consequence of that event, were withdrawn from the patriarchal jurisdiction—viz. 1 Athens, 2 Thebes, 3 Naupactus, 4 Corfu, 5 Patras, 6 Lacedæmon, 7 Argos (Nauplia), 8 Paros and Naxos, 9 Andros, 10 Chalcis (Eubœa), 11 Pharsala, 12 Larissa, 13 Monemvasia. These are all found in the Catalogues given by Philippus Cyprius.

[1] Paparregopoulos, Ἱστορία τοῦ Ἑλληνικοῦ Ἔθνους, IV. pp. 9—12.

and the West in consequence of Saracen, Lombard and Frankish aggressions, stimulated the tendency of the supreme temporal authority to influence and determine elections to the throne of St John Chrysostom. Hence the history of the relations of the two powers, the imperial and the patriarchal, is a record, not perhaps of incessant conflict, but certainly of frequent collisions. The Emperors made no objection to having the forms of election to the patriarchal see by bishops, clergy, and people (the last being represented by the senators) observed with all due dignity, so long as the person of him who obtained election was acceptable to them. Often enough, the election was a mere formality, in which the bishops, clergy and people did not so much ratify, as testify their grateful acceptance of, an imperial nomination. But when the election escaped imperial control, great troubles were certain to arise, and while the Emperor could forcibly depose and imprison a patriarch whom he disliked, the patriarch, or on his behalf the monks, who swarmed in Constantinople, and on whose allegiance the patriarchal power was chiefly based, might by appealing to the people at large call forth turbulent demonstrations of a sort which even a strong ruler would not regard with complete indifference.

The determination of the succession by imperial influence may be said to have been the rule during the millennial existence of the East Roman Empire. After the Turkish Conquest, the patriarch became the chief of the Sultan's Christian subjects, and his position was rather improved than otherwise, for the sovereign, though reserving power to ratify and confirm elections, was disposed to leave those elections in other respects free.

Formal confirmation of election had been exercised by the Christian Emperors, from whose hands the patriarchs received the δεκανίκιον, or jewelled crozier symbolic of governing authority. M. Gedeon refers to Codinus and Phranza for descriptions of the ceremonies of confirmation and investiture[1]. Phranza's account is especially interesting, as it is a record in detail of the manner in which the tradition of the Christian Emperors was perpetuated by the Mohammedan Sultans.

'On the third day after the storming of the city, the Emir held high festival of rejoicing over his victory, and made proclamation that all, both small and great, who had concealed themselves anywhere in the city should come forth, and live in freedom and quietness, also that such as had fled from the city in fear of the siege should return, every man to his own house, and abide, every man in his occupation and religion, even as it had been aforetime. Moreover, he commanded that they should make them a patriarch in accordance with established customs, for the patriarchate was vacant. Then the bishops who chanced to be in the city, and a very few clergy of other orders, and laymen, elected to be patriarch the most learned Georgios Scholarios, who was as yet a layman, and gave him the new name of Gennadios. It was an ancient established custom of the Christian Emperors to present the newly-elected patriarch with a δεκανίκιον (crozier) made of gold and adorned with precious stones and pearls, and a horse selected from the imperial stables, gorgeously harnessed with a saddle and saddle-cloth of royal splendour, white silk and gold being the material of the trappings. The patriarch

[1] Gedeon, Πατριαρχικοὶ Πίνακες, p. 27 f.

returned to his residence accompanied by the senate, and hailed with applauding shouts. Then he received consecration from the bishops in accordance with standing law and custom. Now the patriarch-designate used to receive the δεκανίκιον from the hands of the Emperor after the following manner. The Emperor sat on his throne, and the whole senate was present, standing with heads uncovered. The great prototype of the palace pronounced a blessing and then recited a short series of petitions (μικρὰν ἐκτενήν), after which the grand domestic sang the canticle "Where the presence of the king is, etc. etc." Then, from the opposite side of the choir, the lampadarios recited the "Gloria" and "King of heaven, etc." The canticle being ended, the Emperor rose to his feet, holding in his right hand the δεκανίκιον, while the patriarch-designate, coming forward with the metropolitan of Cæsarea on one side of him and the metropolitan of Heraclea on the other, bowed thrice to the assembly, and then, approaching the sovereign, did obeisance in the manner due to the imperial majesty. Then the Emperor, raising the δεκανίκιον a little, said, "The Holy Trinity, which hath bestowed upon me the Empire, promoteth thee to be patriarch of New Rome." Thus the patriarch was invested with authority by the hands of the Emperor, to whom he returned the assurance of his gratitude. Then the choirs sang "Master, long be thy days" thrice, and after that came the dismissal. The patriarch, coming down, with lights fixed in the imperial candelabra preceding him, found his horse standing ready, and mounted.

'The infidel, therefore, being desirous to maintain, as sovereign lord of the city, the tradition of the Christian princes, summoned the patriarch to sit at meat and confer with him. When the patriarch arrived, the tyrant received him with great honour. There was a long conference, in the course of which the Emir made no end of his promises to the patriarch. The hour for the patriarch's departure having come, the Emir, on giving him leave to retire, presented him with the costly δεκανίκιον, and prayed him to accept it. He escorted the patriarch down to the courtyard, despite his remonstrances, assisted him to mount a horse which he had caused to be made ready, and gave orders that all the grandees of the palace should go forth with the patriarch. Thus they accompanied him to the venerable Church of the Apostles, some going before and some following him. The Emir, you must know, had assigned the precincts of the Church of the Apostles for a residence[1].'

Phranza says that the honours, privileges, and exemptions conferred by Mohammed II. upon Gennadios were intended merely to serve as inducements to the Christians to settle in Constantinople, which had become a desolation. The history of the patriarchs, however, during the reign of Mohammed II., so far as it is known, shows that if the patriarchate fell into an evil plight, this was due not so much to Turkish bad faith as to the prevalence of 'emulations, wrath, strife, seditions, envyings' among the clergy and people. 'Fortunati nimium, sua si bona nossent' is the conclusion one comes to after considering, on the one hand, the ample privileges bestowed upon the patriarchate by the Turkish con-

---

[1] Georgii Phranza *Historia*, III. xi. Phranza, it should be noticed, calls Mohammed II. 'Emir,' not 'Sultan.' The title of 'Sultan' appears not to have been assumed by the Ottoman sovereigns till the sixteenth century.

queror, and on the other, the restless, unsettled state of the Church of Constantinople both under him and under his successors, down to the present day, a clear token whereof is the great number of patriarchal abdications, very few of which have been purely voluntary.

The depositions were not always effected by arbitrary intervention on the part of the secular power. More than once a patriarch was deposed by a synod of metropolitans, which also passed sentence of exile upon him. The execution of the sentence would, of course, be left to the secular authorities.

No doubt much of the disquiet and disorder in the Church of Constantinople during the seventeenth century was due to Jesuit intrigues. But the efforts of the Jesuits would have been comparatively harmless had they not been assisted by the factious spirit rampant among the Greeks. The worst enemies of the Church's peace were to be found among those who were of her own household. With regard to the Turkish Government, we may be permitted to doubt whether it stood in need of any encouragement to perpetrate acts of oppressive intervention, but one cannot be surprised that Sultans and Vizirs, finding themselves appealed to first by one and then by another Christian faction, should have laid hold of the opportunities gratuitously supplied them. If the Christians showed themselves ready to buy the support of the secular power, it was not incumbent upon the secular power, alien in race and religion, to refuse to do business[1].

---

[1] 'The oppression which the Greeks lie under from the Turks, though very bad and dismal in itself, becomes more uneasy and troublesome by their own horrid Quarrels and Differences about the choice of a Patriarch:

Phranza speaks of the bestowal of the patriarchal crozier (τὸ δεκανίκιον or δικανίκιον) as performed by Mohammed II. in imitation of his Christian predecessors. The ceremony of confirmation or investiture, as described by Phranza, appears not to have been retained in practice for very long. The escort of honour from the Porte to the patriarchal residence may have been continued, but the ceremony of the crozier appears in a document of the sixteenth century as an ecclesiastical and no longer a political one[1]. Moreover, it very soon became customary for the patriarchs to take presents to the Porte, instead of receiving them there. The first four patriarchs, says

there being often times several Pretenders among the Metropolitans and Bishops, and they too making an interest, by large summs of mony, in the Vizir, or the other Bassa's, to attain their ends. He who by his mony and his friends has prevailed...will endeavour to reimburse himself and lay the burden and debt, which he has contracted, upon the Church, which must pay for all: while the rest, who envy his preferment...unite their interest and strength to get him displaced, by remonstrating against his injustice and ill management of affairs, and put up fresh petitions to the Turks, and bribe lustily to be heard. The Turks, glad of such an opportunity of gain, readily enough admit their Complaint, and put out and put in, as they see occasion.......When I reflect upon these Revolutions and Changes, I am filled at the same time with amazement and pity, and cannot but put up this hearty prayer to Almighty God...that He would be pleased to inspire the Grecian Bishops with sober and peaceable counsels.' Smith, *An Account of the Greek Church*, pp. 80—83. Thomas Smith, B.D., Fellow of Magdalen College, Oxford, was chaplain to the English Embassy at Constantinople in the reign of Charles II. From the chapter in his book, out of which the above-quoted passages are taken, it appears that he left Constantinople to return to England in 1671 or 1672. He mentions the protection given by the Embassy to the deposed patriarch Methodius III. in 1671.

[1] Manuel Malaxos, *Historia Patriarchica*, p. 192 (Niebuhr. Bonn, 1839).

Manuel Malaxos[1], were elected without making any present to the Sultan, but after the appointment of Mark Xylocaravis, a junta of immigrants from Trebizond offered the Sultan a thousand florins to obtain his support of their opposition to the patriarch, whom they purposed to remove in favour of a fellow-countryman of theirs, one Symeon, a monk. According to Malaxos, 'the Sultan laughed, and then pondered a long while, considering the enviousness and stupidity of the Romans, and their ungodly ways.' Then he confirmed an assertion made by them to the effect that Mark had promised a thousand florins for the confirmation of his election, though the patriarch had neither promised nor given a copper. The Sultan, however, saw an opening to the establishment of such payments as a regular custom. He took the money offered by Mark's enemies and bade them go and elect as patriarch whomsoever they would. A charge of simony was then brought against Mark, who was put on his trial before a synod, condemned, deposed and anathematized. Symeon was then elected and consecrated, but before very long was deposed by order of the Sultan. Once again money had been talking. The Sultan's stepmother, who appears to have been a Christian, was desirous to promote a friend of hers, the metropolitan of Philippopolis, to honour, and at the same time put an end to the scandalous agitations of the Church caused by the strife between the factions of

---

[1] Malaxos, *op. cit.*, p. 102. τοῦτοι οἱ ἄνωθεν τέσσαροι πατριάρχαι, ὁ Σχολάριος, ὁ Ἰσίδορος, ὁ Ἰωάσαφ, καὶ ὁ Ξυλοκαράβης, ἔγιναν χωρὶς νὰ δώσουν τοῦ σουλτάνου κανένα δῶρον· μόνον ἔγιναν, καθὼς καὶ εἰς τὸν καιρὸν τῆς βασιλείας τῶν Ῥωμαίων, ὁποῦ ἐχάριζεν ὁ βασιλεὺς τοῦ πατριάρχου χαρίσματα. Malaxos is one of the chief authorities for the history of the patriarchate in the period A.D 1450—1580.

Symeon and Mark. She therefore brought the Sultan two thousand florins in a silver dish and told him that there was a monk who was her friend, and that she wanted to have him made patriarch. The result of the proposal was an imperial order for the deposition of Symeon, who retired to a monastery. Mark was voted by the synod assembled in the capital, to which he had appealed for revision of his sentence, to the archbishopric of Achrida. Dionysius, the protégé of the Sultan's stepmother, occupied the throne for eight years, and then, in disgust at a false charge of apostasy, though he clearly refuted it, abdicated and retired to a monastery near Cavalla in Macedonia. The synod, in whose presence he had refuted the charge of apostasy, recalled Symeon. It was necessary, however, to make sure of the Sultan's approval, and to this end a deputation presented itself at the Sublime Porte, bringing a thousand florins, and so carrying out in act the charge laid in word against Mark Xylocaravis. But the Defterdar rejected their petition and the proffered douceur. There was an entry in the imperial accounts, he said, showing that the proper amount of the fee was two thousand florins. This, of course, referred to the transaction between the Sultan and his stepmother. Of this matter the members of the synod possibly had no knowledge at the time, but whether they had or not made no difference. There was nothing for it but to sponge up another thousand florins, 'which being done, says Malaxos, 'the Defterdar ceased from troubling[1].'

Thus an evil precedent was set, and henceforth every patriarch was expected to pay a fee for the imperial

[1] Malaxos, p. 112. καὶ ἔτξη εἰρήνευσεν ὁ τευτερτέρης.

confirmation of his election. To this burden another was added by the reckless ambition of a Servian monk, Raphael by name, who procured the final dethronement of Symeon by the conversion of the investiture fee of 2000 florins into an annual ' kharaj' or tribute, the amount of the investiture-fee being now fixed at 500 florins[1]. It was not to be expected, however, that these amounts should never be exceeded. By the time of Jeremias II.'s first election to the patriarchate, viz. A.D. 1572, the investiture fee (πεσκέσιον as Malaxos calls it) was 2000 florins, while the annual ' kharaj' had risen to 4100. In A.D. 1672, as we learn from Paul Ricaut, the English Consul at Smyrna, the debts of the patriarchate amounted to 350,000 piastres, equal to more than £40,000 at the present day; 'the interest of which increasing daily, and rigorously extorted by the Power of the most covetous and considerable Turkish officers, who lend or supply the Money, is the reason and occasion that the Patriarch so often summons all his Archbishops and Bishops to appear at Constantinople, that so they may

[1] Malaxos, l. c. "Εκαμε δὲ ὁ αὐτὸς πατριάρχης [δηλ. ὁ Συμεών] εἰς τὸν θρόνον χρόνους τρεῖς, καὶ ἐπέρνα εἰρηνικῶς...ἀμὴ φθονήσας τοῦτο ὁ τῶν σκανδάλων ἀρχηγὸς καὶ ἐχθρὸς ἡμῶν τῶν Χριστιανῶν, ὁ διάβολος, καὶ ἐφάνη εἰς τὴν μέσιν ἕνας ἱερομόναχος, ὀνόματι 'Ραφαήλ, τοῦ ὁποίου ἦτον ἡ πατρίδα του ἀπὸ τὴν Σερβίαν, καὶ εἶχε μεγάλην φιλίαν καὶ παρρησίαν εἰς τὴν πόρτα τοῦ σουλτάνου, ἔσοντας ὁποῦ ἀγάπουν αὐτὸν οἱ πασιάδες. καὶ...ὑπῆγε καὶ ἐπροσκύνησιν αὐτούς, καὶ...ἐσυμφώνησε καὶ ἔστερξεν ὅτι νὰ δίδει τὸν καθὲν χρόνον εἰς τὴν πόρτα τοῦ σουλτάνου χαράτζιον φλωρία χιλιάδας δύο. καὶ τὸ πεσκέσιον ἔκαμαν νὰ δίδεται ὁπόταν γίνεται νέος πατριάρχης. ἀκούσαντες δὲ τοῦτο οἱ πασιάδες ἐδέχθησαν τὸν 'Ραφαὴλ τὸν φίλον αὐτῶν ἀσπασίως, καὶ ἀναφορὰν ἤγουν ἄρτζη περὶ τούτου τῷ σουλτάνῳ ἔκαμαν. καὶ ἀκούσας τοῦτο ἐχάρη πολλά, καὶ ἐν τῷ ἅμα ἔδωκεν ὁρισμόν, καὶ εὔγαλαν τὸν αὐτὸν κύριν Συμεὼν ἀπὸ τοῦ πατριαρχικοῦ θρόνου. See also the *Historia Patriarchia*, pp. 156, 157, 170, 176, 177, and 193; *Historia Politica*, p. 43, in the same volume of the *Corpus Scriptorum Historiæ Byzantinæ*, Bonn, 1849.

consult and agree on an expedient to ease in some measure the present Burden and Pressure of their Debts; the payment of which is often the occasion of new Demands: For the Turks, finding this Fountain the fresher, and more plentifully flowing for being drained, continually suck from this Stream, which is to them more sweet, for being the Blood of the Poor, and the life of Christians[1].' It was, after all, not so much on the dignitaries and authorities of the Orthodox Church, as upon the parish priests and the poor among the people generally, that the fiscal burdens pressed most heavily. The most helpless had to suffer most. What help, indeed, could they expect when their chief shepherds became robbers?

With ironical respect the Orthodox laity, under the Turkish *régime*, spoke of their bishops as ' δεσποτάδες '— despots. The powers enjoyed by the episcopal order, whose members were made use of by the temporal power as agents of police, were so considerable as to make even an ordinary bishopric an appointment to be coveted—still more a metropolitan see, and most of all the patriarchate[2]. Even apart from the financial opportunities, in the use of which a patriarch or metropolitan could rely on secular assistance, the dignity and honour of 'chief seats in the synagogue' must always have had

[1] Ricaut, *op. cit.* 97—99.

[2] 'The patriarch and the bishops purchased their dignities, and repaid themselves by selling ecclesiastical rank and privileges; the priests purchased holy orders, and sold licenses to marry. The laity paid for marriages, divorces, baptisms, pardons, and dispensations of many kinds to their bishops. The extent to which patriarchs and bishops interfered in family disputes and questions of property is proved by contemporary documents.'— Finlay, *History of Greece*, v. p. 156, cf. p. 150.

considerable attraction for the Greeks, who, even after the Turkish Conquest, esteemed themselves the first of nations[1]. Add to these conditions and circumstances the spirit of jealousy which has been, and still is, the bane of the race—the spirit which gives a Greek army so many generals and so few soldiers[2]—and it is not hard to understand why changes in the occupancy of the patriarchate of Constantinople have been so numerous and frequent[3].

Finlay compares the part played by the Sultans in patriarchal elections with that of the sovereigns of England in appointments to the archbishopric of Canterbury. This comparison, however, is not quite accurate. As a rule, the Sultans have not nominated the successive occupants of the patriarchal throne. Under the Ottoman sovereigns, elections have, if anything, been more free than under their Christian predecessors. But the Padishah must have a list of 'papabili' sent to him, whenever a vacancy occurs in the patriarchate, and he influences the election by notifying to the synod of the 'Great Church' the names of those whom he does *not* wish to see elected. In any case, it is in his power to nullify an election by refusing the necessary 'berat' to the patriarch-designate. The delivery of this document is the formality by which the Sultan confirms the election, invests the person elected with the temporalities of the patriarchal see, and licenses

---

[1] Finlay, *op. cit.*, v. p. 122.

[2] Ἀμείβετο Γέλων τοῖσδε· 'Ξεῖνε Ἀθηναῖε, ὑμεῖς οἴκατε τοὺς μὲν ἄρχοντας ἔχειν, τοὺς δὲ ἀρξομένους οὐκ ἔξειν.' Hdt. VII. 162. The Athenians, however, showed a better spirit at Platæa—see Hdt. IX. 27 *ad fin.*

[3] Finlay finds that 'mutual distrust was a feature in the character of the higher clergy at Constantinople,' *op. cit.* v. 149.

him to exercise his spiritual authority. Above and beyond all this, the autocratic nature of the Sultan's sovereignty enables him to force a resignation or synodical dethronement whenever he thinks fit. Under an absolute despotism like the Sultanate, the ultimate ground of the patriarch's tenure of office must necessarily be the sovereign's pleasure.

The principle was clearly laid down by the Council of Antioch in the fourth century that in every province the metropolitan and his comprovincials must work in concert and by mutual counsel. In the same way, it is a recognized principle of Church government in Orthodoxy that the patriarch should work in concert with his metropolitans. The records of the patriarchate contain evidence enough and to spare that this principle has been, under the Turkish *régime* at any rate, constantly observed. In the latter part of the nineteenth century its observation was brought under the rule that there should always be twelve metropolitans present in the capital to form the 'perpetual' or 'standing administrative council[1].' These twelve metropolitans are

---

[1] A similar arrangement appears to have been in existence in the seventeenth century. 'The patriarch, in the determination of causes brought before him, has the assistance of twelve of the chief Officers belonging to the Patriarchal Church and dignity. These also assist the Archbishop of Heraclea in vesting and crowning him at his Inauguration, and still retain the same high titles as they did before the Turks came among them. These are as it were his standing Council, to whom he refers the great affairs and concerns of religion.' Thomas Smith, *Greek Church*, p. 78. The officials of the patriarchate, however, would be priests, not bishops. A long list of them is given in the 'Euchologion,' pp. 686 f. (Venice, 1891), together with a description of their several functions. More than one of these titles, by its very form, shows that the patriarchate must have paid the imperial court the sincere compliment

not always the same, for six retire every year, having held office as members of the synod or council for two years, and their places are taken by six others. Each of the metropolitans subordinate to the œcumenical throne takes his place on the synod in his turn, according to seniority. It is not, therefore, the patriarch alone, but rather the patriarch in synod, by whom the chief authority in matters ecclesiastical is exercised in the provinces of the Constantinopolitan Church.

This perpetual administrative synod of the patriarchate must be distinguished from the synod which elects the patriarch[1]. The latter consists of lay representatives

of imitation. There can be no doubt as to the origin of such titles as πρωτονοτάριος, καστρήνσιος, ρεφενδάριος, λογοθέτης, δομέστικος, δεπουτάτος, κουβούκλης.

[1] M. Gedeon, in the preface to his Πατριαρχικοὶ Πίνακες, gives an outline of the history of procedure in elections to the patriarchal throne. Nestorius I., successor of Gregory Nazianzen (A.D. 381), and Proclus (A.D. 434), were examples in an early period of succession by virtue of the Emperor's nomination. Chrysostom's election is described by Socrates, *H. E.* VI. 2. Ψηφίσματι κοινῷ ὁμοῦ πάντων, κλήρου τε φημὶ καὶ λαοῦ, ὁ βασιλεὺς αὐτὸν ᾿Αρκάδιος μεταπέμπεται. διὰ δὲ τὸ ἀξιόπιστον τῆς χειροτονίας παρῆσαν ἐκ βασιλικοῦ προστάγματος πολλοί τε καὶ ἄλλοι ἐπίσκοποι, καὶ δὴ καὶ ὁ τῆς ᾿Αλεξανδρείας Θεόφιλος, ὅστις σπουδὴν ἐτίθετο διασῦραι μὲν τὴν ᾿Ιωάννου δόξαν, ᾿Ισίδωρον δὲ ὑπ᾿ αὐτῷ πρεσβύτερον πρὸς τὴν ἐπισκοπὴν προχειρίσασθαι...οἱ μέντοι κατὰ τὰ βασίλεια τὸν ᾿Ιωάννην προέκριναν. ᾿Επειδὴ δὲ κατηγορίας κατὰ Θεοφίλου πολλοὶ ἀνεκίνουν...ὁ προεστὼς τοῦ βασιλικοῦ κοιτῶνος Εὐτρόπιος λαβὼν τὰς ἐγγράφους κατηγορίας ἐπέδειξε τῷ Θεοφίλῳ, εἰπὼν ἐπιλογὴν ἔχειν ἢ χειροτονεῖν ᾿Ιωάννην ἢ τὰς κατ᾿ αὐτοῦ κατηγορίας εἰς ἔλεγχον ἄγεσθαι. Ταῦτα φοβηθεὶς ὁ Θεόφιλος τὸν ᾿Ιωάννην ἐχειροτόνησε. Chrysostom was accordingly consecrated on the 23rd of February, A.D. 398. Germanus was translated from Cyzicus in A.D. 715 ψήφῳ καὶ δοκιμασίᾳ τῶν θεοσεβεστάτων πρεσβυτέρων καὶ διακόνων καὶ παντὸς τοῦ εὐαγοῦς κλήρου καὶ τῆς ἱερᾶς συγκλήτου (Gedeon, p. 16, referring to Scarlati Vizandio, *Constantinopolis*). Leo the Iconoclast seems to have accepted this election without any difficulty, though he found a

as well as of clergy, thus maintaining the old tradition of election by the clergy and people of Constantinople— a tradition which has probably been better observed since the Turkish Conquest than it was previously. In theory, the designation of the patriarch by the votes of vigorous opponent in Germanus, who, however, resigned in A.D. 730. Anastasius (730—754), Constantine II. (754—766) and Nicetas (766—780), all of them εἰκονομάχοι, were court-nominees. Nicephorus I. (A.D. 806— 815), according to Theophanes was elected ψήφῳ παντὸς τοῦ λαοῦ καὶ τῶν ἱερέων, πρὸς δὲ καὶ βασιλέων. The imperial will determined the alternations in Photius' patriarchal career (857—867 and 878—886). M. Gedeon says that κατὰ Φεβρουάριον τοῦ 1059 ὁ αὐτοκράτωρ Ἰσάακιος ὁ Κομνηνός, ψήφῳ τῶν ἀρχιερέων καὶ τοῦ λαοῦ, ἀνέδειξεν οἰκουμενικὸν πατριάρχην τὸν εὐνοῦχον καὶ μοναχὸν Κωνσταντῖνον Λευχούδην, ἄλλοτε πρωτοβεστιάριον καὶ πρόεδρον τῆς συγκλήτου. In November, 1058, Isaac Comnenus had deposed the famous Michael Cerularius. John VIII. (Xiphilinos) was 'called by the Emperor Constantine Ducas to succeed Constantine III.' in 1064, καὶ πάντες ἐπευφήμισαν εἰς τὴν ψῆφον. Germanus II. (1222—1240) is described as προβληθεὶς πατριάρχης ὑπὸ τοῦ αὐτοκράτορος Ἰωάννου Δούκα τοῦ Βατάτζη. On the death of Callistus II. in 1397, Matthew I. ψήφῳ τῆς συνόδου καὶ προβλήσει τοῦ αὐτοκράτορος ἐκλέγεται διάδοχος. See Gedeon, Πατρ. Πιν., pp. 14—16, 255, 259, 262, 263, 268, 282, 290, 322, 327, 328—9, 384, 458. In the *Historia Patriarchica*, pp. 104—107, and the *Historia Politica*, pp. 39—41, we have instances of the Turkish sovereign putting down one and setting up another patriarch, using the bishops and clergy as his instruments. Theoleptos, about A.D. 1514, got himself forced upon the patriarchate by an imperial berat. In 1741, Sultan Mahmud I. issued a firman regulating procedure in patriarchal elections. One requirement was, that testimony to the character of the person elected should be given by the metropolitans of Heraclea, Cyzicus, Nicomedia, Nicæa, and Chalcedon (the 'γέροντες' as they came to be commonly called), otherwise the election would be treated as invalid. M. Gedeon refers in this connection to Sozomen, *Hist. Eccl.* III. 3, where it is recorded that the Arians objected to the appointment of Paul the Confessor (circ. A.D. 340) on the ground that it had taken place παρὰ γνώμην Εὐσεβίου τοῦ Νικομηδείας ἐπισκόπου καὶ Θεοδώρου τοῦ τῆς ἐν Θράκῃ Ἡρακλείας, οἷς ὡς γείτοσιν ἡ χειροτονία διέφερε. —Another imperial firman, issued by Mustapha II. in 1759, required the announcement of elections by means of a sealed report from the electors.— This method of announcing elections is still followed. The firman also an assembly representing the whole Christian population of Constantinople, Roumelia and Asia Minor is admirable[1]. In practice, it has been execrable, simply because of the unlimited licence given to ambition and covetousness. Yet even without the disturbing influence of Mohammedan sovereignty these corrupt passions make themselves felt with destructive effect, as witness the events of the last few years in Cyprus, where party strife has kept the archiepiscopal throne vacant from the summer of 1900 to 1909.

Monastics alone are eligible to the episcopate in the Orthodox Church, and the patriarchal residence in Constantinople may be regarded as a monastery, of which the patriarch is the abbot. Since the beginning of the seventeenth century the Church of St George, in the Fanar quarter on the Golden Horn, has been the patriarch's cathedral. This Church occupies the site of the monastery known as the Petrion or Paulopetrion, which was in existence in the reign of Irene in the

required that every patriarch should pay the expenses of his election, which in the eighteenth century were known to run up on occasion to as much as 50,000 piastres (£6,000). Until 1860 ex-metropolitans and ex-bishops, as well as metropolitans and bishops ἐν ἐνεργείᾳ, used to take part in elections, but since that date the representatives of the episcopal order are all metropolitans. There are now four stages in the process of election; (1) voting by a 'convention' of the metropolitans residing in the capital for the time being, of lay representatives, and plenipotentiaries representing twenty-six of the metropolitical sees; (2) submission of the list of 'papabili' to the Porte; (3) election of *three* from the list as emended by the secular authorities; (4) election of the successor from these three, by the metropolitans present.

[1] The lay electors especially represent Constantinople. The metropolitans who take part, either on the spot, or by sending sealed votes, represent the provinces. M. Gedeon observes that the electors must be native subjects of the Sultan.

eighth century, and was for many years the retreat of the Empress Theodora in the eleventh. It is not a large building, and externally has no beauty to recommend it. Within, the chief and almost the only adornments of any merit are the iconostasion and the pulpit, works of art which Mr Hutton, one of the most recent historians of Constantinople, assigns to the seventeenth century[1]. Most of the buildings of the 'patriarcheion' stand to the west of the church, on ground which rises somewhat steeply—a circumstance which enables the group to make somewhat more of a display than might otherwise have been the case. There is no magnificence, however, about the residence of the most notable ecclesiastic in all Orthodox Christendom—nothing to parallel St Peter's and the Vatican. The difference between the housing of the chief pastors of the Old and the New Rome, the 'servus servorum Dei' and the ' οἰκουμενικὸς πατριάρχης,' is fairly measured by the apparent difference in character between their titles.

Originally, the patriarchal residence was in the neighbourhood of Santa Sophia. After the conquest of the city, Mohammed II. assigned the Church of the Holy Apostles, the burial place of Theodora the wife of Justinian, to Gennadios, but the patriarch, finding the neighbourhood but scantily inhabited by Christians, obtained leave to move his residence to the Church of the Pammakaristos (a special title of the Virgin Mary), which was the cathedral church of the patriarchate for 130 years, viz. A.D. 1456—1586. The Church of the

---

[1] *Constantinople* in the series of 'Mediæval Towns' (London: J. M. Dent); by the Rev. W. H. Hutton, B.D.

Apostles was demolished to make room for the mosque which by its name preserves the memory of Mohammed the Conqueror of Constantinople. In 1586 the Sultan took possession of the Pammakaristos Church and turned it into a mosque. The patriarchal cathedra was then placed for a short time in the church of the 'Panagia of Consolation' or 'Healing' (Παναγία τῆς Παραμυθίας or Θεραπείας), after which it was removed to the Church of St Demetrius in Xyloporta, and thence, in 1601, to its present place[1]. A few icons, books and relics were brought away from the Pammakaristos, and finally deposited in the Church of St George. 'That which they most esteem,' wrote Thomas Smith, chaplain to the Embassy, about 1670, 'is a piece of black Marble; as they pretend, part of that Pillar which formerly stood in the *Prætorium* or Hall of *Pontius Pilate*, to which our Blessed Saviour was tied, when he was whipped; about two foot long, and three or four inches over,... inclosed in brass lattice Grates, that it may not receive prejudice either from devout or sacrilegious persons. For they have a strong imagination, that the dust raised from it, and put into wine, or any way conveyed into the stomach, cures Agues and Fevers almost infallibly. In a brass plate under it I found these six Verses engraven, alluding to the tradition I just now mentioned, which they believe as undoubtedly as if it were Gospell.

> Νῶτον δέδωκας εἰς μάστιγας, Παντάρχα,
> Καὶ πρόσωπον εἰς ῥαπισμάτων ὕβριν.
> Σὴν μαστίγωσιν προσφέρω σοι, οἰκτίρμον,

---

[1] Hutton, *Constantinople*, p. 155. K. N. Satha, Σχεδίασμα περὶ Ἰερεμίου τοῦ Β', σελ. οθ'—πβ'.

Ἵν᾿ ἵλεώς μοι εἴη λατρεύοντί σοι,
Καὶ μάστιγάς σου ἐξ ἐμοῦ ἀποστήσῃς.
Παναγιώτης Νικόσιος εὔχεται.—[1]

In this Church of St George the patriarchs of Constantinople have been formally enthroned for the last three centuries. As the patriarchs are now, and have been for a long time past, taken from the metropolitan episcopate, there is no need of χειροτονία or consecration properly so called. In case of one not already consecrated to the episcopate being elected patriarch, the chief consecrator would be the metropolitan of Heraclea (Erekli on the Sea of Marmora), the origin of whose prerogative lies in the fact that Byzantium, at the time when selected by Constantine to be made the new imperial capital, was included in the district of which Heraclea was the chief town[2]. Even when there is no need of χειροτονία, it is the peculiar function of the metropolitan of Heraclea to place in the hands of the patriarch-designate the δεκανίκιον, δικανίκιον or πατερίτσα, as the patriarchal crozier, a staff terminating in two serpents' heads, is variously termed. This symbol of archipœmenical authority is not indeed the peculiar badge of the patriarch's dignity. Serpent-headed croziers

---

[1] Thomas Smith, *Greek Church*, pp. 60—61.

[2] Gedeon, p. 49. On p. 282, however, in a note, M. Gedeon points out that there have been occasions when the consecration has been performed by another prelate. Photius, for instance, had Gregory of Syracuse for his chief consecrator. Photius was a layman at the time of his election, as were also Nectarius (A.D. 381), Paul III. (A.D. 686), Tarasius (A.D. 784), Nicephorus I. (A.D. 806), Sisinnius II. (A.D. 995) and perhaps John XIII. (A.D. 1315). It was not until after the death of Mohammed II. in 1481 that the practice of translation from a metropolitan see became regularly established. In the course of eleven centuries, under the Christian Emperors, there were not so many as twenty instances of translation.

are carried by the Orthodox episcopate generally, with one notable exception, viz. the Archbishop of Cyprus, whose pastoral staff terminates in a globe. The serpents' heads on the pateritsa remind one of the caduceus of Mercury, and the possibility of a connection between the pateritsa and the caduceus is strongly suggested by the fable preserved in the *Astronomia* of Hyginus. According to this story, Mercury once found two snakes fighting, and separated them with his wand. Thenceforth his wand or staff, encircled or twined about by two snakes, became an emblem of peace[1]. This fable is no doubt only a piece of 'ætiology' designed to account for the fact that the snake-entwined staff was a peaceful emblem. Christian bishops, claiming to stand in the apostolical succession, would have the right to style themselves ambassadors of Christ and messengers of peace[2], and their custom of carrying a serpent-headed staff may have originated from some pictorial representation of Christ, or the Apostles, carrying the caduceus as the emblem of reconciliation between God and mankind.

H. T. F. DUCKWORTH.

---

[1] *Dict. of Greek and Roman Antiquities* (Smith's, second edition), art. Caduceus.

[2] II. Cor. v. 20. ὑπὲρ Χριστοῦ οὖν πρεσβεύομεν, ὡς τοῦ Θεοῦ παρακαλοῦντος δι' ἡμῶν· δεόμεθα ὑπὲρ Χριστοῦ, καταλλάγητε τῷ Θεῷ.

THE PATRIARCHS OF CONSTANTINOPLE

In the first column is given the name of the Patriarch: in the second the date of his Patriarchate: the third shows the page on which his life is narrated in M. I. Gedeon's Πατριαρχικοὶ Πίνακες, royal 8vo, Constantinople, 1890, and the fourth how his official life closed.

Acacios	471—489	198	
Agathangelos	1826—1830	688	deposed
Alexandros	325—340	108	
Alexios	1025—1043	317	
Alypios	166—169	94	
Anastasios	730—754	259	
Anatolios	449—458	188	
Andreas, ap.		82	
Anthimos I	536	223	deposed
Anthimos II	1623	552	resigned
Anthimos III	1822—1824	686	deposed
Anthimos IV	1840, 41	694	deposed
Anthimos IV²	1848—1852	698	deposed
Anthimos V	1841, 42	694	
Anthimos VI	1845—1848	697	deposed
Anthimos VI²	1853—1855	699	
Anthimos VI³	1871—1873	705	resigned
Antonios I	821—832	273	
Antonios II	893—895	294	
Antonios III	974—980	310	resigned
Antonios IV	1389, 90	448	deposed
Antonios IV²	1391—1397	449	
Arsacios	404, 05	161	
Arsenios	1255—1260	389	resigned
Arsenios²	1261—1267	392	deposed
Athanasios I	1289—1293	402	resigned
Athanasios I²	1303—1311	405	resigned
Athanasios II	1450	467	resigned
Athanasios III	1634	559	deposed
Athanasios III²	1652	580	resigned
Athanasios IV	1679	602	deposed
Athanasios V	1709—1711	619	deposed
Athenodoros	144—148	92	
Atticos	406—425	164	

C.

Basileios I	970—974	309	deposed
Basileios II	1183—1187	371	deposed
Callinicos I	693—705	253	blinded
Callinicos II	1688	607	deposed
Callinicos II²	1689—1693	609	deposed
Callinicos II³	1694—1702	611	
Callinicos III	1726	627	
Callinicos IV	1757	648	deposed
Callinicos V	1801—1806	679	deposed
Callinicos V²	1808, 09	681	
Callistos I	1350—1354	426	deposed
Callistos I²	1355—1363	429	
Callistos II	1397	456	
Castinos	230—237	97	
Chariton	1177, 78	369	
Chrysanthos	1824—1826	687	deposed
Clemes	1667	592	deposed
Constantinos I	674—676	248	
Constantinos II	754—766	262	blinded and beheaded
Constantinos III	1059—1063	327	
Constantinos IV	1154—1156	359	
Constantios I	1830—1834	689	resigned
Constantios II	1834, 35	692	deposed
Cosmas I	1075—1081	333	resigned
Cosmas II	1146, 47	353	deposed
Cosmas III	1714—1716	621	resigned
Cyprianos I	1708, 09	617	resigned
Cyprianos I²	1713, 14	621	resigned
Cyriacos I	214—230	96	
Cyriacos II	595—606	236	
Cyrillos I	1612	547	resigned
Cyrillos I²	1621—1623	550	deposed
Cyrillos I³	1623—1630	553	deposed
Cyrillos I⁴	1630—1634	556	deposed
Cyrillos I⁵	1634, 35	560	deposed
Cyrillos I⁶	1637, 38	562	drowned
Cyrillos II	1632	558	deposed
Cyrillos II²	1635, 36	560	deposed
Cyrillos II³	1638, 39	567	deposed
Cyrillos III	1652	579	deposed
Cyrillos III²	1654	582	deposed
Cyrillos IV	1711—1713	620	deposed
Cyrillos V	1748—1751	641	deposed
Cyrillos V²	1752—1757	644	deposed
Cyrillos VI	1813—1818	683	resigned and killed
Cyrillos VII	1855—1860	699	deposed
Cyros	705—711	254	deposed

Demophilos	369—379	126	deposed
Diogenes	114—129	91	
Dionysios I	1467—1472	482	deposed
Dionysios II	1537	504	deposed
Dionysios II[2]	1543—1555	507	
Dionysios III	1662—1665	588	deposed
Dionysios IV	1671—1673	595	deposed
Dionysios IV[2]	1676—1679	599	deposed
Dionysios IV[3]	1683, 84	604	deposed
Dionysios IV[4]	1686, 87	605	deposed
Dionysios IV[5]	1693	610	deposed
Dometios	272—303	98	
Dositheos	1191, 92	375	deposed
Eleutherios	129—136	91	
Epiphanios	520—536	220	
Esaias	1323—1334	417	
Euagrios	369, 70	127	deposed
Eudoxios	360—369	122	
Eugenios I	237—242	97	
Eugenios II	1821, 22	686	
Euphemios	490—496	206	deposed
Eusebios	341, 342	114	Arian
Eustathios	1019—1025	317	
Eustratios	1081—1084	335	deposed
Euthymios I	906—911	296	deposed
Euthymios II	1410—1416	463	
Eutychios	552—565	227	deposed
Eutychios[2]	577—582	231	
Euzoios	148—154	93	
Felix	136—141	91	
Flavianos	447—449	185	killed
Gabriel I	1596	537	
Gabriel II	1657	586	deposed
Gabriel III	1702—1707	614	
Gabriel IV	1780—1785	666	
Gennadios I	458—471	194	
Gennadios II	1454—1456	471	resigned
Georgios I	678—683	250	deposed
Georgios II	1192—1199	376	
Gerasimos I	1320, 21	417	
Gerasimos II	1673—1675	597	deposed
Gerasimos III	1794—1797	673	resigned
Germanos I	715—730	255	resigned
Germanos II	1222—1240	383	
Germanos III	1267	393	deposed
Germanos IV	1842—1845	695	deposed
Germanos IV[2]	1852, 53	699	

Gregorios I (Theologos)	379—381	128	resigned
Gregorios II (Cyprius)	1283—1289	398	resigned
Gregorios III	1443—1450	466	deposed
Gregorios IV	1623	552	deposed
Gregorios V	1797, 98	675	deposed
Gregorios V²	1806—1808	680	deposed
Gregorios V³	1818—1821	684	hanged
Gregorios VI	1835—1840	692	deposed
Gregorios VI²	1867—1871	703	resigned
Hieremias I	1520—1522	500	deposed
Hieremias I²	1523—1527	502	deposed
Hieremias I³	1537—1545	505	
Hieremias II	1572—1579	518	deposed
Hieremias II²	1580—1584	524	deposed
Hieremias II³	1586—1595	531	
Hieremias III	1716—1726	622	deposed
Hieremias III²	1733	631	deposed
Hieremias IV	1809—1813	682	resigned
Ignatios	846—857	278	deposed
Ignatios²	867—878	287	
Isaac	1630	555	deposed
Isidoros I	1347—1350	422	resigned
Isidoros II	1456—1463	479	
Iacobos¹	1679—1683	603	deposed
Iacobos²	1685, 86	605	deposed
Iacobos³	1687, 88	606	resigned
Ioakim I	1498—1502	493	deposed
Ioakim I²	1504, 05	497	
Ioakim II	1860—1863	701	resigned
Ioakim II²	1873—1878	706	
Ioakim III	1878—1884	706	resigned
Ioannes I (Chrysostom)	398—404	141	deposed
Ioannes II	518—520	219	
Ioannes III	566—597	230	
Ioannes IV	582—595	232	
Ioannes V	668—674	247	
Ioannes VI	711—715	254	
Ioannes VII	832—842	274	deposed
Ioannes VIII	1064—1075	328	
Ioannes IX	1111—1134	348	
Ioannes X	1199—1206	377	resigned
Ioannes XI	1275—1282	394	deposed
Ioannes XII	1294—1303	404	resigned
Ioannes XIII	1315	415	resigned

Ioannes XIV	1334—1347	420	deposed
Ioannikios I	1522, 23	502	deposed
Ioannikios II	1646—1648	574	deposed
Ioannikios II^2	1651, 52	575	resigned
Ioannikios II^3	1653, 54	582	deposed
Ioannikios II^4	1655, 56	584	deposed
Ioannikios III	1761—1763	654	deposed
Ioasaph I	1464—1466	481	deposed
Ioasaph II	1555—1565	510	deposed
Ioseph I	1268—1275	393	deposed
Ioseph II	1416—1439	464	
Laurentios	154—166	93	
Leon	1134—1143	350	
Leontios	1190, 91	374	deposed
Lucas	1156—1169	360	
Macarios	1376—1379	439	deposed
Macarios^2	1390, 91	448	deposed
Macedonios I	342—348	118	
Macedonios I^2	350—360	121	
Macedonios II	496—511	209	deposed
Manuel I	1215—1222	383	
Manuel II	1244—1255	388	
Marcos I	198—211	95	
Marcos II	1466, 67	481	deposed
Malthaios I	1397—1410	457	
Malthaios II	1595	536	resigned
Malthaios II^2	1599—1602	541	resigned
Maximianos	431—434	179	
Maximos I	381	131	deposed
Maximos II	1215	382	
Maximos III	1476—1482	485	
Maximos IV	1491—1497	491	deposed
Meletios I	1597—1599	540	locum tenens
Meletios II	1768, 69	661	deposed
Meletios III	1845	696	
Menas	536—552	224	
Methodios I	842—846	277	
Methodios II	1240	387	
Methodios III	1668—1671	592	resigned
Metrophanes I	315—325	104	
Metrophanes II	1440—1443	465	deposed
Metrophanes III	1565—1572	515	deposed
Metrophanes III^2	1579, 80	523	
Michael I	1043—1058	322	
Michael II	1143—1146	351	resigned
Michael III	1169—1177	365	
Michael IV	1206—1212	379	

Nectarios	381—397	133	
Neilos	1380—1388	440	
Neophytos I	1153	358	deposed
Neophytos II	1602, 03	542	deposed
Neophytos II²	1607—1612	545	deposed
Neophytos III	1636, 37	561	resigned
Neophytos IV	1688, 89	608	deposed
Neophytos V	1707	617	deposed
Neophytos VI	1734—1740	634	deposed
Neophytos VI²	1743, 44	638	deposed
Neophytos VII	1789—1794	671	deposed
Neophytos VII²	1798—1801	677	deposed
Nephon I	1311—1314	411	resigned
Nephon II	1486—1489	488	deposed
Nephon II²	1497, 98	492	deposed
Nephon II³	1502	495	resigned
Nestorios	428—431	174	deposed
Nicephoros I	806—815	267	deposed
Nicephoros II	1260, 61	391	
Nicetas I	766—780	263	
Nicetas II	1187—1190	373	deposed
Nicolaos I	895—906	295	deposed
Nicolaos I²	911—925	298	
Nicolaos II	984—995	313	
Nicolaos III	1084—1111	338	
Nicolaos IV	1147—1151	354	resigned
Olympianos	187—198	95	
Onesimos	54—68	89	
Pachomios I	1503, 04	496	deposed
Pachomios I²	1505—1514	498	poisoned
Pachomios II	1584, 85	526	
Paisios I	1652, 53	581	resigned
Paisios I²	1654, 55	583	resigned
Paisios II	1726—1733	628	deposed
Paisios II²	1740—1743	635	deposed
Paisios II³	1744—1748	639	resigned
Paisios II⁴	1751, 54	644	deposed
Parthenios I	1639—1644	569	
Parthenios II	1644, 45	572	deposed
Parthenios II²	1648—1651	576	poisoned
Parthenios III	1656, 57	585	
Parthenios IV	1657—1662	587	resigned
Parthenios IV²	1665—1667	591	
Parthenios IV³	1671	594	deposed
Parthenios IV⁴	1675, 76	598	deposed
Parthenios IV⁵	1684, 85	604	deposed
Paulos I	340, 41	111	deposed

Paulos I²	342—344	117	deposed
Paulos I³	348—350	119	strangled
Paulos II	641—652	243	
Paulos III	686—693	252	
Paulos IV	780—784	265	resigned
Pertinax	169—187	94	
Petros	652—664	245	
Philadelphos	211—214	96	
Philotheos	1354, 55	428	resigned
Philotheos²	1364—1376	431	
Photios	857—867	282	deposed
Photios²	878—886	290	deposed
Phravitas	489, 90	204	
Plutarchos	89—105	90	
Polycarpos I	71—89	90	
Polycarpos II	141—144	92	
Polyeuctos	956—970	307	
Probos	303—315	100	
Proclos	434—447	181	
Procopios	1785—1789	669	deposed
Pyrrhos	638—641	242	deposed
Pyrrhos²	651, 52	245	
Raphael I	1475, 76	484	deposed
Raphael II	1603—1607	543	deposed
Ruphinos	283, 84	98	
Samuel	1763—1768	657	deposed
Samuel²	1773, 74	663	deposed
Sedekion	105—114	91	
Seraphim I	1733, 34	632	deposed
Seraphim II	1757—1761	649	deposed
Sergios I	610—638	238	
Sergios II	999—1019	315	
Sisinios I	425—427	172	
Sisinios II	995—998	313	
Sophronios I	1463, 64	480	deposed
Sophronios II	1774—1780	664	
Sophronios III	1863—1866	702	deposed
Stachys	38—54	89	Rom. xvi. 9
Stephanos I	886—893	293	
Stephanos II	925—928	300	
Symeon	1472—1475	483	resigned
Symeon²	1482—1486	487	deposed
Tarasios	784—806	265	
Theodoros I	676—678	249	deposed
Theodoros I²	683—686	251	
Theodoros II	1213—1215	381	
Theodosios I	1178—1183	369	deposed

Theodosios II	1769—1773	661	deposed
Theodotos I	815—821	272	
Theodotos II	1151—1153	357	
Theoleptos I	1514—1520	499	
Theoleptos II	1585, 86	528	deposed
Theophanes I	1596, 97	538	
Theophanes II	1657	587	deposed
Theophylactos	933—956	303	
Thomas I	607—610	237	
Thomas II	665—668	246	
Timotheos I	511—548	215	
Timotheos II	1612—1621	549	poisoned
Titos	242—272	97	
Tryphon	928—931	300	deposed

The Patriarchs who (in the *Synaxaristes*, G. Ch. Raphtane, Zante, 1868) are numbered with the Saints—οἱ ἐν τοῖς Ἁγίοις—are

Alexander	August 30	Ioseph I	October 30
Anastasios	February 10	Leon	November 12
Anatolios	July 3	Macedonios II	April 25
Antonios III	February 12	Maximianos	April 24
Arsakios	October 11	Maximos I	November 17
Athanasios	October 28	Menas	August 25
Atticos	January 8	Methodios I	June 14
Callinicos	August 23	Metrophanes I	June 4
Callistos	June 20	Nectarios	October 11
Castinos	January 25	Nephon II	August 11
Constantinos	July 29	Nicephoros I	June 2
Cosmas	January 2	Nicolaos II	December 16
Cyriacos	October 27	Nicolaos III	May 16
Cyros	January 8	Paul I	November 6
Epiphanios	August 25	Paul II	August 30
Eutychios	April 6	Photios	February 6
Flavianos	February 16	Polyeuctos	February 5
Gennadios I	November 17	Proclos	November 20
Georgios I	August 18	Sisinios I	October 11
Germanos I	May 12	Stachys	October 31
Gregorios I	January 30	Stephanos I	May 18
Ignatios	October 23	Stephanos II	July 18
Ioannes I	November 13	Tarasios	February 25
Ioannes II	August 25 & 30	Theodoros I	December 27
Ioannes III	February 21	Thomas I	March 21
Ioannes V	August 18	Tryphon	April 19

Ἡ πρώτη στήλη σημειοῖ τὸ ὄνομα τοῦ Πατριάρχου· ἡ δευτέρα, τὸ ἔτος μ. Χ.· ἡ τρίτη τὴν σελίδα ἐν τῇ ἐκδόσει " Μ. Ι. Γεδεών, Πατριαρχικοὶ πίνακες, Κωνστ. 1890." Ἡ τετάρτη δηλοῖ πῶς ἔθετο τέρμα εἰς τὴν πατριαρχίαν του.

Ἀγαθάγγελος	1826—1830	688	παυθεὶς
Ἀκάκιος	471—489	198	
Ἀθανάσιος Ι	1289—1293	402	παραιτηθεὶς
Ἀθανάσιος Ι²	1303—1311	405	παραιτηθεὶς
Ἀθανάσιος ΙΙ	1450	467	παραιτηθεὶς
Ἀθανάσιος ΙΙΙ			
(Παντελλάριος)	1634	559	παυθεὶς
Ἀθανάσιος ΙΙΙ²	1652	580	παραιτηθεὶς
Ἀθανάσιος IV	1679	602	παυθεὶς
Ἀθανάσιος V	1709—1711	619	παυθεὶς
Ἀθηνόδωρος	144—148	92	
Ἀλέξανδρος	325—340	108	
Ἀλέξιος	1025—1043	317	
Ἀλύπιος	166—169	94	
Ἀναστάσιος	730—754	259	
Ἀνατόλιος	449—458	188	
Ἀνδρέας, Ἀπ.			
Ἄνθιμος Ι	536	223	παυθεὶς
Ἄνθιμος ΙΙ	1623	552	παραιτηθεὶς
Ἄνθιμος ΙΙΙ	1822—1824	686	παυθεὶς
Ἄνθιμος IV			
(Βαμβάκης)	1840, 1841	694	παυθεὶς
Ἄνθιμος IV²	1848—1852	698	παυθεὶς
Ἄνθιμος V	1841, 1842	694	
Ἄνθιμος VI			
(Ἰωαννίδης)	1845—1848	697	παυθεὶς
Ἄνθιμος VI²	1853—1855	699	παυθεὶς
Ἄνθιμος VI³	1871—1873	705	παραιτηθεὶς
Ἀντώνιος Ι			
(Κασυματᾶς)	821—832	273	
Ἀντώνιος ΙΙ			
(Καυλίας)	893—895	294	
Ἀντώνιος ΙΙΙ			
(Στουδίτης)	974—980	310	παραιτηθεὶς
Ἀντώνιος IV			
(Μακάριος)	1389, 1390	448	παυθεὶς
Ἀντώνιος IV²	1391—1397	449	

Ἀρσάκιος	404, 405	161	
Ἀρσένιος	1255—1260	389	παραιτηθεὶς
Ἀρσένιος ²	1261—1267	392	παυθεὶς
Ἄττικος	406—425	164	
Βασίλειος I (Σκαμανδρηνὸς)	970—974	309	παυθεὶς
Βασίλειος II (Καματηρὸς)	1183—1187	371	παυθεὶς
Γαβριὴλ I	1596	537	
Γαβριὴλ II	1657	586	παυθεὶς
Γαβριὴλ III	1702—1707	614	
Γαβριὴλ IV	1780—1785	666	
Γεννάδιος I	458—471	194	
Γεννάδιος II	1454—1456	471	παραιτηθεὶς
Γεράσιμος I	1320, 1321	417	
Γεράσιμος II	1673—1675	597	παυθεὶς
Γεράσιμος III	1794—1797	673	
Γερμανὸς I	715—730	255	παραιτηθεὶς
Γερμανὸς II	1222—1240	383	
Γερμανὸς III	1267	393	παυθεὶς
Γερμανὸς IV	1842—1845	695	παυθεὶς
Γερμανὸς IV ²	1852, 1853	699	
Γεώργιος I (Σχολάριος)	678—683	250	παυθεὶς
Γεώργιος II (Ξιφιλῖνος)	1192—1199	376	
Γρηγόριος I (Θεολόγος)	379—381	128	παραιτηθεὶς
Γρηγόριος II (Κύπριος)	1283—1289	398	παραιτηθεὶς
Γρηγόριος III (Μάμμας)	1443—1450	466	παυθεὶς
Γρηγόριος IV (Στραβοαμασείας)	1623	552	παυθεὶς
Γρηγόριος V	1797, 1798	675	παυθεὶς
Γρηγόριος V ²	1806—1808	680	παυθεὶς
Γρηγόριος V ³	1818—1821	684	ἀπαγχονισθεὶς
Γρηγόριος VI	1835—1840	692	παυθεὶς
Γρηγόριος VI ²	1867—1871	703	παραιτηθεὶς
Δημόφιλος	369—379	126	παυθεὶς
Διογένης	114—129	91	
Διονύσιος	1467—1472	482	παυθεὶς
Διονύσιος I ²	1489—1491	490	παυθεὶς
Διονύσιος II	1537	504	παυθεὶς
Διονύσιος II ²	1543—1555	507	
Διονύσιος III (Βάρδαλις)	1662—1665	588	παυθεὶς

Διονύσιος IV (Μουσελίμης)	1671—1673	595	πανθείς
Διονύσιος IV²	1676—1679	599	πανθείς
Διονύσιος IV³	1683, 84	604	πανθείς
Διονύσιος IV⁴	1686, 87	605	πανθείς
Διονύσιος IV⁵	1693	610	πανθείς
Δομέτιος	272—303	98	
Δοσίθεος	1191, 92	375	πανθείς
Ἐλευθέριος	129—136	91	
Ἐπιφάνιος	520—536	220	
Εὐάγριος	369, 70	127	πανθείς
Εὐδόξιος	360—369	122	
Εὐγένιος I	237—242	97	
Εὐγένιος II	1821, 22	686	
Εὐζώιος	148—154	93	
Εὐθύμιος I	906—911	296	πανθείς
Εὐθύμιος II	1410—1416	463	
Εὐσέβιος	341, 42	114	
Εὐστάθιος	1019—1025	317	
Εὐστράτιος	1081—1084	335	πανθείς
Εὐτύχιος	552—565	227	πανθείς
Εὐτύχιος²	577—582	231	
Εὐφήμιος	490—496	206	πανθείς
Ἡσαΐας	1323—1334	417	πανθείς
Θεόδωρος I	676—678	249	πανθείς
Θεόδωρος I²	683—686	251	
Θεόδωρος II (Κωπᾶς)	1213—1215	381	
Θεοδόσιος I	1178—1183	369	πανθείς
Θεοδόσιος II (Μαριδάκης)	1769—1773	661	πανθείς
Θεόδοτος I	815—821	272	
Θεόδοτος II	1151—1153	357	
Θεόληπτος I	1514—1520	499	
Θεόληπτος II	1585, 86	528	πανθείς
Θεοφάνης I (Καρύκης)	1596, 97	538	
Θεοφάνης II	1657	587	πανθείς
Θεοφύλακτος	933—956	303	
Θωμᾶς I	607—610	237	
Θωμᾶς II	665—668	246	
Ἰάκωβος¹	1679—1683	603	πανθείς
Ἰάκωβος²	1685, 86	605	πανθείς
Ἰάκωβος³	1687, 88	606	παραιτηθείς
Ἰγνάτιος	846—857	278	πανθείς
Ἰγνάτιος²	867—878	287	
Ἱερεμίας I	1520—1522	500	πανθείς

Ἰερεμίας Ι²	1523—1527	502	παυθείς
Ἰερεμίας Ι³	1537—1545	505	
Ἰερεμίας ΙΙ (Τρανὸς)	1572—1579	518	παυθείς
Ἰερεμίας ΙΙ²	1580—1584	524	παυθείς
Ἰερεμίας ΙΙ³	1586—1595	531	
Ἰερεμίας ΙΙΙ	1716—1726	622	παυθείς
Ἰερεμίας ΙΙΙ²	1733	631	παυθείς
Ἰερεμίας ΙV	1809—1813	682	παραιτηθείς
Ἰσαὰκ	1630	555	παυθείς
Ἰσίδωρος Ι	1347—1350	422	παραιτηθείς
Ἰσίδωρος ΙΙ	1456—1463	479	
Ἰωακεὶμ Ι	1498—1502	493	παυθείς
Ἰωακεὶμ Ι²	1504, 1505	497	
Ἰωακεὶμ ΙΙ	1860—1863	701	παραιτηθείς
Ἰωακεὶμ ΙΙ²	1873—1878	706	
Ἰωακεὶμ ΙΙΙ	1878—1884	706	παραιτηθείς
Ἰωάννης Ι (Χρυσόστομος)	398—404	141	παυθείς
Ἰωάννης ΙΙ (Καππαδόκης)	518—520	219	
Ἰωάννης ΙΙΙ	566—577	230	
Ἰωάννης ΙV (Νηστευτὴς)	582—595	232	
Ἰωάννης V	668—674	247	
Ἰωάννης VΙ	711—715	254	
Ἰωάννης VΙΙ (Παγκρατίον)	832—842	274	παυθείς
Ἰωάννης VΙΙΙ (Ξιφιλῖνος)	1064—1075	328	
Ἰωάννης ΙΧ (Ἀγαπητὸς)	1111—1134	348	
Ἰωάννης Χ (Καματηρὸς)	1199—1206	397	παραιτηθείς
Ἰωάννης ΧΙ (Βέκκος)	1275—1282	394	παυθείς
Ἰωάννης ΧΙΙ (Κοσμᾶς)	1294—1303	404	παραιτηθείς
Ἰωάννης ΧΙΙΙ (Γλυκὺς)	1315	415	παραιτηθείς
Ἰωάννης ΧΙV (Καλέκας)	1334—1347	420	παυθείς
Ἰωαννίκιος Ι	1522, 23	502	παυθείς
Ἰωαννίκιος ΙΙ (Λίνδιος)	1646—1648	574	παυθείς
Ἰωαννίκιος ΙΙ²	1651, 52	575	παραιτηθείς
Ἰωαννίκιος ΙΙ³	1653, 54	582	παυθείς

Ἰωαννίκιος II⁴	1655, 56	584	παυθείς
Ἰωαννίκιος III			
(Καρατζᾶς)	1761—1763	654	παυθείς
Ἰωάσαφ I (Κόκκας)	1464—1466	481	παυθείς
Ἰωάσαφ II	1555—1565	510	παυθείς
Ἰωσὴφ I	1268—1275	393	παυθείς
Ἰωσὴφ I²	1283	397	
Ἰωσὴφ II	1416—1439	464	
Καλλίνικος I	693—705	253	τυφλωθείς
Καλλίνικος II			
(Ἀκαρνὰν)	1688	607	παυθείς
Καλλίνικος II²	1689—1693	609	παυθείς
Καλλίνικος II³	1694—1702	611	
Καλλίνικος III	1726	627	
Καλλίνικος IV	1757	648	παυθείς
Καλλίνικος V	1801—1806	679	παυθείς
Καλλίνικος V²	1808—1809	681	
Κάλλιστος I	1350—1354	426	παυθείς
Κάλλιστος I²	1355—1363	429	
Κάλλιστος II			
(Ξανθόπουλος)	1397	456	
Καστῖνος	230—237	97	
Κλήμης	1667	592	παυθείς
Κοσμᾶς I			
(Ἱεροσολυμίτης)	1075—1081	333	παραιτηθείς
Κοσμᾶς II	1146, 47	353	παυθείς
Κοσμᾶς III	1714—1716	621	παραιτηθείς
Κυπριανὸς I	1708, 09	617	παραιτηθείς
Κυπριανὸς I²	1713, 14	621	παραιτηθείς
Κυριακὸς I	214—230	96	
Κυριακὸς II	595—606	236	
Κύριλλος I			
(Λούκαρις)	1612	547	παραιτηθείς
Κύριλλος I²	1621—1623	550	παυθείς
Κύριλλος I³	1623—1630	553	παυθείς
Κύριλλος I⁴	1630—1634	556	παυθείς
Κύριλλος I⁵	1634, 35	560	παυθείς
Κύριλλος I⁶	1637, 38	562	πνιγείς
Κύριλλος II			
(Κονταρῆς)	1632	558	παυθείς
Κύριλλος II²	1635, 36	560	παυθείς
Κύριλλος II³	1638, 39	567	παυθείς
Κύριλλος III			
(Σπανὸς)	1652	579	παυθείς
Κύριλλος IV	1711—1713	620	παυθείς
Κύριλλος V			
(Καράκαλος)	1748—1751	641	παυθείς

Κύριλλος V²	1752—1757	644	παυθείς
Κύριλλος VI (Σερμπετσόγλους)	1813—1818	683	φονευθείς
Κύριλλος VII	1855—1860	669	παυθείς
Κῦρος	705—711	254	παυθείς
Κωνσταντῖνος I	674—676	248	
Κωνσταντῖνος II	754—766	262	τυφλωθείς καὶ ἀποκεφαλισθείς
Κωνσταντῖνος III (Λευχούδης)	1059—1063	327	
Κωνσταντῖνος IV (Χλιαρηνὸς)	1154—1156	359	
Κωνστάντιος I	1830—1834	689	παραιτηθείς
Κωνστάντιος II	1834, 35	692	παυθείς
Λαυρέντιος	154—166	93	
Λέων	1134—1143	350	
Λεόντιος	1190, 91	374	παυθείς
Λουκᾶς	1156—1169	360	
Μακάριος	1376—1379	439	παυθείς
Μακάριος²	1390, 91	448	παυθείς
Μακεδόνιος I	342—348	118	παυθείς
Μακεδόνιος I²	350—360	121	
Μακεδόνιος II	496—511	209	παυθείς
Μανουὴλ I (Σαραντηνὸς)	1215—1222	383	
Μανουὴλ II	1244—1255	388	
Μάρκος I	198—211	95	
Μάρκος II (Ξυλοκαράβης)	1466, 67	481	παυθείς
Ματθαῖος I	1397—1410	457	
Ματθαῖος II	1595	536	παραιτηθείς
Ματθαῖος II²	1599—1602	541	παραιτηθείς
Μαξιμιανὸς	431—434	179	
Μάξιμος I	381	131	παυθείς
Μάξιμος II	1215	382	
Μάξιμος III	1476—1482	485	
Μάξιμος IV	1491—1497	491	παυθείς
Μεθόδιος I	842—846	277	
Μεθόδιος II	1240	387	
Μεθόδιος III (Μορώνης)	1668—1671	592	παραιτηθείς
Μελέτιος I (Πηγᾶς)	1597—1599	540	τοποτηρητὴς
Μελέτιος II	1768, 69	661	παυθείς
Μελέτιος III (Πάγκαλος)	1845	696	
Μηνᾶς	536—552	224	
Μητροφάνης I	315—325	104	
Μητροφάνης II	1440—1443	465	παυθείς

Μητροφάνης III	1565—1572	515	πανθείς
Μητροφάνης III²	1579, 80	523	
Μιχαὴλ I	1043—1058	322	
Μιχαὴλ II (Κουρκούας)	1143—1146	351	
Μιχαὴλ III (τοῦ Ἀγχιάλου)	1169—1177	365	
Μιχαὴλ IV (Αὐτωρειανὸς)	1206—1212	379	
Νεκτάριος	381—397	133	
Νεῖλος	1380—1388	440	
Νεόφυτος I	1153	358	πανθείς
Νεόφυτος II	1602, 03	542	πανθείς
Νεόφυτος II²	1607—1612	545	πανθείς
Νεόφυτος III	1636, 37	561	παραιτηθείς
Νεύφυτος IV	1688, 89	608	πανθείς
Νεόφυτος V	1707	617	πανθείς
Νεόφυτος VI	1734—1740	634	πανθείς
Νεόφυτος VI²	1743, 44	638	πανθείς
Νεόφυτος VII	1789—94	671	πανθείς
Νεόφυτος VII²	1798—1801	677	πανθείς
Νεστόριος	428—431	174	πανθείς
Νήφων I	1311—1314	411	παραιτηθείς
Νήφων II	1486—1489	488	πανθείς
Νήφων II²	1497, 98	492	πανθείς
Νήφων II³	1502	495	παραιτηθείς
Νικήτας I	766—780	263	
Νικήτας II (Μουντάνης)	1187—1190	373	πανθείς
Νικήφορος I	806—815	267	πανθείς
Νικήφορος II	1260, 61	391	
Νικόλαος I (Μυστικὸς)	895—906	295	πανθείς
Νικόλαος I²	911—925	298	
Νικόλαος II (Χρυσοβέργιος)	984—995	313	
Νικόλαος III (Γραμματικὸς)	1084—1111	338	
Νικόλαος IV (Μουζάλων)	1147—1151	354	παραιτηθείς
Ὀλυμπιανὸς	187—198	95	
Ὀνήσιμος	54—68	89	
Παΐσιος I	1652, 53	581	παραιτηθείς
Παΐσιος I²	1654, 55	583	παραιτηθείς
Παΐσιος II (Κιομουρτζόγλους)	1726—1733	628	πανθείς
Παΐσιος II²	1740—1743	635	

Παΐσιος II³	1744—1748	639	παραιτηθείς
Παΐσιος II⁴	1751, 52	644	παυθείς
Παρθένιος I			
(Γέρων)	1639—1644	569	
Παρθένιος II			
(Ὀξύς)	1644, 45	572	παυθείς
Παρθένιος II²	1648—1651	576	δηλητηριασθείς
Παρθένιος III	1656, 57	585	
Παρθένιος IV			
(Μογιλάλος)	1657—1662	587	παραιτηθείς
Παρθένιος IV²	1665—1667	591	παυθείς
Παρθένιος IV³	1671	594	παυθείς
Παρθένιος IV⁴	1675, 76	598	παυθείς
Παρθένιος IV⁵	1684, 85	604	παυθείς
Παῦλος I	340, 41	111	παυθείς
Παῦλος I²	342—344	117	παυθείς
Παῦλος I³	348—350	119	ἀποπνιγείς
Παῦλος II	641—652	243	
Παῦλος III	686—693	252	
Παῦλος IV	780—784	265	παραιτηθείς
Παχώμιος I	1503, 04	496	
Παχώμιος I²	1505—1514	498	δηλητηριασθείς
Παχώμιος II			
(Πατέστος)	1584, 85	526	παυθείς
Περτίναξ	169—187	94	
Πέτρος	652—664	245	
Πλούταρχος	89—105	90	
Πολύευκτος	956—970	307	
Πολύκαρπος I	71—89	90	
Πολύκαρπος II	141—144	92	
Πρόβος	303—315	100	
Πρόκλος	434—447	181	
Προκόπιος	1785—1789	669	παυθείς
Πύρρος	638—641	241	παυθείς
Πύρρος²	651, 52	245	
Ῥαφαὴλ I (Σέρβος)	1475, 76	484	παυθείς
Ῥαφαὴλ II	1603—1607	543	παυθείς
Ῥουφῖνος	283, 84	98	
Σαμουὴλ¹	1763—1768	657	παυθείς
Σαμουὴλ²	1773, 74	663	παυθείς
Σεδεκίων	105—114	91	
Σεραφεὶμ I	1733, 34	632	παυθείς
Σεραφεὶμ II	1757—1761	649	παυθείς
Σέργιος I	610—638	238	
Σέργιος II	999—1019	315	
Σισίνιος I	425—427	172	
Σισίνιος II	995—998	313	

Στάχυς	38—54	89	Ῥωμ. xvi. 9
Στέφανος I	886—893	293	
Στέφανος II	925—928	300	
Συμεὼν	1472—1475	483	παραιτηθεὶς
Συμεὼν [2]	1482—1486	487	παυθεὶς
Σωφρόνιος I (Συρόπουλος)	1463, 64	480	παυθεὶς
Σωφρόνιος II	1774—1780	664	
Σωφρόνιος III	1863—1866	702	παυθεὶς
Ταράσιος	784—806	265	
Τιμόθεος I	511—548	215	
Τιμόθεος II	1612—1621	549	δηλητηριασθεὶς
Τίτος	242—272	97	
Τρύφων	928—931	300	παυθεὶς
Φῆλιξ	136—141	91	
Φιλάδελφος	211—214	96	
Φιλόθεος	1354, 55	428	παραιτηθεὶς
Φιλόθεος [2]	1364—1376	431	
Φλαβιανὸς	447—449	185	φονευθεὶς
Φραυῖτας	489, 90	204	
Φώτιος	857—867	282	παυθεὶς
Φώτιος [2]	878—886	290	παυθεὶς
Χαρίτων	1177, 78	369	
Χρύσανθος	1824—1826	687	παυθεὶς

Οἱ ἐν τοῖς Ἁγίοις καταλεγόμενοι Πατριάρχαι (Συναξαριστής, Γ. Χ. Ῥαφτάνη, Ζάκυνθος, 1868) εἰσὶν οἱ ἀκόλουθοι.

Ἀθανάσιος	Ὀκτωβρίου 28	Κῦρος	Ἰανουαρίου 8
Ἀλέξανδρος	Αὐγούστου 30	Κωνσταντῖνος	Ἰουλίου 29
Ἀναστάσιος	Φεβρουαρίου 10	Λέων	Νοεμβρίου 12
Ἀνατόλιος	Ἰουλίου 3	Μακεδόνιος Β΄	Ἀπριλίου 25
Ἀντώνιος Γ΄	Φεβρουαρίου 12	Μαξιμιανὸς	Ἀπριλίου 4
Ἀρσάκιος	Ὀκτωβρίου 11	Μάξιμος Α΄	Νοεμβρίου 17
Ἀττικὸς	Ἰανουαρίου 8	Μεθόδιος Α΄	Ἰουνίου 14
Γεννάδιος Α΄	Νοεμβρίου 17	Μηνᾶς	Αὐγούστου 25
Γεώργιος Α΄	Αὐγούστου 18	Μητροφάνης Α΄	Ἰουνίου 4
Γερμανὸς Α΄	Μαΐου 12	Νεκτάριος	Ὀκτωβρίου 11
Γρηγόριος Α΄	Ἰανουαρίου 30	Νήφων Β΄	Αὐγούστου 11
Ἐπιφάνιος	Αὐγούστου 25	Νικηφόρος Α΄	Ἰουνίου 2
Εὐτύχιος	Ἀπριλίου 6	Νικόλαος Β΄	Δεκεμβρίου 16
Θεόδωρος Α΄	Δεκεμβρίου 27	Νικόλαος Γ΄	Μαΐου 16
Θωμᾶς Α΄	Μαρτίου 21	Παῦλος Α΄	Νοεμβρίου 6
Ἰγνάτιος	Ὀκτωβρίου 23	Παῦλος Β΄	Αὐγούστου 30
Ἰωάννης Α΄	Νοεμβρίου 13	Πολύευκτος	Φεβρουαρίου 5
Ἰωάννης Β΄	Αὐγούστου 25 κ. 30	Πρόκλος	Νοεμβρίου 20
Ἰωάννης Γ΄	Φεβρουαρίου 21	Σισίνιος Α΄	Ὀκτωβρίου 11
Ἰωάννης Ε΄	Αὐγούστου 18	Στάχυς	Ὀκτωβρίου 31
Ἰωσὴφ	Ὀκτωβρίου 30	Στέφανος Α΄	Μαΐου 18
Καλλίνικος	Αὐγούστου 23	Στέφανος Β΄	Ἰουλίου 18
Κάλλιστος	Ἰουνίου 20	Ταράσιος	Φεβρουαρίου 25
Καστῖνος	Ἰανουαρίου 25	Τρύφων	Ἀπριλίου 19
Κοσμᾶς	Ἰανουαρίου 2	Φλαβιανὸς	Φεβρουαρίου 16
Κυριακὸς	Ὀκτωβρίου 27	Φώτιος	Φεβρουαρίου 6